OCCASIONAL PAPER 208

Yemen in the 1990s
From Unification to Economic Reform

Klaus Enders, Sherwyn Williams, Nada Choueiri,
Yuri Sobolev, Jan Walliser

INTERNATIONAL MONETARY FUND
Washington DC
2002

Production: IMF Graphics Section
Figures: IMF Graphics Section
Typesetting: Danielle Bujosa, Choon Lee

Library of Congress Cataloging-in-Publication Data

Yemen in the 1990s : from unification to economic reform/ Klaus Enders …
[et al.] — Washington, D.C.: International Monetary Fund, 2001.

p. cm. — (Occasional paper; 208)

Includes bibliographical references.
ISBN 1-58906-042-3

1. Yemen—Economic conditions. 2. Yemen—Economic policy.
I. Enders, K. II. Occasional paper (International Monetary Fund) ; 208.

HC415.34.Y466 2001
338.9533—dc21

20011051781

Price: US$20.00
(US$17.50 to full-time faculty members and
students at universities and colleges)

Please send orders to:
International Monetary Fund, Publication Services
700 19th Street, N.W., Washington, D.C. 20431, U.S.A.
Tel.: (202) 623-7430 Telefax: (202) 623-7201
E-mail: publications@imf.org
Internet: http://www.imf.org

recycled paper

Contents

Figures

Section

The following symbols have been used throughout this paper:

. . . to indicate that data are not available;

n.a. to indicate not applicable;

— to indicate that the figure is zero or less than half the final digit shown, or that the item does not exist;

– between years or months (i.e., 1997–98 or January–June) to indicate the years or months covered, including the beginning and ending years or months;

/ between years or months (i.e., 1997/98) to indicate a crop or fiscal (financial) year.

"Billion" means a thousand million; "trillion" means a thousand billion.

Minor discrepancies between constituent figures and totals are due to rounding.

The term "country," as used in this paper, does not in all cases refer to a territorial entity that is a state as understood by international law and practice; the term also covers some territorial entities that are not states, but for which statistical data are maintained and provided internationally on a separate and independent basis.

Preface

Most of the material presented in this Occasional Paper was originally prepared as background for discussions in the IMF Executive Board. It has been updated to take account of developments through early 2001. The authors are grateful to the Yemeni authorities for extensive discussions and comments and for their assistance in providing data and other source material.

This Occasional Paper has benefited from valuable analytical analyses from David Moore, Rodney Ramcharan, and Manmohan Singh. The authors are grateful for valuable comments from the staff in the Middle Eastern Department as well as the World Bank. The authors would also like to express their appreciation for valuable research assistance that was provided by Aminata Toure and for careful and patient secretarial assistance from Anne-Barbara Hyde, Wilma Gonzalez Buenaobra, Rochelle Gittens, and Melissa Wills. The authors are also indebted to the External Relations Department, to Mike Treadway who edited the paper, and to Gail Berre who coordinated its production and publication.

The opinions expressed are solely those of the authors and do not necessarily reflect the views of the International Monetary Fund, the Executive Directors, or the Yemeni authorities.

List of Abbreviations

ARC	Aden Refinery Company
CanOxy	Canadian Occidental Petroleum
CBY	Central Bank of Yemen
CMEA	Council of Mutual Economic Assistance
CPI	Consumer Price Index
CSF	Civil Service Fund
CSO	Central Statistics Organization
DSA	Debt Sustainability Analysis
GAVTT	General Authority for Vocational and Technical Training
GIA	General Investment Authority
GPC	General People's Congress
GST	General Sales Tax
HBS	Household Budget Survey
HC	High Commission
HDI	Human Development Index
HIPC	Highly Indebted Poor Country
HNS	Harmonized Nomenclature System
IDA	International Development Agency
IMF	International Monetary Fund
KUFPEC	Kuwait Foreign Petroleum Exploration Company
LCCD	Local Councils for Cooperative Development
LMIS	Labor Market Information System Database
LNG	Liquefied Natural Gas
LPG	Liquefied Petroleum Gas
MENA	Middle East and Northern Africa
MOLVT	Ministry of Labor and Vocational Training
MOP	Ministry of Planning
MPH	Ministry of Public Health
NGO	Non Governmental Organization
NPC	Nimir Petroleum Company
NPEC	Nimir Petroleum Exploration Company
NPV	Net Present Value
PAR	Poverty Assessment Review
PDRY	People's Democratic Republic of Yemen
PEC	Public Electricity Corporation
PTC	Public Telephone Corporation
RGDI	Real Gross Domestic Income
RGDP	Real Gross Domestic Product
RO	Repurchase Operations
SFD	Social Fund for Development
SWF	Social Welfare Fund
TFP	Total Factor Productivity
TIN	Taxpayer Identification Number
TPCS	Tax on Production, Consumption, and Services
TPO	Technical Privatization Office

UNCTAD	United Nations Conference on Trade and Development
UNHCR	United Nations High Commissioner for Refugees
WEO	World Economic Outlook
WTO	World Trade Organization
YAR	Yemen Arab Republic
YBRD	Yemen Bank for Reconstruction and Development
YCIOM	Yemeni Company for Investment in Oil and Mineral Resources
YFZPA	Yemen Free Zones Public authority
YPC	Yemen Petroleum Company
YRG	Yemeni Reform Group
YSP	Yemeni Socialist Party

I Overview

The decade of the 1990s was surely one of the most dramatic periods in Yemen's rich history. Unification of the two Yemens, rapid development of an oil sector, and a radically changed external environment fundamentally transformed the opportunities and challenges the Yemeni people face. This paper summarizes economic developments in Yemen during the 1990s, takes stock of the many structural changes in the economy during the decade, and identifies reforms that are needed if Yemen is to move to a path of rapid and sustainable growth, reduce rampant poverty, and responsibly manage the highly volatile economic rents from its oil wealth. It is hoped that this paper will contribute to the ongoing debate in Yemen on the appropriate development strategy for the coming years.

Section II summarizes the main political and exogenous events that shaped the decade. The decade began with the unification of the Yemen Arab Republic (YAR, or North Yemen) with the People's Democratic Republic of Yemen (PDRY, or South Yemen). The YAR had emerged in the 1960s as the republican successor to the medieval regime of the *imam*; the socialist PDRY had its origins in the struggle for independence in the British colony and protectorates around Aden in 1967. Only a few months after unification Yemen experienced a major shock: the onset of the second Persian Gulf crisis led to the return of about three quarters of a million Yemeni workers from the Gulf states, challenging a fragile socioeconomic fabric already weakened by a severe two-year drought. The development of the country's oil fields during the same period may have been the element that kept Yemen away from the brink. Oil exports provided a new and growing source of foreign exchange earnings, even if fluctuations in world oil prices added a new vulnerability.

The strains from these developments eventually led to a brief civil war in 1994, following an attempt at secession by elements of the former PDRY leadership. It was only after the secessionists were defeated militarily—and as the new constitutional system providing for a multiparty democracy, a free press, and an essentially market-based economic system took hold—that the political consensus could be forged for the urgent economic reforms that had been delayed since unification. In 1995 Yemen initiated an economic reform program, supported by the IMF as well as by the World Bank and other institutions and countries, aimed at strengthening the foundations of a market-based and private sector–driven economy, integrated into world markets and operating in a context of broad financial stability. This approach underpins government policy today.

The first priority of reform was obviously to restore macroeconomic stability, which was threatened by large fiscal imbalances; by price distortions resulting from the attempt to suppress excess demand through price, foreign exchange, and interest rate controls; and by a huge debt overhang arising largely, but not solely, out of the former PDRY's debt to the Soviet Union. Section III describes the emerging macroeconomic policy mix. Fiscal policy was obviously key, and in light of the importance of oil for government revenue, it is assessed also from an intertemporal perspective, given the fact that Yemen has only limited proven reserves.

Although stabilization policy was highly successful, structural reforms faced greater difficulties and greater resistance and were more severely constrained by Yemen's limited administrative capacity. Section IV describes the progress on structural reform to date, pointing to impressive success in liberalizing the exchange and trade regime and lifting price controls, but also to a huge unfinished agenda in tax and budget management reform, privatization, and civil service reform. Deep-rooted obstacles to economic growth, notably including weaknesses in the judicial system and governance, have barely been touched; reform in these areas, perhaps more than in others, will have to emerge from and be shaped by civil society itself.

Section V looks at some of the "formal" social safety net measures put in place to protect the most vulnerable segments of society not only against the adverse effects of certain reform measures (notably the reduction in generalized subsidies), but also—and probably more important—against the often brutal exogenous shocks that Yemeni society has had to absorb. These included not only the return of expatriate workers in 1990–91 and the dislocations from the civil war in 1994, but more recently the collapse of oil prices in 1998. No data exist to gauge the scope of traditional, often tribal- or religious-based, social support systems. Such systems likely remain far more important than formal systems and must have been at the core of Yemen's ability to absorb the workers returning from the Gulf region.

Finally, Section VI looks at the Yemeni economy's performance in terms of growth and inflation, social indicators, and saving and investment balances; the analysis also compares Yemen's record with that in other, similar countries. Clearly, during the second half of the 1990s, performance improved on all three fronts—remarkably so for macroeconomic stability, but considerably less so for social indicators. This reflects several factors: the return to political stability and peace, oil sector developments that were on the whole favorable, and the first fruits of reforms. But in order to build on these achievements, an even greater focus on growth and poverty reduction will be needed. The Yemeni authorities have therefore embarked on preparing a comprehensive poverty reduction strategy, in the context of the next Five-Year Plan (2001–06) and in broad consultation with civil society. The plan was launched in early 2001. It is hoped that this paper can contribute to formulating such a strategy by providing some of the needed background and by drawing some first lessons from Yemen's adjustment experience to date.

II External Environment: Politics, Oil, and Debt

Economic developments in Yemen in the 1990s were driven largely by dramatic changes in the political sphere—in particular, by unification and civil war—and by external events, chief among which was the Gulf crisis at the beginning of the decade. A third major influence was the massive debt overhang inherited from the previous political regimes.

Political Developments: Unity, Gulf Crisis, Civil War, and Democracy

Unification of North and South Yemen in early 1990 opened a decade of dramatic sociopolitical and economic change. As in the unification of Germany, a larger and broadly market-based economy (the YAR) absorbed a smaller, centrally planned economy (the PDRY). At the time of unification, the population of the YAR was estimated at 10.4 million, and that of the PDRY at 2.4 million (Dunbar, 1992); their GDPs were $5.4 billion and $1.3 billion, respectively.[1]

Also as in the German case, unification had been a long-standing aspiration of the Yemeni people in both states and became possible mainly through the effects of *perestroika* in the Soviet Union on its ally, the socialist PDRY. On the economic side, a reduction in financial and technical assistance from the Soviet bloc, combined with declining workers' remittances—a mainstay of the PDRY, accounting for about half of government revenue in the late 1980s—created pressures for a rethinking of the PDRY's development strategy in the mid-1980s. Although the PDRY had achieved respectable improvements in education and other social indicators (more so than the YAR),[2] the economy was in a dismal state as a result of failed socialist reforms in agriculture, fisheries, and port activity. Large Soviet-financed investments in the Shabwah oil field, discovered in 1986, added half a billion dollars to the PDRY's staggering debt (largely to the Soviet Union and her allies), but the oil facilities remained unfinished, and production was limited to 10,000 barrels a day (b/d), which was trucked to the decrepit refinery in Aden.[3] On the political side, the last years of the PDRY saw some liberalization of political activity and the press but were also marked by instability within the political leadership of the country, with violent internal struggles in 1986.

The YAR, in contrast, had witnessed a measure of political stability with some consolidation of central control—even over traditional tribal areas—as well as a measure of economic development despite limited progress in education and health. Oil exploration was in private hands, and discoveries in 1984 quickly led to development of a major oil field (Marib). Production began in 1987, with most of the output exported through a pipeline, reaching about 195,000 b/d in the early 1990s. Although the YAR, like the PDRY, was dependent on workers' remittances, its foreign debt averaged a relatively manageable 60 percent of GDP, well below the PDRY's 180 percent of GDP, during 1987–89.

Development of oil resources was another important catalyst for unification. The nearly simultaneous oil discoveries in the YAR and the PDRY were in adjacent areas, and development and further exploration required settling of outstanding border issues. The first fruits of this effort were a bilateral agreement demilitarizing the border zone in 1988, along with an easing of bilateral travel restrictions and the activation of common institutions, notably the Supreme Yemeni Council, formally in place since 1982. The dynamics set in motion were such that, in late 1989, a "historic agreement" was reached, calling for a draft constitution for a unified Yemen to be presented to both parliaments within six months and a referendum to be held six months thereafter. A unity government was formed in early 1990, and a

[1]These estimates are based on the two countries' national accounts using official exchange rates, which were well below parallel market rates in both countries.

[2]Illiteracy in the PDRY was reduced from 97 percent in 1967, when the PDRY was formed, to 59 percent in 1985; at that point the YAR's illiteracy rate was still 80 percent (Dunbar, 1992).

[3]Shabwah was closed down in 1994 after disappointing results, mainly due to the inappropriate recovery methods introduced in the late 1980s.

year later an impressive majority in both parts of the country approved a new constitution by popular referendum. The new constitution provided for basic political freedom (for both women and men), including the right to organize and vote and the right of private ownership, and establishing *sharia* (Muslim law) as the principal (but not sole) source of law.

Early on, however, severe strains developed to challenge the newfound unity. Most important, during the Gulf crisis in late 1990, Saudi Arabia—home to the bulk of Yemeni migrant workers, who made up an estimated 17 percent of the Saudi workforce—decided to end the visa and sponsorship exemptions traditionally enjoyed by Yemenis living and working there. As a result, an estimated three-quarters of a million workers returned to Yemen (Dunbar, 1992). Another roughly 50,000 workers returned from other Gulf states. Although most of the repatriated migrants returned to their hometowns and villages, some 60,000 had to be put in refugee camps. The returnees initially lived off their savings, but the loss in remittances and of official assistance from the Gulf states (about $200 million a year in the late 1980s) and the need to accommodate some three-quarters of a million returnees contributed to a rapid deterioration in economic balances, contracting economic activity and fueling inflation. A severe drought during 1990–91 added to the adversity.

Other economic (and political) strains resulted from the way the two very different economic systems were merged. The two civil services were simply added together, with 50–50 sharing of all posts between the former YAR and the former PDRY services, reflecting a similar sharing of the top leadership posts. Harmonization of wage scales at the higher level prevailing in the YAR added to pressures on the public finances. Tensions quickly arose over policy issues—for example, over what education policy to pursue. Hasty attempts to roll back the PDRY's redistribution of farmland, and the slow restitution of real estate nationalized under the PDRY to business owners who had fled, led to dissatisfaction among farmers and the business community. The bloated bureaucracy fueled a rise in governance problems. Many southerners were concerned about certain aspects of traditional YAR society such as the strong tribal influence and the greater circumscription of the role of women; many northerners had similar misgivings about what was perceived as non-Islamic behavior in the south. As a result, the leadership remained largely divided among north-south lines, with southern representatives often abstaining from joint cabinet meetings. Each side largely preserved control over its former armed forces.

At the same time, the introduction of democracy led to a flourishing of political parties (more than 40 of which emerged) and newspapers across a broad political spectrum. In the first unified election in 1993, the electorate largely voted along traditional north-south lines (Kostiner, 1996). The General Peoples' Congress (GPC), which included much of the former YAR's leadership, emerged as the dominant political force, winning nearly half of the available seats. The newly formed Islamic Yemeni Reform Group (YRG), or Islah, came in a distant second, closely followed by the Yemeni Socialist Party (YSP). The YSP was made up largely of the former PDRY leadership and won most seats in the south. There were also a large number of independents and small parties. Although a coalition government including the GPC, the YRG, and the YSP was formed, the election results led to growing estrangement between the southern and northern leaderships, with each focused on the rebuilding of its regional power base. This was also fueled by the development of a southern oil field (Masila), which came on stream in 1993. This field initially produced 40,000 b/d, which was trucked to Aden; output rose to 150,000 b/d as a central processing unit and a pipeline to the Indian Ocean were completed in 1994. Despite many attempts—notably by other Arab states—to mediate between the two sides, the declaration of an independent southern state by parts of the YSP leadership in 1994 triggered a civil war. The war ended with the defeat of the southern forces a few months later, at considerable cost to lives and property.

The new constitution adopted in September 1994 provided for direct popular election of the president. A new government comprising only GPC and Islah representatives was formed and, in 1995–96, was able to reach a broad consensus to start the needed economic and administrative reforms. New elections in April 1997 were boycotted by the YSP and gave the GPC an absolute majority, with Islah again the second-largest party, followed by a number of smaller parties and independents. This time the GPC alone formed the government, although the cabinet included a few independents (the prime minister among them). President Ali Abdullah Saleh also instituted a Consultative Council, including members of the YRG, the YSP, and the GPC along with eminent tribal leaders and other representatives of civil society. The council has no legislative or executive mandate except to debate the major issues and submit recommendations to the president; however, it plays an important role in mediating, for example, differences between parliament and the executive.

In September 1999 President Saleh won another five-year mandate in Yemen's first contested presidential election, running against another GPC member. The YRG refrained from putting up a candidate, and other opposition parties were unable to muster the 10 percent of votes in parliament needed to field a presidential candidate.

Yemen's Emergence as an Oil Producer

From a regional perspective, Yemen is a minor player in the oil market: estimated proven oil reserves and production levels in 1998–99 were 0.6 percent and 1.8 percent, respectively, of Middle East totals. The oil sector in Yemen is characterized by little government intervention and is instead dominated by large international oil companies, which manage exploration and production. Oil production began in 1987 in the Marib concession, held by a consortium of companies including Hunt, Exxon, and Yukong. In 1993 the second major block, Masila, operated by Canadian Occidental Petroleum (CanOxy), came on stream, giving a major boost to oil output growth (Table 1). As oil production continued to increase at an average annual rate of about 3 percent throughout the rest of the decade (Figure 1), Yemen's economy became highly oil-dependent. The share of oil in real GDP nearly doubled, from 10.7 percent in 1992 to 20.2 percent in 1999, and government crude oil export revenues as a share of GDP increased eightfold over the same period.

Inception and Evolution of Exploration Agreements

Although oil exploration had taken place in Yemen as early as in the late 1930s, it accelerated in the 1970s, when eight agreements were signed with oil companies to conduct exploration, mostly in the Hadramout and Tihama areas. Between 1982 and 1991 Yemen signed about ten additional exploration and production agreements,[4] including agreements for the five blocks currently producing oil: Marib, Masila, Jannah, Shabwah, and Ayad. The contracts in each case were fairly similar. Exploration commitments were specified,[5] in addition to cost oil percentages and profit-sharing ratios, and signing bonuses were granted in most cases.[6] The share of cost oil was usually around 30 percent, and profit sharing was on average about 20 percent for the company.[7]

Three agreements signed in the 1980s eventually led to oil discoveries, which were quite substantial in two cases.[8] The remaining agreements for the blocks producing oil today were signed in the early 1990s. By the mid-1990s foreign interest in the Yemeni oil sector had diminished, mainly because of the civil war and the relatively low success rate of previous explorations (primarily due to geological difficulties). As the government realized that, without additional foreign investment, oil production would decline in the near future, it began to offer better financial terms to interested oil companies and eased the terms of existing contracts on a case-by-case basis. A major change implemented in the contracts was one allowing the share of cost oil to be periodically revised in light of movements in world oil prices.

In 1995–96, to provide better incentives to oil companies investing in small fields, the Yemeni government renegotiated deals with Nimir Petroleum Company and CanOxy. The new financial terms allowed the oil companies to recover their initial exploration expenses over a shorter period.[9] For the

[4]See *Arab Oil and Gas Directory,* various issues; some information can also be found on the World Wide Web site of the Ministry of Oil and Mineral Resources (www.momr.gov.ye).

[5]For example, contracts specified which activities would be undertaken in the exploration phase, such as the numbers of wells to be drilled and the kind and amount of seismic data to be produced and analyzed. Funds committed in the exploration phase, generally on the order of tens of millions of dollars, were also stated.

[6]Cost oil is the amount recoverable by the operator per year to cover expenses during the appraisal and exploration period as well as operating costs.

[7]As an illustration, assume that production is at 100,000 b/d, the share of cost oil is 50 percent, and profit sharing is 20–80 in favor of the government. The company then receives 50,000 b/d as cost oil plus 20 percent of the remaining 50,000 b/d, or 10,000 b/d, as profit, while the government receives 40,000 b/d.

[8]The first was signed in September 1981 with the U.S. company Hunt Oil over a 16,890-square-kilometer area located in what was then North Yemen, in the onshore Tihama area (the Marib block). In addition to shares of cost oil and profit distribution, the terms of the agreement specified a 10 percent royalty to the government on the fraction of production in excess of 100,000 b/d. In September 1986 a consortium consisting of CanOxy and Athens-based Consolidated Contractors International Company was awarded two onshore tracts in the Masila region of South Yemen. These tracts, totaling 35,548 square kilometers, turned in the second most important oil findings in Yemen after Marib. In April 1987 the South Yemeni government awarded Total of France the 15,827-square-kilometer East Shabwa concession, located northeast of Aden. A consortium consisting of Total, Hunt Oil/Exxon, the Kuwait Foreign Petroleum Exploration Company (Kufpec), Mashinoimport, and Zarubezhgeologia signed an agreement in 1990 with the Yemeni Company for Investment in Oil and Mineral Resources for the exploration of Jannah, a tract of land in northern Yemen measuring 2,372 square kilometers, with a signature bonus of $6 million. The following year Nimir Petroleum Company (NPC) signed an exploration agreement for the Ayad block, also in northern Yemen, obtaining a much larger signature bonus of $27 million and a production bonus of $5 million at a rate of output exceeding 50,000 b/d. Oil had been found in the Ayad block earlier in the 1980s, but the company that held the concession at the time later relinquished it.

[9]In the revised agreement with CanOxy, for example, costs would be recovered out of 50 percent of crude oil produced instead of the previous 28 percent. The original 10 percent flat royalty rate was replaced with a sliding scale, rising from 3 percent on production up to 25,000 b/d to 10 percent on production exceeding 100,000 b/d. Under its revised agreement, NPC would collect 70 percent of revenue generated on production up to 25,000 b/d as cost oil (instead of the previous 24 percent). Once that allocation has been made, the company would pay the government 3 percent as a royalty, and the remaining profit would be split evenly between NPC and the government. Similarly, in early 2000 the government finalized amendments raising companies' profit share to the share in the production-sharing agreement with the Norwegian company DNO, which operates Howarim (Block 32).

Table 1. Selected Economic Indicators, 1990–99

	1990	1991	1992	1993	1994	1995	1996	1997	1998	1999
					(Change in percent)					
Production and prices										
Nominal GDP at market prices	41.2	18.6	27.0	23.8	28.4	67.1	43.7	21.5	0.4	24.3
Real GDP at market prices	. . .	–2.1	4.8	0.4	–3.6	7.9	2.9	8.1	5.3	3.8
Real non-oil GDP	. . .	–1.5	8.0	–0.1	–9.6	5.5	0.5	8.2	5.9	3.2
Real oil GDP	. . .	–5.7	–15.9	4.3	43.7	20.0	13.5	7.5	2.7	6.2
Consumer price index (annual average)	33.5	44.9	50.6	62.4	71.3	62.5	40.0	4.6	11.5	8.0
Crude export oil price (weighted average, US$ per barrel)	22.1	19.8	19.7	15.9	15.4	16.9	20.3	18.5	11.6	18.7
					(In percent of GDP)					
Government finance										
Total revenue and grants	19.8	23.1	16.1	14.9	12.8	19.5	35.9	32.8	26.4	31.8
Oil revenue	7.5	9.4	4.7	4.2	3.7	9.3	25.1	22.1	13.8	19.8
Non-oil revenue	11.2	12.6	11.1	10.5	8.9	9.8	10.5	10.1	12.2	11.1
Grants	1.1	1.0	0.3	0.1	0.3	0.3	0.3	0.6	0.4	0.9
Total expenditure	32.3	30.1	28.9	29.5	29.0	25.6	39.8	34.7	32.7	32.1
Current	23.6	26.1	25.5	26.0	26.4	22.5	33.2	27.9	26.6	26.5
Development	8.7	4.0	3.4	3.5	2.6	3.1	6.6	6.8	6.1	5.6
Overall balance including grants (cash basis)	–11.7	–5.6	–11.7	–13.9	–15.7	–5.2	0.6	–1.8	–7.9	–0.4
Overall balance excluding grants (commitment basis)	–13.6	–8.0	–13.1	–14.8	–16.4	–6.4	–4.2	–2.5	–6.7	–1.2
					(12-month change in percent of initial broad money)					
Monetary data										
Broad money	35.1	18.8	27.6	35.4	34.7	20.4	8.6	10.7	11.7	13.8
Credit to nongovernment sector	36.4	21.5	7.2	15.8	69.0	28.0	–29.4	46.6	54.2	15.0
Benchmark deposit interest rate (percent)	6.5	6.5	6.5	6.5	6.5	20.0	25.0	11.0	15.0	18.0
Velocity (non-oil GDP/M2)	1.5	1.5	1.5	1.4	1.2	1.7	1.9	2.0	2.2	2.1
					(In millions of U.S. dollars)					
External sector										
Exports, f.o.b.	1,384	1,197	1,095	1,167	1,824	1,937	2,263	2,274	1,501	2,466
Of which										
Crude oil	1,203	1,011	819	834	1,615	1,735	1,976	1,945	1,229	2,131
Imports, f.o.b.	–1,726	–1,897	–1,891	–2,087	–1,522	–1,948	–2,294	–2,407	–2,228	–2,440
Services (net)	–739	–661	–852	–917	–475	–411	–370	–470	–398	–489
Private remittances and transfers (net)	1,241	1,078	1,071	1,067	1,117	1,104	1,188	1,256	1,254	1,314
Capital account (net)	356	88	–36	74	–641	–876	–397	34	–154	11
Overall balance	–65	–803	–1,283	–1,008	–779	–38	–625	116	–463	320
					(In millions of U.S. dollars)					
Central bank own gross foreign reserves[2]	424	680	323	147	357	525	937	1,152	853	1,351
In months of imports[2]	2.8	4.2	2.2	0.9	2.9	3.1	4.6	5.3	4.2	6.0
As percent of base money	8.6	12.5	4.9	1.7	3.0	19.0	73.2	103.5	79.3	112.3
As percent of M2	6.8	9.2	3.4	1.2	2.1	12.5	48.8	53.7	41.7	62.7
Current account, including grants (in percent of GDP)	–3.1	–10.7	–13.2	–16.1	5.6	2.8	1.7	0.3	–3.7	2.9
Current account, excluding grants (in percent of GDP)	–4.4	–12.2	–13.8	–16.5	4.5	2.2	0.7	–1.0	–4.6	1.5
Debt service ratio, obligation basis[3]	46.7	91.3	89.1	80.8	46.8	42.1	31.9	12.6	17.0	10.5
Official external debt, before rescheduling[3]	9,915	10,323	10,541	10,735	10,876	11,017	11,135	5,359	5,373	5,490
(In percent of GDP)	105.7	129.5	127.9	138.5	167.1	170.1	173.2	81.2	85.3	80.4
Terms of trade (1996=100)	122.3	113.0	107.4	91.8	85.5	85.3	100.0	100.7	69.5	114.1
Exchange rate (free market, eop) (YRls/US$)	17.5	29.7	42.7	67.8	101.0	127.1	126.9	130.5	141.7	159.7
Real effective exchange rate (1996=100)[4]	. . .	. . .	. . .	. . .	. . .	76.2	100.0	109.7	119.5	107.1

Sources: Yemeni authorities; IMF staff estimates and projections.

[1]EBS/99/98 (6/15/99).

[2]Gross reserves minus commercial bank foreign exchange deposits held with the central bank. Imports are for the current year, and exclude oil and gas sector imports. Short-term debt by remaining maturity; excludes private debt for which data is not available.

[3] Public- and publicly guaranteed debt including central bank foreign liabilities. Debt service ratios in percent of exports of goods and services and reflecting reschedulings in 1996 and 1997 under the auspices of the Paris Club.

[4]Based on the free market rate.

Figure 1. Actual and Projected Crude Oil Production and Government Share
(In millions of barrels a year)

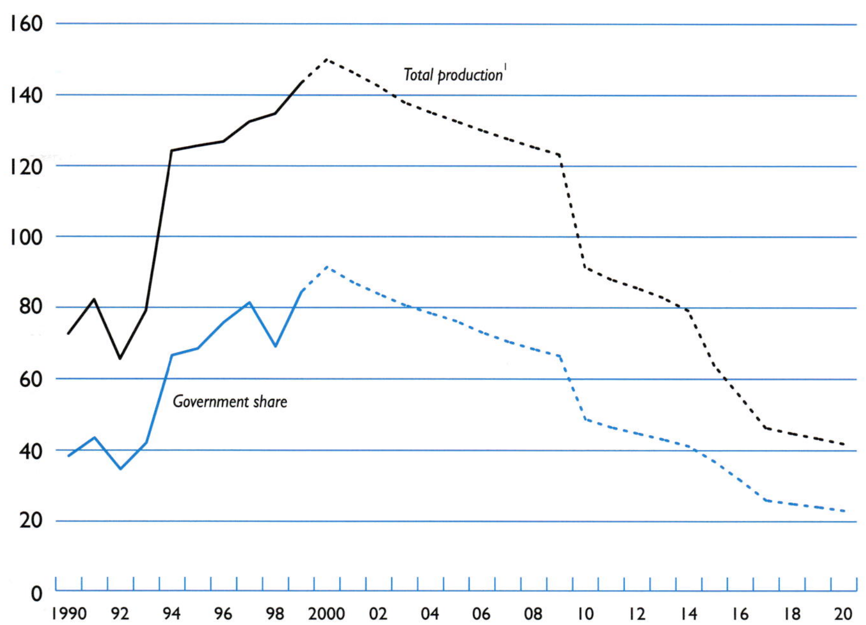

Sources: Ministry of Oil and Mineral Resources; Ministry of Finance; IMF staff estimates.
[1]Dashed lines indicate projections based on proven recoverable reserves as of the end of 1999, excluding natural gas reserves.

new agreements signed in 1996 and onward, the starting point for the sliding scale of the profit-sharing formula was increased from 20 percent to 30 percent, and the share of cost oil was increased from about 30 percent to between 50 and 75 percent. That share was to be decreased, however, once the oil company had recovered its initial costs and entered into the operational phase. As a result of these better terms, the number of new companies in the oil sector increased significantly. During 1996–99, 20 exploration blocks were awarded (see Statistical Appendix Table A.11). As of February 2000 more than 26 oil companies were conducting exploration operations in Yemen on a total of 30 blocks. Most had finished their seismic surveys and were drilling exploration wells. More recently, the authorities have moved away from their traditional approach of negotiating concessions on a bilateral basis and embarked in late 1999 on road shows in London and Houston, inviting a new round of bids for the development of seven blocks. About 15 companies seemed interested, but none was ready to make a formal commitment, possibly because they were awaiting important discoveries in the current exploration operations.

Production Prospects

According to the Petroleum Exploration and Production Board, Yemen's remaining recoverable reserves of oil stood at 2.8 billion barrels at the end of April 2000, for a production horizon of about 18 years at the current level of output.[10] Production increased from an average of 389,000 b/d in 1999 to about 434,000 b/d on average in 2000. The main increase came from the Jannah and Shabwah blocks, where large investments in infrastructure are taking place. Unless relatively large new fields come on stream, however, oil production is expected to start declining from 2001 onward at an approximate aver-

[10]Of these reserves, 413 million barrels are located in the Marib block, 1,410 million in the Masila block, 181 million in the Shabwah block, 281 million in the Jannah block, 107 million in the Ayad block, and 25 million in the Howarim block.

age rate of 3 percent a year, as fields in both Marib and Masila start drying up.[11]

Refining

Yemen has two state-owned refineries, in Aden and in Marib. The refinery in Aden was constructed in 1954 by British Petroleum and later nationalized by the PDRY. It is currently entirely state-owned and operated by the Aden Refinery Company (ARC). Initial capacity was about 150,000 to 170,000 b/d, but obsolescence of its equipment and other inefficiencies had reduced the refinery's capacity to about 110,000 b/d by 1990, and it sustained further significant damage during the civil war in 1994. The facility refines only about 70,000 b/d currently, producing an array of petroleum products (including gasoline, fuel oil, kerosene, and diesel fuel) mainly for the domestic market. The Marib refinery was constructed much later, in 1986, specifically to refine oil extracted in that block. Operated by Yemen Hunt Oil Company, its capacity is a much lower 10,000 b/d, and it mostly supplies the local market.

Under pricing arrangements introduced in early 1999, refineries pay the international price for crude oil delivered out of the government's share in production (through the Yemen Oil and Gas Corporation) and charge the Yemen Petroleum Corporation (YPC) international prices for refined products.[12] The Ministry of Finance transfers to the YPC the difference between its payments to the refineries and its sales (at administratively fixed prices for most products).

The renovation of the Aden refinery has been plagued with problems, including disagreements over how much capacity to restore. In May 1998 the Council of Ministers approved, in principle, the privatization of the refinery, and in January 2000 preparations for its privatization began.

The Role of Crude Oil in the Yemeni Economy

The bulk of Yemeni crude oil production has always been exported, and oil accounted for 80 to 90 percent of total exports over the period 1994–99 (Figure 2). Companies export their entire share, which averaged about 43 percent of production in the second half of the 1990s; the government sells about two-thirds of its share abroad. The second half of 1999 was an exceptionally favorable period for the Yemeni government, as both the government's oil share and oil prices increased; the rise in its share was mainly due to the high oil prices, which allowed the government to negotiate cost oil shares that were substantially lower than usual.

Over the course of the decade, Yemen's dependence on oil to generate exports and budget revenues increased quite sharply, both in absolute terms and compared with some other nonmajor oil-producing countries (Figure 2). By the second half of the 1990s, Yemen's dependence on oil exceeded, for example, that of the Syrian Arab Republic, and it was higher than Egypt's throughout the decade.[13] A simple simulation exercise highlights the extent to which Yemen has become more vulnerable to oil price movements. Table 2 shows the effect of a unit decrease in the export price of crude oil on government and export revenues for the countries in Figure 2 and for the Islamic Republic of Iran and for Saudi Arabia, assuming unchanged production levels and profit-sharing

[11]Masila is currently the country's most productive block. Production there started in July 1993 at an initial rate of 40,000 b/d and by 1999 reached 207,000 b/d on average. CanOxy reported that operating costs of the Masila fields were under $1 a barrel in 1999; it also invested about $60 million in continued field development for that year. However, if no new discoveries are made, Masila's production could begin to decline in 2001 by an average of 9,000 b/d a year. Marib, the country's second-largest and oldest production field, peaked in 1994 at 185,000 b/d; average production has since declined at a rate of about 14,000 b/d a year. This trend decline is expected to continue over the medium term, albeit at a slower pace. Without further investment for secondary or tertiary extraction, Marib's output could decline to levels below 40,000 b/d by 2005. Jannah is the most promising block of those that emerged in the late 1990s. Production started in 1996 at about 4,000 b/d and rapidly rose to reach 48,000 b/d in 1999. Output rose further, to about 68,000 b/d in 2001, and to keep on increasing annually by 5,000 to 6,000 b/d for the near term. Shabwa came on stream in December 1997, and its output is expected to reach 27,000 b/d in 2000, from a current level of 17,000 to 18,000 b/d. This increase is owed to the development of two recently discovered fields on its tract, and this new level should be sustained in the near term. Some production took place in the Ayad block from 1988 to early 1990, when Technoexport operated the block. NPC took over in 1991 and resumed production in 1992 at a low level of 5,000 b/d. The civil war in Yemen caused the suspension of NPC's operations, and production (at a low rate of 1,000 b/d) resumed only in 1997, after amendment of the terms of agreement with the government. Given the difficult geological conditions in the Ayad tract, production is expected to decline steadily over the near term. Howarim, Block 32, is the sixth and latest block to produce oil in Yemen. As previously noted, it is operated by the Norwegian company DNO and came on stream in early 2001, with initial production from two wells in the Tasour field of about 5,000 to 7,000 b/d. Other exploration blocks (S1, S2, 9, and 15) yielded oil that added about 380 million barrels to recoverable reserves; production could start within a couple of years.

[12]The formulas used by the two refineries differ. YPC pays the Marib refinery average monthly prices quoted on the Mediterranean market; however, it pays the ARC daily prices quoted by Platts Marketscan News from the Rotterdam market, plus a premium of $17 a ton. The premium supposedly reflects remuneration for shipping services but may also include an explicit subsidy to compensate for the refinery's inefficiency.

[13]Data on government crude oil revenues for Egypt (measured by crude oil receipts of the state petroleum company) were not available for fiscal years 1989/90, 1991/92, and 1992/93 (the data reported in Figure 2 correspond to fiscal years). For both Syria and Yemen, the fiscal year is the same as the calendar year; for Egypt, 1990 refers to data for fiscal year 1989/90, and so on.

Figure 2. Republic of Yemen and Selected Comparators: Crude Oil Exports and Revenue[1]

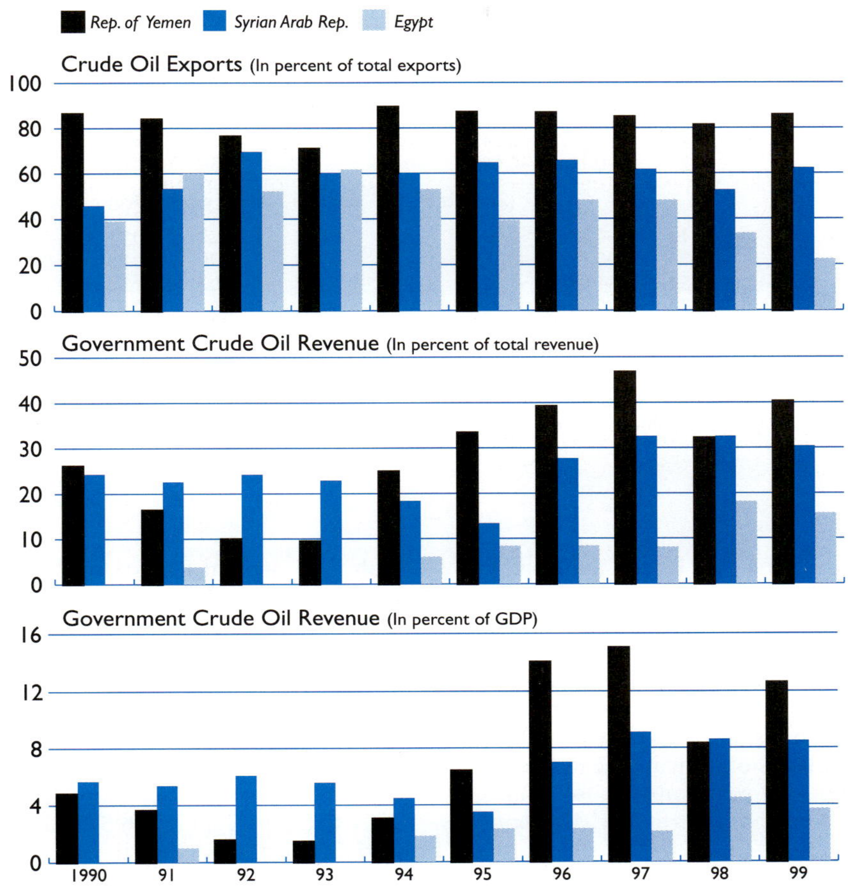

Sources: Ministry of Oil and Mineral Resources; IMF staff estimates.
[1]Comparator countries are nonmajor oil exporters in the Middle East region.

arrangements for each year. For example, a one-dollar drop in the oil price in 1999 would have resulted in a drop in budget revenue of 0.68 percent of GDP in Yemen, more than in any other country in the sample except Saudi Arabia. It would have reduced exports by 1.67 percent of GDP, considerably more than for any of the other sample countries.

More generally, Table 3 summarizes key volatility measures of oil-related macroeconomic aggregates for Yemen and the other countries in Table 2, and for Jordan, a non-oil exporter in the region. Terms-of-trade volatility in the 1990s was much higher for the oil exporters than for Jordan; the difference is clearly due to volatility in oil prices. Yemen's terms-of-trade volatility was similar to that of other oil exporters in the region but was associated with higher-than-average income volatility. Indeed, in Yemen as in Iran, the volatility of GDP is not much below that of the terms of trade; for Saudi Arabia and Egypt, in contrast, GDP is far less volatile than the terms of trade.[14] Yemen's terms-of-trade variability is also associated with relatively higher volatility of government rev-

[14]Unstable correlation patterns between trade price indices and output have often been observed in data for both developed and developing countries. For example, see Backus and Crucini (2000).

Table 2. Sensitivity to Oil Price Changes, 1990–99
(In percent of GDP)

	1990	1991	1992	1993	1994	1995	1996	1997	1998	1999
(1) Effect of US$1 decrease in the oil export price on budget revenues[1]										
Egypt	n.a.	–0.05	n.a.	n.a.	–0.12	–0.16	–0.14	–0.11	–0.31	–0.36
Iran	–0.45	–0.44	–0.46	–1.51	–1.09	–0.98	–0.81	–0.81	–0.65	–0.67
Saudi Arabia	–1.46	–1.74	–1.7	–1.71	–1.54	–1.43	–1.32	–1.57	–1.4	–1.12
Syria	–0.26	–0.3	–0.34	–0.37	–0.28	–0.21	–0.37	–0.5	–0.76	–0.53
Yemen	–0.23	–0.18	–0.08	–0.09	–0.2	–0.38	–0.69	–0.81	–0.71	–0.68
(2) Effect of US$1 decrease in the oil export price on exports[1]										
Egypt	–0.18	–0.31	–0.26	–0.28	–0.23	–0.22	–0.21	–0.18	–0.15	–0.11
Iran	–0.98	–0.78	–0.75	–1.12	–1.23	–0.96	–0.85	–0.84	–0.84	–0.74
Saudi Arabia	–1.58	–1.88	–1.96	–2.33	–2.3	–2.02	–1.58	–1.54	–1.82	–1.48
Syria	–0.72	–0.78	–0.92	–0.93	–0.81	–0.91	–0.83	–0.86	–0.88	–0.83
Yemen	–0.66	–0.89	–0.75	–1.12	–2.9	–2.55	–1.78	–1.59	–1.62	–1.67

Source: IMF staff estimates.

[1]Assumes unchanged production and sharing patterns between the government and oil companies. Because of different classifications for each country, the results should only be interpreted as broadly indicative of trends.

enue from oil than in Syria and Egypt, and high oil price variability could therefore have a greater negative impact on Yemen. In part, this reflects the fact that, under the cost-sharing agreements with the oil companies, oil revenue accruing to the government does not change linearly with oil prices. The lower the oil price, the more oil is needed to pay for oil production costs, and thus less oil is available to the government. Hence falling oil prices also cause a fall in oil volumes received by the government. The opposite holds true for rising oil prices.

Fluctuations in real gross domestic income (RGDI) are another way to capture the impact of oil price volatility on the Yemeni economy, adjusting fluctuations in real gross domestic product (RGDP) for terms-of-trade effects (see IMF, 2000):

$$RGDI = RGDP + \textit{terms-of-trade effect}.$$

The terms-of-trade effect adjusts the volume of production, measured by RGDP, for changes in the purchasing power of income generated by that production.[15] Simple calculations show that in 1990–99 the volatility of RGDI reached 0.23, or more than double RGDP volatility. In 1998, following the large drop in oil prices, the 30 percent decline in the terms of trade for Yemen was associated with a 15 percent decline in RGDI. The 61 percent improvement in the terms of trade the following year led to a 59 percent increase in RGDI (changes in RGDP for these two years were 5.3 percent and 3.8 percent, respectively).

Recent episodes illustrate Yemen's growing budgetary vulnerability. The collapse in oil prices in 1998 was accompanied by a dramatic decline in government export revenue from 15 percent of GDP in 1997 to 8.5 percent in 1998. In that instance, because of rising cost oil shares, the price decline was aggravated by a 17 percent reduction in the government share of the total volume of oil production. By the same token, in 1999, with the rapid rise in oil prices and an increasing government share in oil production, oil export revenue reached 12.7 percent of GDP. The 1998–99 swing in prices also pointed to costs in adjusting expenditure. Given Yemen's limited access to foreign financing, avoiding inflationary deficit financing requires sharp adjustments to expenditure in times of low oil prices. Yet much expenditure is already predetermined by long-term decisions and cannot be cut at short notice. In 1998 the government coped with the unexpected revenue shortfall by stopping development projects on an ad hoc basis, not always consistent with spending priorities. Moreover, wage increases were delayed and granted only after the recovery of oil prices in 1999. Although difficult to quantify, the economy likely suffered costs, for example from the unavailability of unfinished schools and infrastructure as well as more indirect effects on investment and saving.

[15]In other words, the terms-of-trade effect = $NX/P - (X/Px - M/Pm)$, where NX is the nominal trade balance, P is a price deflator for the trade balance (the consumer price index is used here as a proxy), X and M are nominal exports and imports, respectively, and Px and Pm are their respective price deflators.

Table 3. Oil-Related Volatility in the Economy, Compared with Other Oil Exporters in the Region
(In millions of Yemeni Rials)

	Crude Export Price[1]	Terms of Trade[1]	Oil Exports, Share of GDP[2]	Budget Revenues from Crude Oil, Share of GDP[2]	Real GDP[1]
			(Major oil exporters)		
Saudi Arabia	0.17	0.16	3.7	4.7	0.05
Iran	0.18	0.2	3.7	5.5	0.12
			(Other oil exporters)		
Egypt	0.2	0.31	1.4	1.2	0.1
Syria	0.17	0.1	1.9	1.9	0.16
Yemen	0.18	0.17	11.6	5.2	0.1
			(Non-oil exporters)		
Jordan	...	0.07	...	...	0.15

Source: IMF staff estimates.

[1]The volatility for crude export price, terms of trade, and real GDP was calculated as the standard deviation of the natural logarithms of the corresponding annual values over the period 1990–99.

[2]The volatility for the GDP shares of oil exports and budget oil revenues was calculated as the standard deviation of the corresponding annual values.

Prospects for Gas Production

Yemen's proven natural gas reserves are about 15 trillion cubic feet,[16] or roughly 1 percent of the Middle East total. So far, however, few facilities for recovering and utilizing gas associated with oil-producing wells have been installed. Liquefied petroleum gas (LPG) equivalent in energy content to about 30,000 b/d of crude oil is currently produced in the Marib block each year, fully covering domestic consumption.

After the civil war, the government signed a joint contract establishing the Yemen Liquefied Natural Gas Company, a partnership of Hunt, Exxon, Yukong, and Total of France with the public General Gas Corporation of Yemen, which retained 26 percent of the venture. The project stipulates the construction of a two-train liquefaction plant with a capacity of 5.3 million tons per year, and facilities for supplying the liquefied gas to local power stations and industrial factories. The initial expenditure is estimated at about $2.6 billion but could reach $5 billion if the cost of shipping the LPG to foreign markets is factored in. In addition, a gas line with a capacity of 100 million to 250 million cubic feet a day is to be constructed to supply the capital, Sana'a, with gas for local consumption, and the maximum possible volume of gas is to be extracted for both domestic consumption and export. The agreement between the government and the foreign companies with holdings in the project is set to expire 25 years after the start of exports.

The launching of the LPG project has been delayed so far by a lack of secured markets in which to sell the gas. The East Asian crisis in 1997–98 temporarily dimmed the prospects of finding markets for LPG in that region. Even with the upturn of the economic situation in East Asia, however, Yemen faces strong competition from Oman and Qatar, which already have LPG infrastructure in place, with room to expand existing plants, if necessary. However, despite the fact that no definite gas sales contracts have yet been signed, Yemen LPG recently decided to invite bids for the execution of the project (including the plant, pipeline, and long-lead items) starting in 2001. Three years would be needed to complete construction of the plant.

External Debt

Of the many burdens inherited by the unified Yemen, the crushing external debt was among the

[16]About 13.5 trillion cubic feet in the form of associated and nonassociated gas is concentrated in the Marib block; the rest is found in the Jannah block. Recent discoveries in Block S1 could add some 2 trillion cubic feet to this stock.

heaviest. By the end of 1990, unified Yemen's medium- and long-term external public and publicly guaranteed debt amounted to an estimated $9.9 billion (equivalent to 106 percent of GDP; Table 4). Of this, $6.4 billion (valued at the official exchange rate) was owed to member countries of the former Council of Mutual Economic Assistance (CMEA), with Russia accounting for 97 percent.[17] Yemen's debt-service obligations for 1990 were estimated at $696 million (equivalent to 47 percent of exports of goods and nonfactor services) on a commitment basis. However, actual debt-service payments were on the order of $426 million, as debt service to the former CMEA and certain Middle Eastern countries and financial institutions had been in abeyance since mid-1990.

In 1991 the government began to explore the possibilities for normalizing the arrears situation and obtaining debt relief. Following the temporary interruptions in 1990, debt-service payments to all regional multilateral institutions were resumed. The government's policy was to fully service its contractual obligations to international multilateral creditors and to give debt-servicing priority to those bilateral and regional multilateral creditors who continued to provide resources for development.[18] For the former CMEA creditors, the policy was to seek a write-off of all obligations relating to the military debt of the former PDRY and a rescheduling of principal and a write-off of interest obligations on civilian debt.[19]

In 1993 Germany forgave Yemen's $46 million debt to the former German Democratic Republic, but there were no negotiations with Middle Eastern or other former CMEA countries, except Russia, to seek ways to address Yemen's external indebtedness. Although an agreement was reached with the Russian authorities in early 1993 on the magnitude of the ruble stock of debt, differences persisted over the currency and exchange rate to be used in valuing and servicing the debt. In late 1994 Russia offered to cancel Yemen's debt in return for a cash payment equivalent to 10 percent of the stock of debt outstanding plus the accumulated interest arrears, valued at the exchange rate at the time the debt was contracted. Although the Yemeni government wished to resolve the Russian debt issue, the financial resources available at the time or in prospect were not sufficient to meet those terms.

In 1994, all debt service to multilateral creditors became current, but shortfalls continued in debt-service payments to bilateral creditors.[20] By the end of 1995, Yemen's public and publicly guaranteed external debt (including capitalized interest) had risen to about $11.0 billion, or 170 percent of GDP, of which $6.8 billion was owed to Russia. Over the same period, the stock of official external arrears reached an estimated $6.4 billion, of which $4.8 billion consisted of arrears to Russia.

In February 1996 the government requested debt relief from its Paris Club bilateral creditors and intensified its efforts to reach an agreement on debt relief with Russia and other bilateral official and commercial creditors. On September 24, 1996, the Paris Club creditors reached an agreement with Yemen on a flow rescheduling on Naples terms.[21] The debt relief applied to medium- and long-term public and publicly guaranteed external debt contracted before the January 1, 1993, cutoff date and entailed a 67 percent reduction in the net present value of consolidated debt, encompassing outstanding debt-service arrears as of the end of August 1996 and obligations falling due between September 1, 1996, and June 30, 1997.[22] This provided debt-service relief in the amount of $93 million for the remaining months of 1996. The participating creditor countries also agreed in principle to consider the matter of Yemen's debt-service payments falling due after June 30, 1997, and relating to loans contracted before January 1, 1993.

Following the September 1996 Paris Club meeting, the Yemeni authorities communicated to all other bilateral creditors requests to negotiate debt relief on terms at least as favorable as those granted by the Paris Club creditors. In particular, intense direct contacts with Russia were initiated in late 1996.[23]

On September 17, 1997, Russia reached an agreement with the Paris Club creditors on its participation in the Paris Club and, in line with the provisions of the agreement, agreed to provide debt relief to Yemen on Paris Club terms. The agreement applied to the totality of Russian claims on Yemen, including

[17]The debt of the former PDRY to the former Soviet Union was inherited by the unified Yemen and Russia, respectively.

[18]Given the difficult external debt position, the government's external borrowing policy was to avoid new borrowing on commercial terms, to carefully consider any new concessional borrowing, and to provide government guarantees only on supplier credits for food imports.

[19]Debt obligations to the former CMEA creditors were viewed largely as "political" rather than "economic" debt.

[20]External debt-service obligations during 1994–95 were estimated at $1.8 billion on a commitment basis, but only $205 million was paid.

[21]The participating creditor countries were Denmark, France, Germany, Italy, Japan, the Netherlands, the United Kingdom, and the United States.

[22]The 1996 agreement did not include late interest; by the end of 1996 this amounted to $542 million, 90 percent of which was owed to Russia.

[23]By the end of 1996, the stock of Yemen's external debt stood at $11.1 billion, or 173 percent of GDP, and the stock of external arrears reached $7.0 billion. Debt to Russia, evaluated at the loan contracting exchange rate of 0.6 ruble to the dollar, accounted for 62 percent of Yemen's total debt and 77 percent of its amortization and interest arrears.

Table 4. Balance of Payments, 1990–99

(In millions of U.S. dollars)

	1990	1991	1992	1993	1994	1995	1996	1997	1998	1999
Current account	–292	–849	–1,091	–1,248	366	183	106	23	–230	195
Current account excluding oil company transactions	–370	–669	–516	–520	375	–135	–143	–153	–541	–193
Goods and services	–1,080	–1,361	–1,648	–1,837	–173	–422	–401	–602	–1,124	–464
Trade balance	–341	–700	–796	–920	302	–11	–31	–133	–727	25
Exports, f.o.b.	1,384	1,197	1,095	1,167	1,824	1,937	2,263	2,274	1,501	2,464
Of which										
Crude oil	1,203	1,011	819	834	1,615	1,735	1,976	1,945	1,229	2,131
Imports, c.i.f.	–1,726	–1,897	–1,891	–2,087	–1,522	–1,948	–2,294	–2,407	–2,228	–2,440
Of which										
Food	–554	–550	–489	–499	–427	–687	–915	–916	–787	–807
Of which										
Wheat and flour imports	. . .	. . .	. . .	. . .	–274	–433	–617	–484	–374	–378
Services, net	–739	–661	–852	–917	–475	–411	–370	–470	–398	–489
Income	–454	–566	–514	–478	–579	–499	–682	–631	–359	–655
Of which										
Oil company profits	–284	–290	–265	–244	–393	–324	–541	–554	–301	–599
Interest income, net	22	25	17	6	4	16	29	47	40	43
Current transfers	1,241	1,078	1,071	1,067	1,117	1,104	1,188	1,256	1,254	1,314
Of which										
Workers' remittances, net	1,071	841	989	1,013	1,043	1,064	1,123	1,157	1,191	1,223
Capital and financial account	356	88	–36	74	–641	–876	–397	34	–207	–74
Financial account excluding oil company transactions	84	–390	–754	–829	–657	–626	–123	109	–11	364
Oil sector direct investment, net	–131	282	718	903	16	–218	–60	–138	–267	–319
Trade credits, net	. . .	–12	12	–51	29	36	104	–16	–117	–119
Medium- and long-term loans, net	84	–678	–762	–771	–685	–694	–521	–66	–64	27
Private capital, net	. . .	. . .	. . .	. . .	. . .	. . .	80	255	240	337
Errors and omissions[1]	–129	–42	–156	165	–504	655	–334	60	–27	199
Financing	65	803	1,283	1,008	779	38	625	–116	463	–320
Net reserves, official and banks (increase –)	–205	–158	380	99	–79	–713	–37	–297	317	–459
Official net reserves	44	–272	332	144	–149	–260	–294	–27	330	–467
Commercial banks net reserves	–249	114	48	–45	69	–453	257	–270	–13	8
Memorandum items:										
Current account including grants (percent of GDP)	–3.1	–10.7	–13.2	–16.1	5.6	2.8	1.7	0.3	–3.7	2.9
Of which										
Official grants (percent of GDP)	1.2	1.6	0.5	0.4	1.1	0.6	0.9	1.4	0.9	1.3
Central bank own gross foreign reserves[3]	424	680	323	147	357	525	937	1,152	853	1,351
(Months of imports)[4]	2.8	4.2	2.2	0.9	2.9	3.1	4.6	5.3	4.2	6.0
Official external debt[5]	9,915	10,323	10,541	10,735	10,876	11,017	11,135	5,359	5,373	5,490
Official external debt (percent of GDP)[5]	105.7	129.5	127.9	138.5	167.1	170.1	173.2	81.2	85.3	80.4
Debt service (percent of exports of goods and services)[5]										
Obligation basis	46.7	91.3	89.1	80.8	46.8	42.1	31.9	12.6	17.0	10.5
Actual	28.6	17.9	17.2	13.2	3.3	6.6	8.7	10.3	14.0	8.3
Change in outstanding Fund credit (US$ millions), increase (+)	. . .	. . .	. . .	. . .	. . .	. . .	120.6	129.8	84.5	73.5

Sources: Central Bank of Yemen; and IMF staff estimates and projections.

[1]For the period until 1996, includes private capital.

[2]Represents full settlement of overdue obligations to non-Paris Club official bilateral creditors under discussion to ensure comparable treatment and commercial debt subject to IDA debt buyback.

[3]Includes central bank SDR holdings, foreign exchange held abroad, foreign securities, gold, silver, and foreign currencies, excludes commercial bank required foreign exchange reserves with the central bank against their foreign currency deposits.

[4]Imports are c.i.f. for current year and exclude oil sector imports.

[5]Public- and publicly guaranteed debt including central bank foreign liabilities. Debt and debt service reflect the 1996 and 1997 Paris Club reschedulings, including the 80 percent upfront discount provided by the Russian Federation.

capitalized interest. Also, for purposes of treatment within the Paris Club, the agreement entailed an 80 percent upfront discount to be applied on the date of signature of an Agreed Minute.[24] The Agreed Minute negotiated in November 1997 between Yemen and its Paris Club creditors (including Russia) provided a 67 percent reduction (in net present value terms) of consolidated public and publicly guaranteed external debt contracted before January 1, 1993, and encompassing outstanding debt-service arrears as of the end of October 1997 (including late interest); principal due from November 1, 1997, up to October 31, 2000; and interest obligations (excluding late interest) falling due from July 1, 1999, to October 31, 2000.[25] This provided immediate debt relief in the amount of $6.0 billion, of which $5.9 billion was for arrears reduction.

In addition, the authorities requested assistance under the IDA Debt Reduction Facility in executing buybacks of the remaining commercial debt, which had been in default since 1991. Yemen's total commercial debt eligible for the IDA facility amounted to $695 million, of which $415 million consisted of principal and the rest of interest arrears. Of the principal, about $342 million was owed to Russian creditors and the rest to creditors from 51 other countries. Under the proposed buyback operation, all interest arrears were to be forgiven. The principal arrears were to be bought back at a fixed price after an initial reduction of 80 percent was applied to the stock of Russian commercial debt in line with the provisions of the September 17, 1997, agreement on Russia's participation in the Paris Club.[26] A grant in the amount of $15.1 million was approved in November 1999, and a buyback offer of 10 cents on the dollar of outstanding principal was launched.[27]

The multiyear debt relief provided under the 1997 Paris Club rescheduling substantially reduced Yemen's external debt burden. Total official external debt declined from $11.1 billion (173 percent of GDP) at the end of 1996 to $5.5 billion (80 percent of GDP) by the end of 1999, and the stock of amortization and interest arrears was reduced from $7.0 billion to $1.2 billion.[28] Over the same period, external debt-service obligations declined from 32 percent of exports of goods and nonfactor services to 11 percent.

In early 2000 the government undertook a debt sustainability analysis in collaboration with IMF and World Bank staffs. The analysis was based on the stock of public and publicly guaranteed external debt outstanding as of the end of 1999 and assumed full use of traditional debt relief mechanisms, in particular a stock-of-debt operation on Naples terms in the near future. The results indicate that Yemen's external debt position would remain sustainable over the medium term, with the stock of debt and the ratio of debt-service payments to exports of goods and nonfactor services projected to decline further (after taking into account expected new borrowing), to $5.4 billion (64 percent of GDP) and 7.8 percent, respectively, by 2005. The analysis also indicated that Yemen would not be eligible for special assistance under the enhanced Highly Indebted Poor Countries Initiative.

[24]Determination of the rate of discount was based on the fact that Yemen is an IDA-only country (that is, it is eligible for World Bank Group borrowing only from that organization's concessional lending affiliate, the International Development Association), for which Russia was the largest military creditor among the Paris Club creditors. Russia's agreement to the discount was based on the official Soviet Gosbank exchange rate of 0.6 ruble to the dollar and a conversion rate of the transferable ruble (in which the original claims were denominated) of 1 ruble to the dollar.

[25]As of the end of 1999, the bilateral agreements implementing the Agreed Minute had been signed with all Paris Club creditors except France.

[26]This ensured comparable treatment with the official debts, included in the Paris Club agreement, owed by the government of Yemen to the Russian government. As a consequence, the effective buyback price for the "Russian debt" component of this operation was 2 cents on the dollar of the principal amount of eligible debt.

[27]Of this amount, $1 million was intended for incidental costs related to closing the operation, auditing the records, and protecting against exchange rate fluctuations.

[28]Implementation of the commercial debt buyback operation would further reduce the stock of external debt-service arrears to $760 million, which represents arrears to non–Paris Club bilateral creditors from whom the Yemeni authorities have requested debt relief on terms comparable with those obtained from the Paris Club.

III Macroeconomic Policy During 1990–99

The macroeconomic policy mix in Yemen in the first half of the 1990s differed radically from that in the second. Unification of the YAR and the PDRY in 1990 joined two countries each of which already faced considerable macroeconomic policy challenges of its own in the late 1980s. The budget deficits of the YAR ranged from 15 to 20 percent of GDP in 1988 and 1989, about two-thirds of which were financed by the central bank, keeping inflation in double digits. In the centrally planned economy of the PDRY, the fiscal deficit exceeded 50 percent of GDP in both 1988 and 1989, of which 25 to 30 percent was domestically financed. (Price controls kept official inflation subdued, however.) Unification added new problems related to the merger of the two civil services and tax systems as well as the large number of publicly operated enterprises in the southern governorates. Since unification had resulted from negotiation between two sovereign governments, each of which received equal weight in the new joint government, many conflicts inherent in the different economic philosophies were resolved only after the 1994 civil war.[29] The Gulf crisis of 1990 also added strains to both public and private financial balances in the early 1990s, with the return of workers from the Gulf countries and the drying up of most external financial assistance. Faced with financial crisis, after some early price liberalization efforts during 1990–91, the authorities centered the macroeconomic policy mix in the first half of the decade around attempts to manage financial imbalances through direct control of the economy, affecting in particular imports, the exchange rate, interest rates, and investment. The attempt to defend the nominal exchange rate led to a sharp appreciation in terms of the real effective exchange rate in the first half of the 1990s (Figure 3). As it became increasingly clear that multiple exchange rates and foreign exchange controls were intensifying the negative impacts of external shocks, in 1993–94 the authorities took some partial steps to achieve positive real interest rates and more realistic exchange rates.

Figure 3. Real and Nominal Effective Exchange Rates
(Index, August 1996 = 100)

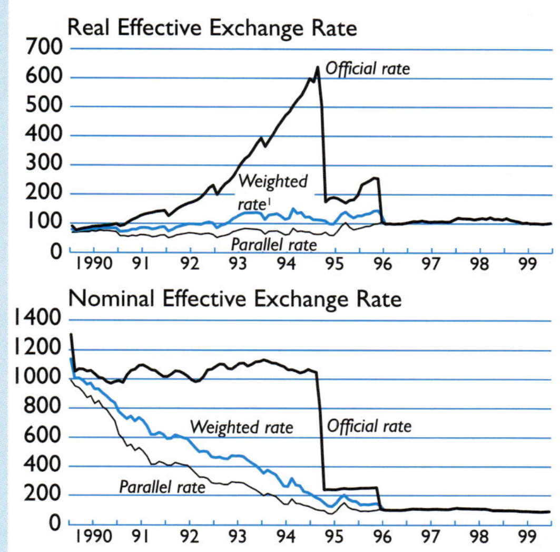

Source: IMF, *Information Notice System.*
[1]Derived by applying assumptions about the shares of various external transactions taking place at either the parallel or the official exchange rate.

However, it was only during 1995–99 that the implementation of the reform program, with assistance from the IMF and the World Bank, slowly transformed the economy into one of the more open and market oriented in the region. This process was supported by rising oil revenue and the return of internal and external stability. Efforts to improve fiscal balances were essential to these achievements, as was

[29]In this respect, the Yemeni experience differs from German unification. In Germany, practically all laws and regulations of the market economy of the Federal Republic of Germany were immediately adopted in the formerly centrally planned east, and many high-ranking East German civil servants lost their jobs.

Figure 4. Government Revenue from Oil and Taxes

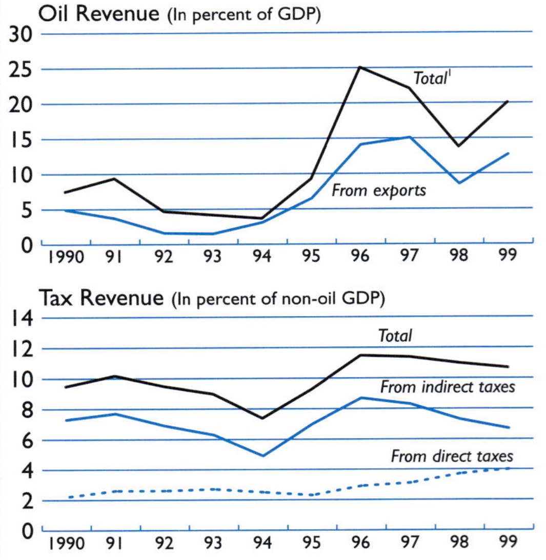

Source: Data provided by the Yemeni authorities.
[1]Net of petroleum subsidies.

Figure 5. Customs Revenue
(In percent)

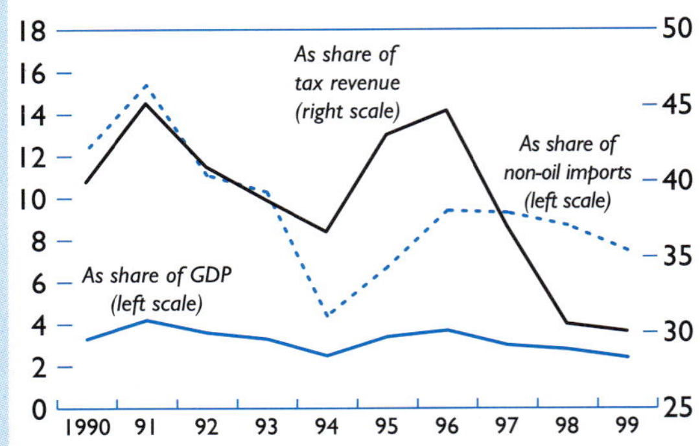

Source: Data provided by the Yemeni authorities.

the adoption of a unified floating exchange rate system, which helped to broadly stabilize the real exchange rate at levels well below the earlier peaks. However, the large swing in oil prices in 1998 and 1999 served as a reminder of the fragility of macroeconomic balances in a country that depends heavily on revenue from crude oil exports. The government's ongoing reform program therefore aims at preserving a larger share of the oil revenue to cushion swings in oil prices, and at enhancing growth of the non-oil economy by encouraging investment and improving education.

Crisis, Controls, and Stagnation: Macroeconomic Policies During 1990–94

Public Finances

Between 1990 and 1994, limited efforts were made to address Yemen's severe structural fiscal problems. Large and rising implicit subsidies for domestic petroleum products and wheat imports weighed heavily on public finances, the customs base was eroding, and taxes collected on goods and services were declining as a percentage of GDP (Figures 4 and 5). An already large civil service was granted large wage increases, albeit below levels that would generate rampant inflation. The resulting financial pressures motivated the maintenance of controls, which in turn further aggravated the fiscal imbalances and deterred private sector activity. After 1994 the newly constituted government was thus left with a large backlog of economic reforms as well as the task of repairing the physical damage of the war and mending the rift between north and south.

The large fiscal deficits were at the core of the severe internal and external imbalances in 1990–94 (Table 1; Figure 6). With the exception of 1991, the deficit on a commitment basis remained above 12 percent of GDP between 1990 and 1994. Because loan disbursements dried up almost entirely in the years after the Gulf crisis of 1990 and the dissolution of the Soviet Union, these deficits were largely financed by the accumulation of external arrears or were simply monetized, and inflation accelerated from 34 percent in 1990 to 71 percent in 1994.

Overall revenue dwindled from 20 percent of GDP in 1990 to 13 percent in 1994 (Table 5). Both declining oil revenue and declining tax revenue contributed to these developments. Oil revenue suffered from the decline in oil prices, the impact of the multiple exchange rate system, and the rising importance of domestic refining. Oil and gas revenue, which by the time of unification amounted to 7.5 percent of GDP and 40 percent of budget revenue, deteriorated after peaking at 9.4 percent of GDP in 1991. In 1994 oil revenue was only 3.7 percent of

Figure 6. Fiscal Balance and Civil Service Wage Bill

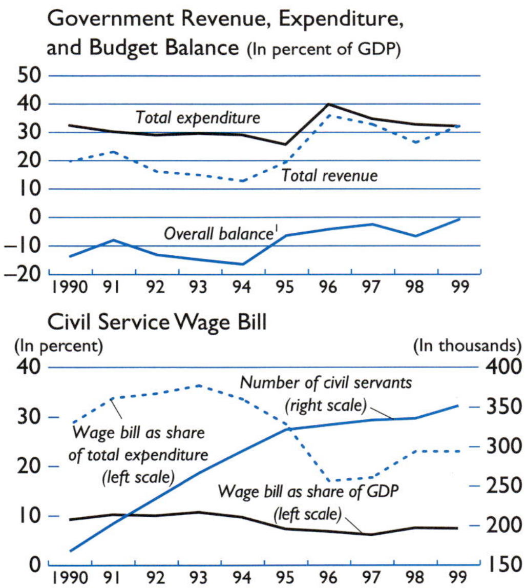

Source: Data provided by the Yemeni authorities.
[1]On a commitment basis, excluding grants.

GDP and represented only 30 percent of budget revenue.

Some of the decline in oil revenue can be explained by the fall in oil prices from $22 a barrel in 1990 to $15 a barrel in 1994. In addition, oil production at Marib, Yemen's major field in the early 1990s, fell by 10 percent in 1992 following technical problems. The widening gap between the market-based parallel exchange rate and the official exchange rate also contributed to the decline of oil revenue as a share of GDP.[30] Receipts were credited to the budget at the official exchange rate and thus assumed a declining share of the overall economy, in which most other external transactions took place at the parallel rate. The revenue loss to the budget resulting from use of the official rate also implied subsidies for those products whose importation was financed at the official rate, particularly wheat and petroleum products. The implicit subsidies, including those for domestic petroleum product sales, reached 13 percent of GDP in 1996.

Finally, following the Gulf crisis, the government increased oil deliveries to domestic refineries to substitute for previously imported petroleum products. At the same time, domestic petroleum prices were increased by 30 to 50 percent in 1990. As a result, domestic oil revenue surged in 1991 and continued to exceed export revenue until 1994, when exports increased as the Masila field came on stream for its first complete year and the Aden refinery was damaged during the civil war, disrupting domestic deliveries. Because domestic petroleum prices remained unchanged during 1992–94, their value dropped to about 10 percent of international prices (evaluated at the parallel exchange rate), reflecting a rising subsidy for domestic consumption of petroleum products. This policy implied increasing incentives for smuggling, further eroding the oil revenue base.

The fall over time in indirect tax revenue as a share of non-oil GDP was partially compensated by rising direct tax revenue as a share of non-oil GDP. The latter largely reflected the rising government wage bill as a share of GDP as well as bracket creep in the progressive tax system in a high-inflation environment.

Public expenditure was dominated by the heavy weight of the civil service wage bill (Figure 6). As noted earlier, the public workforces of the YAR and the PDRY were merged upon unification, and the pay scale in the south was adjusted to the higher level of the north. Moreover, many civil servants received allowances for moving from the former PDRY capital of Aden to Sana'a, the former YAR capital and capital of the unified country. The government also reinstated a policy that guaranteed employment to all university graduates and employees of public enterprises. In 1991–94 the government conceded sizable pay raises to public employees, which kept the wage bill on the order of 10 to 11 percent of GDP.[31] Between 1990 and 1993 the share of wages in total expenditure rose from 29 percent to 36 percent, largely at the expense of development expenditure, whose share fell from 27 percent to 12 percent. Defense spending ranged between 8.4 percent and 8.9 percent of GDP between 1990 and

[30]At the end of 1994, the official rate of YRls 12.01 to the dollar was about one-eighth of the parallel rate of YRls 103 to the dollar.

[31]Despite nominal increases on the order of 25 to 30 percent, wages did not keep pace with inflation, which accelerated from 34 percent to 71 percent in the same period. The fact that the wage bill as a share of GDP remained stable while real wages declined reflects the large differences between the GDP deflator and the consumer price index (CPI). The GDP deflator gave a higher weight to official transactions, recorded at the stable official exchange rate, than did the CPI. Comparisons with later years should be made cautiously because of substantial adjustments in the calculation of national accounts after the unification of exchange rates.

Table 5. Central Government Finance, 1990–99

(In percent of GDP)

	1990	1991	1992	1993	1994	1995	1996	1997	1998	Prel. 1999
Total revenue and grants	19.8	23.1	16.1	14.9	12.8	19.5	35.9	32.8	26.4	31.8
Total revenue	18.7	22.0	15.8	14.7	12.6	19.2	35.6	32.2	26.0	30.9
Oil and gas revenue	7.5	9.4	4.7	4.2	3.7	9.3	25.1	22.1	13.8	19.8
Crude oil exports	4.9	3.7	1.6	1.5	3.1	6.5	14.1	15.1	8.5	12.7
Domestic oil and gas[1]	2.6	5.7	3.1	2.7	0.5	2.9	11.0	7.0	5.2	7.1
Non-oil revenue	11.2	12.6	11.1	10.5	8.9	9.8	10.5	10.1	12.2	11.1
Tax revenue	8.2	9.2	8.8	8.5	6.9	8.0	8.4	8.2	9.2	8.0
Direct	1.9	2.3	2.4	2.5	2.4	2.0	2.1	2.2	3.1	3.0
Indirect	6.3	6.9	6.4	6.0	4.6	6.0	6.3	5.9	6.1	5.0
Nontax revenue	3.0	3.5	2.3	2.0	1.9	1.9	2.1	2.0	3.0	3.0
Grants (cash)	1.1	1.0	0.3	0.1	0.3	0.3	0.3	0.6	0.4	0.9
Total expenditure and net lending	32.3	30.1	28.9	29.5	29.0	25.6	39.8	34.7	32.7	32.1
Current expenditure	23.6	26.1	25.5	26.0	26.4	22.5	33.2	27.9	26.6	26.5
Civilian wages and salaries	9.2	10.2	10.0	10.7	9.7	7.3	6.8	6.1	7.5	7.4
Materials and services	1.9	2.0	2.4	1.7	1.8	1.5	2.3	2.9	3.0	3.1
Development O and M	0.0	0.0	0.0	0.0	0.0	0.0	0.0	0.2	0.2	0.2
Agriculture and road maintenance funds	0.0	0.0	0.0	0.0	0.0	0.1	0.3	0.3	0.3	0.2
Defense	8.4	8.9	8.9	8.3	9.7	6.7	5.6	6.0	6.1	5.8
Interest obligations[2]	2.4	2.9	1.9	2.6	2.9	1.5	3.3	2.3	3.7	4.1
Transfers and subsidies	1.7	2.2	2.4	2.7	2.3	4.9	14.6	9.3	5.2	5.1
Subsidies	0.0	0.0	0.0	0.0	0.0	3.4	13.0	7.7	3.0	2.5
Petroleum cash subsidies[1]	. . .	. . .	. . .	. . .	. . .	1.0	5.3	2.9	. . .	2.0
Wheat and flour subsidy[3]	0.0	0.0	0.0	0.0	0.0	2.3	7.4	4.5	3.0	0.4
Financial support electricity	0.0	0.0	0.0	0.0	0.0	0.0	0.3	0.3	0.0	0.0
Current transfers	1.7	2.2	2.4	2.7	2.3	1.5	1.6	1.6	2.2	2.7
Other current expenditure	0.0	0.0	0.0	0.0	0.0	0.4	0.3	0.7	0.5	0.6
Development expenditure	8.7	4.0	3.4	3.5	2.6	3.1	6.6	6.8	6.1	5.6
Net lending	0.0	0.0	0.0	0.0	0.0	0.0	0.0	0.0	0.0	0.0
Overall balance (commitment)	–12.4	–7.0	–12.8	–14.7	–16.2	–6.1	–3.9	–1.9	–6.3	–0.2
Overall balance (commitment, excluding grants)	–13.6	–8.0	–13.1	–14.8	–16.4	–6.4	–4.2	–2.5	–6.7	–1.2
Overall balance (cash)	–11.7	–5.6	–11.7	–13.9	–15.7	–5.2	0.6	–1.8	–7.9	–0.4
Financing	11.5	6.0	11.9	14.1	15.8	5.2	–0.7	1.8	7.9	0.0
External (net)	2.7	1.6	0.2	0.2	0.1	–0.2	0.4	0.3	1.2	2.3
Domestic (net)	8.8	4.4	11.7	13.9	15.7	5.3	–1.1	1.5	6.7	–2.3
Bank	8.8	4.4	11.7	13.9	15.7	5.1	–1.5	–0.1	3.3	–4.4
Central bank	9.1	4.1	11.3	14.0	16.1	4.6	–2.5	–3.4	3.1	–4.8
Commercial banks	–0.3	0.3	0.4	–0.2	–0.4	0.5	0.9	3.2	0.2	0.4
Nonbank	0.0	0.0	0.0	0.0	0.0	0.2	0.4	1.6	3.4	2.1
Pension funds	0.0	0.0	0.0	0.0	0.0	0.0	0.0	0.0	3.3	1.2
Public enterprises	0.0	0.0	0.0	0.0	0.0	0.0	0.0	0.0	0.0	0.6
Others	0.0	0.0	0.0	0.0	0.0	0.2	0.4	1.6	0.2	0.3
Discrepancy	–0.3	0.4	0.2	0.2	0.2	0.0	–0.1	0.0	0.0	–0.4
Memorandum items:										
Primary balance (commitment)[4]	–11.2	–5.1	–11.2	–12.2	–13.5	–4.9	–0.9	–0.1	–3.0	2.9
Public sector savings[5]	–4.9	–4.1	–9.7	–11.3	–13.9	–3.3	2.4	4.3	–0.6	4.4
Non-oil balance (commitment, excluding grants)	–18.5	–11.7	–14.7	–16.3	–19.6	–12.9	–18.3	–17.6	–15.2	–13.9
Tax revenue, as percent of non-oil GDP	9.5	10.2	9.5	9.0	7.4	9.3	11.5	11.4	11.0	10.7
Direct	2.2	2.6	2.6	2.7	2.5	2.3	2.9	3.1	3.7	4.0
Indirect	7.3	7.7	6.9	6.3	4.9	7.0	8.7	8.3	7.3	6.7
Taxes on goods and services	2.3	2.3	2.4	2.2	1.6	2.4	3.0	3.5	4.1	3.1
Custom duties, as percent of non-oil imports	12.3	15.4	11.1	10.3	4.4	6.7	9.4	9.3	8.7	7.5
Average oil price for government exports ($/bbl)	. . .	. . .	. . .	. . .	15.5	17.3	18.3	18.2	13.1	16.3
Net domestic oil revenue[6]	2.6	5.7	3.1	2.7	0.5	1.8	5.7	4.1	5.2	5.1
GDP (at market prices in billions of YRls)	122.1	144.8	183.9	227.7	292.3	488.5	702.1	852.9	855.9	1,063.6
Social expenditures (in percent of GDP)[7]	. . .	. . .	. . .	. . .	. . .	. . .	4.6	5.8	8.8	9.3

Sources: Ministry of Finance; Ministry of Planning; and IMF staff estimates.

[1] 1990–95: Revenues net of subsidies.

[2] Profit transfers from the Central Bank of Yemen were netted out against interest payments to the CBY until 1998.

[3] Until the unification of exchange rates, subsidies were implicit by applying a preferential exchange rate to wheat and flour imports.

[4] Revenue excluding grants, net of expenditures excluding interest obligations.

[5] Primary cash balance excluding grants and development expenditures.

[6] Domestic oil revenue net of cash petroleum subsidies.

[7] Comprises spending on wages, salaries, materials, services, capital in the education and health sectors, and spending by the social welfare fund.

1993, with a sharp increase to 9.7 percent of GDP in 1994 due to the civil war. Moreover, many of the money-losing public enterprises relied on government transfers, reflected in the rise of current transfers from 1.7 percent to 2.7 percent of GDP between 1990 and 1993.

Monetary and Exchange Rate Controls

To contain the spillovers from the fiscal imbalances to the external account, the authorities maintained a "hybrid" foreign exchange system. This involved a large and relatively free parallel exchange market—with occasional ad hoc attempts to tighten control over it—and a highly administered exchange system for certain (including official) transactions involving quantity rationing and a highly appreciated currency (see Section IV). Thus there was little scope to formulate an independent monetary policy in the period immediately following unification. Rapid expansion of net domestic assets was driven by the need to provide financing for the budget, given the absence of nonbank financing.

Commercial banks were reluctant to lend to the nongovernmental sector, given the absence of effective recourse within the legal system for the timely recovery of overdue loans. Accordingly, banks preferred to deposit their resources with the central bank for on-lending to the government, at a remuneration of 1.5 percentage points above the banks' average cost of funds.

The continued existence of separate interest rate structures after unification posed special problems for the monetary authorities. Although the authorities were seeking to establish a unified system based on the structure of the market-based former YAR, the National Bank of Yemen—the only commercial bank (state owned) in the South—was allowed to set its own rates as an interim measure. Statutory interest rates in this period were very low, and real rates were highly negative (Figure 7). This discouraged the mobilization of savings, facilitated inefficient consumption and investment choices, and put further pressure on the foreign exchange market. Indeed, foreign currency deposits doubled from 1991 to 1992, while Yemeni rial deposits increased by only 15 percent. Also, negative real interest rates continued to encourage financial disintermediation, as the absence of controls in the parallel financial market for rials spurred growth in this market at the expense of the banking sector.[32]

[32]The informal financial market was dominated by moneychangers, the largest of whom accepted deposits from the public (see Section IV).

Figure 7. Interest Rates
(In percent a year)

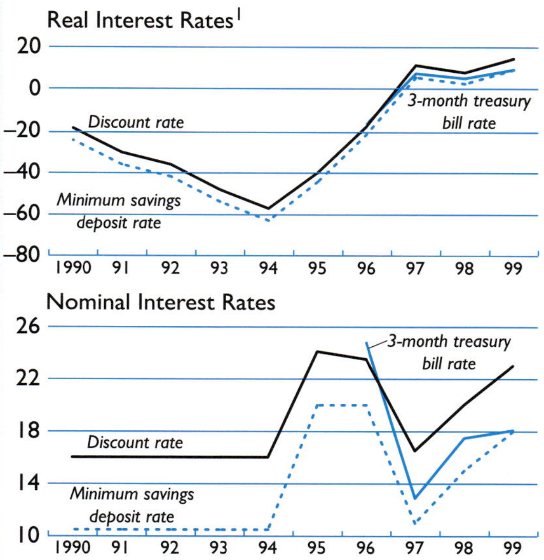

Source: Data provided by the Yemeni authorities.
[1]Nominal rates minus inflation, as measured by the consumer price index.

Partial Liberalization of the Exchange and Interest Rates

During 1993–94 economic structures became more unified and conducive to national macroeconomic policymaking, and the authorities increasingly recognized the need for strong corrective fiscal policy action, establishment of positive real interest rates, and unification of exchange rates at a realistic level. However, initial reform efforts remained partial, and extensive controls remained. In particular, the real appreciation of the currency accelerated, undercutting efforts to contain the fiscal and external imbalances. For example, faced with a growing gap between the free market parallel rate and various official rates in November 1994, the authorities introduced a "managed official parallel market rate" at YRls 84 to the dollar, to be "guided" by a committee of moneychangers and commercial bank representatives under the supervision of the central bank, taking into account market indicators. This attempt to manage the parallel market failed, however, and already by the end of 1994 the rial had depreciated on the unofficial parallel market to 100 to the dollar.

To allow a greater role of market forces in financial intermediation, the authorities took some steps to improve competitiveness in the banking sector. First, they adopted a more liberal policy toward licensing of bank branches, removing the monopoly of the National Bank of Yemen in the south. Second, the central bank began strengthening prudential regulation and supervision (see Section IV). In particular, the banking system's vulnerability to depreciation of the rial had to be addressed to prepare for liberalization of the exchange rate. The largest commercial bank, the Yemen Bank for Reconstruction and Development (YBRD), had built up sizable foreign currency deposits, but its net foreign assets position was negative. Unification of the exchange rate at a realistic level would thus trigger large valuation losses. This bank's problem was addressed by the government assigning most of this debt to the public sector enterprises for which the (foreign) credits had been opened, thus shifting the vulnerability to the corporate sector. The foreign liability position of the central bank was also large, mainly reflecting deposits from foreign governments prior to unification, outstanding liabilities related to oil imports, and short-term liabilities to foreign banks.

Reform and the Return of Stability and Growth During 1995–99

A new phase of postunification macroeconomic policymaking began in early 1995. By this time the political situation had stabilized, and the new government embarked upon a program of macroeconomic adjustment and structural reform with support from the World Bank and the IMF. The program included strong fiscal adjustment measures, liberalization of most interest rates, and reform of the exchange rate system, including in 1996 the elimination of the official exchange rate and unification of exchange rates at the free market level, and the adoption of a floating rate regime.

Fiscal improvements during the second half of the 1990s were the basis for the gradual return of some measure of macroeconomic stability to Yemen. Integrating the official and parallel exchange rates helped reduce the subsidy bill and, combined with rising government oil exports, strongly boosted revenue. As a result, the fiscal imbalance declined from 6 percent of GDP in 1995 to 2 percent in 1997. However, as a stark reminder of Yemen's oil dependence, macroeconomic stability suffered a blow in 1998 with the collapse of oil prices, and the budget deficit rose once again to 6 percent of GDP. The reverse outcome was then observed in 1999, when a surge in oil prices led to a balanced budget and a substantial strengthening of the external position.

Revenue

Total revenue increased from 19 percent of GDP in 1995 to 32 percent in 1999, in large part because of improving oil revenue. Following the enforcement problems encountered during the 1994 civil war, the government also improved its tax collection and introduced several simplifying reforms to tax and customs laws, which contributed to a rising ratio of tax revenue to non-oil GDP. Because of the rising oil share in GDP, the ratio of taxes to total GDP remained roughly flat.

Rising production and prices as well as the stepwise unification of exchange rates in July 1996 raised oil export revenue accruing to the budget from 3 percent of GDP in 1994 to 15 percent of GDP in 1997. The volume of crude oil available to the government for domestic deliveries and exports almost doubled between 1993 and 1997, partly because overall production rose, and partly because concession holders had recouped their investment costs, reducing their share in production. Moreover, the stepwise adjustment of the official exchange rates to the parallel market rate substantially raised the value of oil revenue recorded in Yemeni rials, while eliminating the implicit subsidization of certain economic activities resulting from preferred access to foreign exchange.

Domestic oil revenue increased from 3 percent of GDP in 1995 to 7 percent in 1999. Exceptionally high domestic revenue in 1996 resulted in large part from a settlement of excess cost recovery charges with one of the oil companies, yielding an amount equivalent to 2.3 percent of GDP. Rising international prices and the unification of the exchange rates also contributed. Although exchange rate unification removed one source of implicit subsidization, transactions among the government, oil refineries, and distributors remained opaque and involved nonmarket-based transfer prices and free inputs. Only beginning in 1999 was pricing of all wholesale transactions based on world prices.[33] Therefore domestic revenue has to be evaluated together with the subsidy payments to arrive at a clear picture of domestic efforts. As the memorandum item in Table 5 shows, the resulting measure of net domestic oil revenue has risen steadily over time.

Tax revenue rose strongly, to 11.5 percent of non-oil GDP in 1996, but then began to erode slowly, reaching 10.7 percent of non-oil GDP in 1999. The initial strengthening of tax revenue was a consequence of exchange rate unification, economic recov-

[33]As a result, the government is now indifferent between exporting oil and selling it to domestic refineries; meanwhile the implicit consumption and production subsidies have become transparent cash subsidies.

ery, and several tax reforms undertaken in 1995 and 1996 (see Section IV). Higher exchange rates applied to import valuation, and the recovery of the economy was followed by higher import volumes; these factors, together with the simplification of the tariff structure and concomitant improvements in customs administration, led to a rebound of customs revenue to more than 9 percent of non-oil imports in 1996. Taxes on goods and services also benefited from increased economic activity, a widening of the tax base, and a higher tax elasticity after some specific taxes were replaced with ad valorem taxes. Direct tax revenue rose with a simplification of the corporate income tax at a single 35 percent rate. After 1996, direct taxes and—until 1999—taxes on goods and services continued to rise faster than non-oil GDP, but a decline in customs revenue pulled down overall revenue growth. Direct taxes benefited from the rising share of government wages in GDP, improving business income tax revenue after the 1996 rate unification, improving economic conditions, and an increase in top tax rates in 1999. Taxes on goods and services grew strongly after their base was broadened in 1996, but fell as a share of non-oil GDP after the 1999 tax amendments changed a number of tax rates. The poor performance at customs likely reflects the rising importance of smuggling, continuing weaknesses in administration, and to a certain extent the elimination of import surcharges in 1998.

Expenditure

Large swings in government expenditure were driven by the move to unify exchange rates and by related subsidy reform. After the unification of exchange rates over 1995–96, the implicit subsidies on wheat, flour, and petroleum products through the below-market exchange rate were replaced by explicit cash subsidies. In 1996 these subsidies rose to 13 percent of GDP because of a widening gap between domestic and international prices. In later years, however, these subsidies declined when domestic prices were moved closer to world market prices, and wheat and flour subsidies were eliminated entirely by mid–1999 (see Section IV). The civil service wage bill declined to 6 percent of GDP in 1997 as wage increases were kept below inflation, and despite rising currency costs for foreign workers (mainly teachers) paid in foreign exchange. However, following large wage increases in 1998–2000, the civil service wage bill has recently been on the rise again. These increases largely reflected the implementation, phased in over three years, of a teachers' law passed by parliament in 1998 that granted 100 percent wage increases to workers in education, where the majority of civil servants are employed. Similar wage increases were granted to health workers. Defense spending declined from 6.7 percent of GDP in 1995 to less than 6 percent in 1999. Development expenditure doubled as a percentage of GDP in 1996, but was cut back in 1998 and early 1999 after the fall in oil prices.

Fiscal Balance

The financing of the government deficit through central bank credit remained a critical source of macroeconomic instability. Although disbursements of foreign grants and loans on the order of 2 percent of GDP resumed in 1996, the government continued to face large amortization obligations; hence net external financing remained small until rescheduling agreements were reached with Paris Club creditors in 1996–97. To develop sources of noninflationary financing and deepen the financial system, a market for treasury bills was introduced in 1995, and the central bank subsequently closed its term deposit facility for banks and pension funds in order to channel resources into this market (see Section IV). Thus, in 1996 and 1997 the government reduced its indebtedness to the central bank, financing its deficits by accumulating arrears to wheat importers as well as through increasing treasury bill sales to commercial banks and nonbanks. However, as oil revenue shrank dramatically in 1998, the government had to borrow 3 percent of GDP from the central bank, and the concomitant expansion in the money supply resulted in an immediate spurt of inflation. Fortunes were reversed in 1999, and inflation fell as rising crude oil revenues led to a balanced budget, permitting the government to reimburse almost 5 percent of GDP to the central bank.

Monetary and Exchange Rate Policy

The use of monetary policy instruments became more flexible, responding to macrofinancial conditions. In the context of the reform program, in 1995 the central bank unified the reserve requirement at a rate of 25 percent, without remuneration, for all rial deposits. This requirement was lowered to 15 percent in December 1996 and to 10 percent in December 1997. A rate of remuneration of 5 percent on these deposits was initiated in December 1996 and rose the following year to equal the benchmark deposit rate. In December 1997 the reserve requirement on foreign currency deposits was lowered from 25 percent to 15 percent, and the rate of remuneration was set at half a percentage point less than the rate received on the central bank's deposits abroad. The higher reserve requirements for foreign currency deposits and the much lower rate of remuneration on these deposits reflected the central bank's objective to stem the trend of increasing dollarization of the economy and to enhance the attractiveness of the rial as a store of value. Undoubtedly, however, such discriminatory measures induced capital flight. The effectiveness of reserve requirements as an instrument of monetary policy might have been hampered by the less than full implementation of the penalties for shortfalls. Although the central bank can impose a maximum daily penalty of 5 percent, in practice this figure lies in the 0.5 to 2.0 percent range. The central bank used credit ceilings as an instrument of monetary policy in the early postunification period, but this instrument was hardly effective then and subsequently lost all importance.[34]

Two sharp real depreciations took place in early 1995 and mid-1996 (Figure 3). The second of these reflects the nominal depreciation that occurred at the time of unification of the exchange rates. The first, however, was the result of a partial reform of the exchange rate system implemented at the time, including the elimination of special official rates and the depreciation of the only remaining official rate from YRls 12 to YRls 50 to the dollar.

With the move to a floating exchange rate system, which was maintained throughout the period, the rial broadly stabilized in real effective terms; some small appreciation in real terms between the end of 1996 and the end of 1999 partly reflected a reluctance to tolerate substantial variability in the exchange rate. Indeed, exchange rate stability remains, in the eyes of the public, the main yardstick of the success of government policy. Accordingly, through interest rate policy, moral suasion, and the regular auctioning of foreign exchange to moneychangers and banks, the central bank attempted to stabilize the exchange rate in times of turmoil. In part, its intervention also reflected an attempt to smooth sharp seasonal peaks in demand for foreign exchange (especially around the Ramadan and Hajj seasons), given the limited depth of the private market. For example, reflecting the impact of low oil prices on macroeconomic performance in 1998, the central bank employed its limited monetary tools to ease the pressure on the exchange rate. It raised the official benchmark interest rate (to 3.5 percent a year in real terms) and ended the remuneration on foreign currency deposits at the central bank, but still had to spend half of its reserves to limit the rial's depreciation during 1998 to 7 percent against the dollar. Only in early 1999 did the authorities allow a faster rate of depreciation, coupled with further interest rate tightening.

In light of sharply improved macroeconomic balances in the latter half of 1999, the central bank initiated a gradual lowering of benchmark interest rates. As a result, the rial showed a modest depreciation in real terms in 1999, reversing some of the appreciation of 1998.

Preserving the Oil Wealth: A Long-Term View of Yemen's Fiscal Policy Stance

For oil-exporting countries, the management of finite oil wealth adds to the complexity of fiscal policymaking. Yemen derives a significant share of government revenue from oil exports and oil-related economic activity. Unless further exploration activities result in new discoveries, however, most of the country's proven recoverable oil resources—estimated at 2.8 billion barrels in April 2000—will be depleted within 18 years.[35] Figure 1 in Section II showed the amount of crude oil accruing to the government, after subtraction of cost oil and the oil producer's profit share, between 1990 and 2020. Under these projections, the government's crude oil share was expected to peak in 2000 and drop steeply after 2009 with the exhaustion of the Marib field. Unless revenue from the non-oil economy replaces oil revenue in future years, achieving long-run sustainability implies saving a portion of today's oil revenue in the form of financial assets, human capital, or infrastructure. In practice, it is highly uncertain whether spending the country's oil wealth on education and infrastructure will boost growth sufficiently for the tax revenue generated from additional growth to sustain government spending.[36]

Fiscal policy decisions must rely on an estimate of oil wealth, that is, the present value of all future government revenue to be generated by extracting crude oil. However, calculating oil wealth at any given point in time is subject to considerable uncertainty. It depends notably on forecasts of future oil prices, oil production, and interest rates. Oil prices change in unpredictable ways. Statistical tests of their movements generally have difficulty rejecting the hypothesis that oil prices do not systematically return to a long-run average and that the current price is the

[34]For example, a ceiling on credit growth was set at 50 percent in 1996, a year in which credit actually fell. In early 1997 credit growth ceilings were once more set at 25 percent, and again these ceilings were not binding. The central bank has not renewed these ceilings since then, but prefers to keep open the option to impose new ceilings should extreme circumstances warrant them.

[35]Estimates of recoverable resources vary widely and are changing rapidly. In particular, a recent treaty settling border issues with Saudi Arabia may boost exploration activity and thus the likelihood of discovering additional resources. The following discussion should therefore be interpreted as only illustrative of broad orders of magnitude.

[36]A discussion of the relationship between sustainability and government investment policies can be found in Easterly and Fischer (1990).

best predictor of future prices.[37] As a result, small changes in the current price could lead to large changes in estimated oil wealth, because a price change today would lead to revisions in all future prices. New information on oil reserves, extraction rates, and discount factors as well as technological developments also affect estimates of a country's oil wealth and permanent income. Therefore, oil wealth estimates underlying long-run policy decisions must be adapted frequently to new information regarding prices, oil reserves, crude oil extraction rates, and long-run interest rates.

A simple rule to ascertain the long-run sustainability of consumption out of oil wealth can be derived from the permanent income theory of consumption.[38] This rule prescribes that, in each period, governments should consume at most the real interest they receive on their total wealth.[39] From the perspective of consumption possibilities, the permanent income model treats oil wealth and other forms of wealth as equivalent. Hence consumption in excess of permanent income would result in a decline in total wealth over time. In more practical terms, this concept of government wealth proxies the ability of governments to sustain current levels of spending in real terms. Preserving wealth thus means preserving the ability to deliver to future generations the same level of public services (health, education, and other services) available to the current generation.

The permanent income framework can be extended to account for growth of the population. Yemen's annual population growth exceeds 3 percent. If the government aims at preserving wealth per capita, it must adjust its consumption for the expanding population. The reason for maintaining wealth per capita is that it allows keeping the same stream of income per capita over time and thus constant government expenditure per capita. If it is assumed that the population will continue to grow at 3 percent a year, the government needs to save an additional 3 percent of wealth each year to keep wealth per capita at the same level. Returning to the example above, at a 4 percent real interest rate with a population growing at 3 percent a year, Yemen should consume only 1 percent of its wealth each year and save the remaining 3 percent interest earnings to keep wealth per capita constant.

Apart from oil and financial assets, the non-oil sector provides an additional source of income for the government. Revenue generated by a non-oil sector that is expanding in per capita terms could over time replace revenue from exploiting oil. In allocating consumption over time, the government should thus take into account the expected future growth in non-oil revenue. However, additional non-oil revenue must be generated by growth in non-oil GDP per capita, not by an increasingly heavy tax burden. The latter would not reflect growing overall resources but would simply change the distribution of wealth between the public and the private sector. Growth of the non-oil sector could be driven by investment in infrastructure or human capital, as well as by increased factor productivity. However, as outlined earlier, such investment would have to generate tax revenue sufficient to replace oil revenue in order to sustain fiscal spending. Since the impact of infrastructure and human capital investment on tax revenue is indirect and therefore difficult to ascertain, the subsequent discussion is largely limited to the conversion of oil wealth into financial wealth.

To analyze past Yemeni fiscal policy from an intertemporal perspective, this section concludes with a few calculations, based on a permanent income framework, to estimate sustainable consumption on the assumption that the government keeps wealth per capita derived from oil constant over time. These calculations do not consider how future growth of non-oil GDP per capita could enhance the government's revenue base (rather, they implicitly assume that non-oil revenue per capita remains constant), and thus they may understate sustainable consumption.[40] Optimal consumption is derived in each year (starting in 1990) for the current and future years, assuming that oil prices remain constant at current levels. For example, optimal consumption out of oil wealth for 1998 is derived under the assumption that oil prices from 1998 onward remain at $11.90 a barrel, Yemen's 1998 average oil export price. This assumption corresponds to the hypothesis that the current price is the best predictor of future prices, that is, that oil price shocks are permanent. Furthermore, the calculations assume that Yemen's oil wealth is limited to the amount of proven recoverable reserves estimated today (2.8 billion barrels). Other important assumptions are a 4 percent real interest rate and a population growth rate of 3 percent in 1999, de-

[37]Pindyck (1999) was able to reject the unit root hypothesis only after considering more than 70 years of data. Cashin, Hong, and McDermott (1999) find that petroleum price shocks are infinitely persistent. A survey of the stochastic properties of oil prices can also be found in Engel and Valdes (2000).

[38]The literature on this subject includes Tersman (1991); Liuksila, Garcia, and Bassett (1994); Chalk (1998); and Alier and Kaufman (1999).

[39]This assumes that a government is neither more nor less impatient to consume resources than implied by the interest rates prevailing on international capital markets.

[40]At 1999 wealth levels, assuming annual total factor productivity (TFP) growth of 1 percent would add about 1 percent of GDP to sustainable consumption. However, during the 1990s estimated TFP growth was negative (see Section VI).

clining to 2.5 percent in 2005 and 1.5 percent in 2050. The calculations also incorporate Yemen's initial net financial wealth, which is assumed to be equivalent to its foreign indebtedness. Under these assumptions, oil wealth at the beginning of 1999 stood at about 280 percent of 1999 GDP, or $1,080 per capita. Net total wealth, after subtracting external debt, was $13.3 billion, or $765 per capita.

The calculations show that, in the early 1990s, the level of consumption out of oil wealth, as a percentage of GDP, consistent with preserving oil wealth per capita was virtually nil. It would have been necessary to save almost the entire oil revenue to preserve wealth per capita, because population growth rates, partly reflecting the return of expatriates, were high and close to the assumed real interest rate of 4 percent. Moreover, the country entered unification with a debt stock of roughly $11 billion. As a result, sustainable consumption of oil wealth was only between 0.1 percent and 0.5 percent of GDP. The rescheduling agreement of 1996 reduced external debt by about one-third and, together with declining population growth rates and somewhat higher oil prices, permitted higher consumption out of oil wealth after 1996. Sustainable consumption levels rose to 1.8 percent of GDP in 1997. However, the example of 1998 clearly shows that revaluing oil wealth at current prices would necessitate large adjustments of consumption levels. The fall in oil prices in 1998 resulted in a drop in oil wealth, because future production is evaluated at current prices, and thus sustainable consumption fell to 1.0 percent of GDP in that year. Hence following the permanent income rule would result in sizable fiscal adjustments. At 1999 oil prices, oil wealth consumption of 2.4 percent of GDP would be sustainable. This level would rise to about 3.5 percent in the long run with the assumed decline in population growth rates to 1.5 percent.

The calculation of sustainable consumption out of oil wealth raises the question of how the government's actual policies stacked up against that benchmark. For that purpose, budgetary outcomes must be translated into consumption out of oil wealth. The government budget constraint can be summarized as follows:

$$OR_t + TR_t + rA_{t-1} - C_t - I_t = A_t - A_{t-1},$$

where OR stands for the total value of oil production accruing to the government, TR for tax revenue net of transfers (such as subsidies), A for net financial wealth, C for government consumption, and I for government net investment after subtracting the depreciation of existing capital. Transfers must include the subsidies for domestic petroleum products implied by charging less than world market prices, even if these subsidies do not appear directly in the budget.[41] Moreover, investment figures must be adjusted for assumed depreciation. The equation can be rewritten as;

$$TR_t - C_t + rA_{t-1} = A_t - A_{t-1} + I_t - OR_t;$$

that is, government non-oil saving (the left-hand side of the equation) equals the change in total public wealth (including financial wealth, infrastructure, and oil in the ground).

Hence, if non-oil saving were zero, total wealth would be unchanged—as prescribed by the permanent income framework for the case of zero inflation and zero population growth. Positive non-oil saving would be required for a growing population. The major difficulty in applying this concept lies in estimating *net* investment, because depreciation levels are unknown. To overcome this problem, only two extreme cases are discussed, providing upper and lower bounds. The first assumes that depreciation equals investment (that is, that net investment is zero), and the second that depreciation is zero (that is, that gross investment equals net investment).

In the event, consumption out of oil wealth between 1990 and 1999 was much higher than can be sustained. As Figure 8 demonstrates, the difference between optimal government non-oil saving and actual saving was large, between 10 percent and 25 percent of GDP. The results indicate that, under the assumptions made, Yemen has spent on average each year some 10 percent to 25 percent of GDP more than can be sustained, and that, up to today, oil revenue has not been converted into sufficient amounts of wealth to sustain such expenditure, even if all development expenditure is counted as net addition to wealth.

Again, the analysis above is subject to great uncertainty regarding future oil and gas resources, as well as in its general assumptions. Yemen still has territory whose oil and gas potential remains unexplored, and future technologies could render currently inaccessible reserves available. Moreover, the large proven gas reserves, which could last for at least 25 years at a rate of LPG production exceeding 5 million tons annually, could prove another important source of revenue. However, developing the capacity to produce LPG is expensive and may produce limited revenue for the government until potential investors have recouped their costs. Another uncertainty surrounds non-oil growth and growth strategies: the analysis implicitly assumes that the return to the government from investing in financial assets will be higher than

[41]The reasoning is as follows: oil wealth is evaluated at world market prices and, hence, domestic consumption depletes that wealth by the volume consumed evaluated at world market prices, not at administered prices.

Figure 8. Government Non-Oil Saving and National Wealth

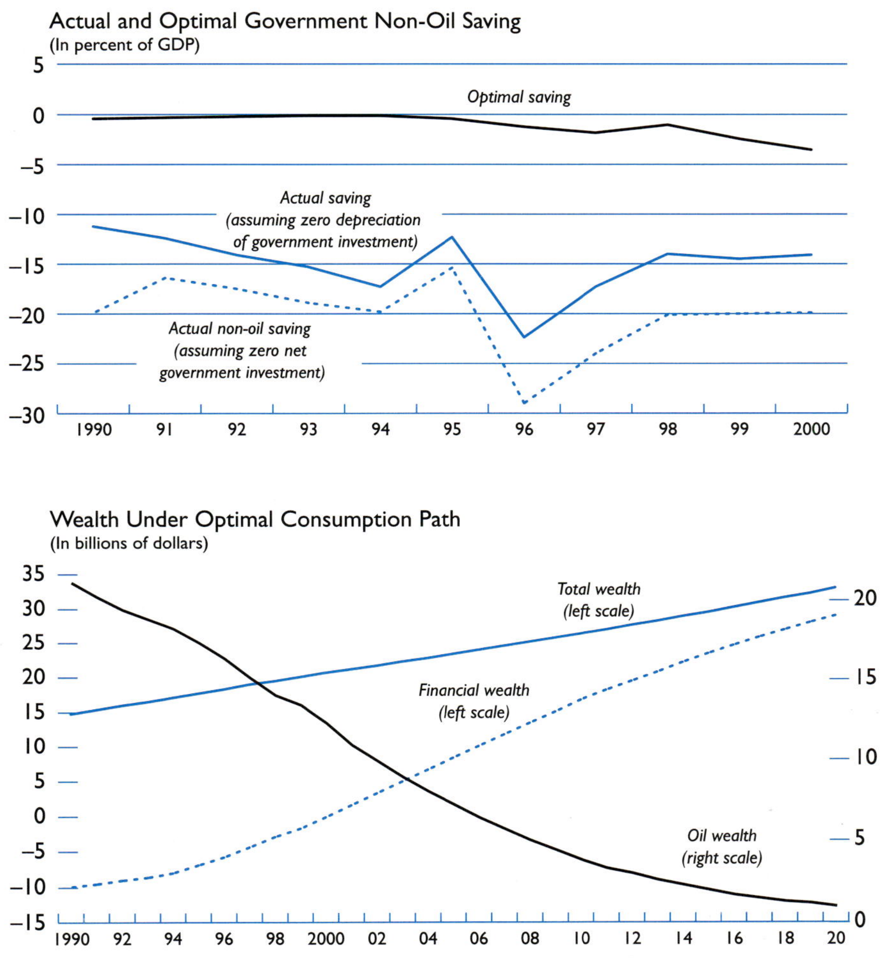

Sources: Data provided by the Yemeni authorities; IMF staff estimates.

returns from investing in other assets. It ignores the fact that some government consumption, especially in health and education, has contributed to building human capital and thus potential future non-oil growth. This, in return, could boost future government revenue from the non-oil economy. Similarly, structural reform may eventually bring about positive TFP growth. However, despite increasing budgetary allocations to the education sector, the limited progress to date in improving social indicators, and low non-oil per capita growth, may indicate that too much oil wealth has thus far been used to support current consumption rather than the accumulation of human or physical capital.

IV Microeconomic Reforms

In the 1960s the end of the reign of the *imam* in the north of Yemen brought about the establishment of a republic, which took first steps toward introducing a modern, market-oriented commercial and civil law. At the same time, the socialist government that took power in the south following the end of the British mandate established a legal regulatory system based on central planning and extensive government control over production. Thus the unification of the country in 1990 required the merging of two very different legal systems. The product was a complex and ineffective regulatory environment, combining elements of modern Western law with *sharia* and tribal law, and at the onset of the 1990s an array of controls covered all economic sectors. For a large set of commodities, prices were administratively fixed by the government, to keep basic consumer and input prices low and to suppress inflation.

As discussed in Section III, multiple exchange rates and interest controls were in place, the latter mainly to control credit in the economy. Quantitative import controls, such as bans and licensing, were used to protect domestic agricultural and industrial activities, while export bans (mainly on fish and unprocessed leather) aimed to maintain supply at low prices. Other laws allowed the government to enforce domestic and external trade monopolies. The Agencies Law and the Trade and Supply Law effectively protected certain monopolistic activities, and the government tolerated such private monopolistic structures as the trucking cartel (Ferzah) and the shipping agents' cartel in Aden, or even supported such practices through entry restrictions in various forms. The Investment Law gave the government discretion to approve projects as well as wide-ranging control over their implementation. This economic and legal environment failed to attract much investment, especially foreign investment. Hence an important component of the reform program of 1995 was regulatory reform.

Foreign Exchange Regime and Foreign Trade Reforms

On July 1, 1990, the foreign exchange and trade systems of the former PDRY and the former YAR were unified using the system of the latter. However, as part of an attempt to contain growing financial imbalances through administrative controls, a complex system of segmented foreign exchange markets, ad hoc administrative measures aimed at curbing "speculative" activity, and wide-ranging trade restrictions was maintained through 1995.

The Foreign Exchange System

At the time of unification, the foreign exchange market in Yemen comprised official and parallel markets. The official market was limited to government external transactions and covered crude oil and petroleum products, official receipts and payments, and external debt-service payments. The official exchange rate applied to allocations of foreign exchange by the central bank to the private sector for imports of wheat, flour, rice, and LPG under government tender, as well as for special purposes such as officially approved medical treatment or study abroad. The central bank prepared indicative foreign exchange budgets in parallel with commodity budgets prepared by the Ministry of Supply and Trade. All other external transactions occurred through the parallel market, which was operated by moneychangers and lacked legal status until January 1, 1993. At that time a law was enacted establishing regulations for money changing operations, including licensing, capital, and reporting requirements, with oversight powers assigned to the central bank. The law also established a parallel market oversight committee consisting of commercial banks, moneychangers, business community representatives, and an observer from the central bank.

Commercial banks operated in the foreign exchange market only as agents of the central bank and were permitted to buy or sell foreign exchange only for the accounts of their customers with the central bank. Their opening of foreign currency accounts for residents and nonresidents was subject to a long list of restrictions on the sources and uses of the funds. Commercial banks were prohibited from participating in the parallel market or from transacting with each other in foreign exchange and were required to use the official exchange rate in accounting and foreign exchange transactions with their customers.

At the time of unification, the exchange rate in the parallel market was YRls 13 to the dollar, compared with YRls 12 to the dollar in the official market. On April 1, 1991, the exchange rate for imports of wheat, flour, and rice was increased to YRls 16 to the dollar; on January 1, 1992, the customs valuation rate for all imports (except petroleum products, wheat, flour, and at that time rice) was increased to YRls 18 to the dollar. On May 1, 1992, an incentive rate of YRls 18 to the dollar was introduced for purchases of rials by bilateral and multilateral assistance agencies and foreign embassies, as well as for imports by the government and public sector enterprises. All of these constituted multiple currency practices.[42] On November 15, 1994, the parallel market oversight committee introduced an "official" parallel foreign exchange market for purchases of foreign exchange for self-financed imports at an exchange rate of YRls 84 to the dollar.[43] The central bank enforced the official parallel market rate by mandating that commercial banks could open letters of credit only if the importer provided documentary evidence that the foreign exchange had been purchased at the official parallel rate. By the end of 1994 the free market rial had depreciated by 700 percent from its May 1990 level and stood at 103 to the dollar. In early 1995 the main official exchange rate was changed to YRls 50 to the dollar (from YRls 12), while the free market rate rose further to around YRls 125 to the dollar. To limit the depreciation of the rial at the free market rate, the central bank from time to time suspended the operations of moneychangers, pushing foreign exchange transactions in the parallel market underground.

The exchange system was free of surrender requirements or taxes and subsidies on purchases or sales of foreign exchange. With the exception of local payments for hotel bills and airline tickets by foreign nationals, which had to be made in foreign currency, there were no prescriptions of currency requirements.

In January 1996 the authorities began a two-staged process of unification and liberalization of the foreign exchange market. In the first stage the official rial was devalued from 50 to 100 to the dollar, and all other official rates were eliminated (Figure 9). This rate continued to apply only to budget accounting, customs valuations, and transactions between the central bank and the Ministry of Finance. Commercial and specialized banks were allowed to participate fully in the parallel market, and foreign exchange regulations were amended to eliminate provisions inconsistent with free market operations. The prohibition on the issuing of letters of credit unless the foreign exchange was purchased in the official parallel market was eliminated, and the issuing of letters of credit for public sector enterprises and purchasing of foreign exchange from foreign oil companies was shifted from the central bank to the commercial banks. The government also eliminated the multiple currency practice related to wheat and flour imports by delinking the subsidy payment from the foreign exchange transaction.[44]

Figure 9. Nominal Rial-Dollar Exchange Rates

(In Yemeni rials to the dollar)

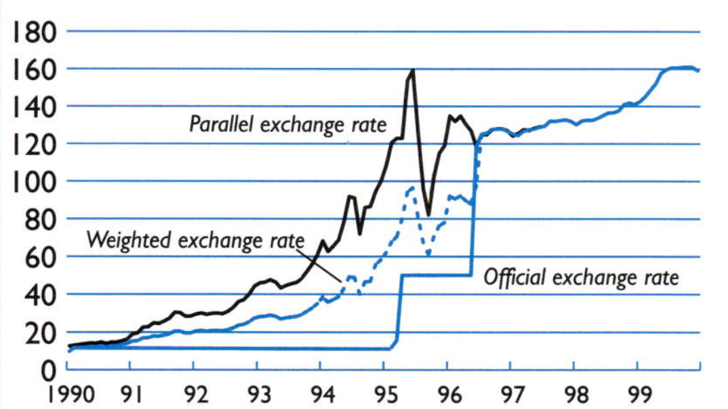

Sources: Data provided by the Yemeni authorities; IMF staff estimates.

Following a short transition period under a dual rate system, full unification of the foreign exchange market was implemented on July 1, 1996, and an independently floating exchange rate regime was adopted. All government and central bank transactions, including customs valuations, began to use the unified market rate, thus completing the second liberalization stage by August 1, 1996. Finally, in December 1996 Yemen formally accepted the obligations under Article VIII, Sections 2, 3, and 4, of the IMF Articles of Agreement, and since then it has maintained a foreign exchange system free of exchange restrictions on current or capital account transactions.

---

[42]The incentive rate was increased to YRls 25 to the dollar on July 1, 1993, and imports by the government and public sector enterprises, as well as imports of LPG, were moved to the parallel market. Subsequently, commercial banks were allowed to operate in the parallel market on behalf of their customers, but this permission was withdrawn on June 7, 1994, with the objective of containing the depreciation in the parallel market.

[43]In addition, there was a diplomatic rate of YRls 5 to the dollar for staff working in Yemeni embassies abroad.

[44]Importers of wheat and flour were required to purchase foreign exchange at the free market rate, and payment of a rial subsidy to the importers was made by the Ministry of Finance upon transfer of ownership of the imported wheat to domestic distributors. The rial subsidy was eliminated in June 1999.

The central bank is empowered to conduct exchange rate policy and aims to maintain an independently floating exchange rate regime by limiting its interventions in the foreign exchange market to the smoothing of volatility. If the central bank had intervened in the market between 1996 and early 2000 (virtually always as a seller), it would have invited open bids from commercial banks and large moneychangers to buy dollars, and it would have sold to the highest bidder.

The Moneychangers Section of the central bank is responsible for the licensing and inspecting of moneychangers. The number of licensed moneychangers has declined from 260 in 1996 to 170 at present, of which 71 are located in Sana'a. A handful of large moneychangers account for up to 90 percent of transactions in the market. Moneychangers are not part of the banking sector, and their balance sheets are not included in the monetary survey, although their foreign exchange and rial accounts with commercial banks are. Moneychangers are supposed to report their transactions volume to the central bank, but currently fewer than one-fifth comply. Some of the moneychangers who have significant capital are reportedly involved in informal deposit taking and lending operations, which are not legal and are usually not recorded. The interest rate charged by moneychangers is estimated to include a premium of up to 15 percentage points over the lending rate quoted by commercial banks.

No firm data are available on the average daily volume of transactions in the foreign exchange market, but the underlying transactions for private current account activities are estimated by the central bank to be on the order of $1.0 billion to $1.5 billion annually on both the buy and the sell side. A fully functioning interbank wholesale market encompassing both spot and forward transactions among banks and moneychangers has not yet developed.[45] The retail spot market continues to be centered largely on the moneychangers, who provide easy and efficient transactions at very narrow spreads. According to central bank estimates, moneychangers account for about 60 to 70 percent of all transactions in the foreign exchange market; the commercial banks account for the rest. Currently there is no clearinghouse for foreign exchange transactions, but commercial banks are considering establishing one, as noncash instruments would then grow in importance, which would shift the balance in favor of commercial banks and away from the moneychangers.

[45]Available information indicates that neither the central bank nor other market participants are involved in forward or derivative operations.

All transactions, including those for budget accounting purposes, now use the market rate, although not all supply and demand for foreign exchange is channeled through the foreign exchange market; certain transactions go through the central bank. These mainly include oil export proceeds, foreign loans and grants, and public sector debt-service payments, thus affecting the foreign exchange reserves of the central bank rather than the market rate. The central bank publishes its daily exchange rate by calculating an average from a sampling of rates from a group of large moneychangers and commercial banks; the central bank then uses this rate for its official transactions such as government debt service and budget accounting. Individual commercial banks usually call large moneychangers to sample the market rates that day and refer to them for their own transactions.

Both foreign and domestic banks are allowed to freely conduct all foreign and domestic currency operations. Effective January 15, 1996, commercial and specialized banks were required to observe prudential regulations regarding their currency exposure and to begin reporting their positions. Open positions (both oversold and overbought) are limited to 25 percent of the bank's capital for all foreign currencies and 15 percent for any one currency. Banks report their daily open positions to the central bank at the end of each week, although the central bank checks only the last day's position against the limit.

Foreign Trade

Upon unification, the foreign trade regime (adopted from the former YAR) was inward oriented, characterized by import prohibitions (through a positive import list),[46] licensing, and a mean nominal tariff on the order of 27 percent. Virtually all imports required licenses from the Ministry of Supply and Trade, and the importation of certain products required the permission of particular government agencies.[47] The annual commodity and foreign exchange budgets provided the basis for issuing import licenses. These budgets gave priority to imports of foodstuffs, medicines, petroleum products, and inputs for production. Imports of petroleum products were reserved for the YPC and the Aden refinery.

[46]A positive import list is one in which only those items listed may be imported; a negative list is one in which only those items listed may not be imported.

[47]The only exceptions were the importation of equipment by foreign oil companies; the importation of spare parts to meet emergency needs of manufacturing enterprises, subject to an annual limit of $50,000 for each enterprise; and the importation of machinery and spare parts worth up to $40,000 by Yemeni nationals returning from abroad to set up a small business. In the latter case, authorization from the Ministry of Supply and Trade was required, and the payment had to be made out of expatriated foreign exchange savings.

Foreign exchange for both private and official transactions had to be purchased at the official exchange rate from the central bank, which also had to approve its availability.

Imports were subject to a customs duty under a tariff structure, which incorporated 15 bands with tariff rates ranging from 5 to 200 percent. In addition to the applicable customs duty, imports were subject to numerous taxes and surcharges, including an earthquake damage reconstruction tax, a Ministry of Finance surcharge, a Chamber of Commerce surcharge, and a Health Department surcharge.

Beginning August 1, 1990, the authorities permitted the self-financing of licensed imports through foreign exchange obtained from the parallel market. A commercial bank guarantee equivalent to 2 percent of the value of the imports was required for an import license to be issued. Commercial banks were then authorized to open letters of credit for holders of import licenses, provided that the full foreign exchange value of the imports was deposited with a commercial bank. All importers holding an import license for wheat, flour, rice, or LPG could obtain the necessary foreign exchange from the central bank at the special official rate (see above), which also served as the customs valuation rate. In January 1991 the 100 percent import deposit requirement was reduced to 50 percent for commercial imports and to 25 percent for industrial imports; it was finally abolished altogether in January 1992.

In May 1993 the positive import list was replaced by a negative list, which included 63 categories of items competing with domestically produced goods. Import licensing remained in effect because of foreign exchange shortages. The government assigned priorities among import categories and granted licenses only up to a ceiling for each category. Export bans, such as the temporary ban on exports of fish in 1994, were imposed from time to time on commodities considered to be in short supply in the domestic market.

From January to March 1996, a comprehensive reform of the tariff and trade system was implemented; this was aimed at reducing effective protection, enhancing the economy's allocational efficiency and growth prospects, and facilitating its integration into the world economy. The main elements of the reform included the following:

- All import bans maintained for economic reasons were abolished except for those covering fresh fruit, vegetables, and coffee.[48]
- All import licensing by the Ministry of Supply and Trade was eliminated except for wheat, flour, and petroleum products.
- The 15-band tariff structure was replaced with a 4-band structure, with tariff rates of 5, 10, 15, and 30 percent ad valorem.[49]
- The tariff reform was accompanied by excise tax harmonization whereby excise taxes on industrial inputs and a production tax on local manufacturers applied uniformly to imported and domestic products.
- A phaseout of import fees and surcharges was initiated, and by September 1997 all had been eliminated.
- Duty exemptions for imports by the government and public sector enterprises were abolished.
- No new discretionary project-related import duty exemptions were to be granted except under the Investment Law.
- All government controls over exports were eliminated except those in place for security, public health, religious, or environmental reasons.[50]

One month following the unification of the exchange system on July 1, 1996, the customs valuation rate was unified with the market exchange rate. To mitigate the one-time price increase effect of the customs rate devaluation on politically sensitive imports, tariff rates were reduced at that time for imports of seven basic food items and medicines. In October 1997 the maximum tariff was further reduced by 5 percentage points, to 25 percent, and tariff rates on inputs for production were lowered from 10 percent and 15 percent to 5 percent. Tariffs for goods prone to smuggling were also reduced on a selective basis.

In March 1998 the government began a phased elimination of the remaining import bans maintained for economic reasons, replacing them with the maximum tariff. By the end of 1999 the importation of 14 categories of fruits and vegetables had been liberalized, and the remaining import bans were removed in 2000.

These trade reforms brought the trade regime closer to standard international rules. Consequently, in 1999 the government initiated the process of accession to the World Trade Organization (WTO). Following the granting of observer status at the WTO in 1999, the government is working toward full membership.

[48]In addition to coffee, import bans continued to apply to 21 categories of fruit and vegetables classified according to the four-digit Harmonized Nomenclature System code, introduced in October 1997. Importation of the following items was prohibited for security, religious, or environmental reasons: weapons and explosives, narcotics, pork and pork products, alcohol, and rhinoceros horn.

[49]A special tariff rate of 70 percent applied to tobacco and tobacco products for revenue reasons.

[50]Export licensing is required for statistical purposes, and the Ministry of Fisheries limits the export of certain categories of seafood products. Exports of antiques and archeological items exceeding $100 in value are prohibited.

Table 6. Middle Eastern and North African Countries: Trade Restrictiveness Rating

Index Rating	1	2	3	4	5	6	7	8	9	10
	OPEN				MODERATE		RESTRICTIVE			
Country	Djibouti Qatar U.A.E	Bahrain Yemen	Mauritania	Kuwait Oman	Saudi Arabia	Jordan	Algeria Lebanon Pakistan	Egypt Morocco Sudan Tunisia	—	Iran Syria

Source: IMF, Trade Policy Information database.

Under the reformed tariff structure, the mean tariff rate was reduced from 27 percent to 12 percent. This, together with the elimination of import bans, licensing, and other nontariff trade barriers, reduced Yemen's trade restrictiveness index from 10 (closed or very restrictive) at the time of unification to 2 (open) by the end of 1999 (Table 6).[51]

Tax Reform

Taxes on Income and Profits

The 1991 income tax law specified an individual income tax with four brackets. Tax rates on wages, salaries, and rental income varied between 3 percent for the lowest bracket and 16 percent for the top bracket (22 percent for nonresidents). Because of high inflation, however, by the end of 1994 virtually all taxpayers were in the highest (16 percent) bracket, and the income tax had become essentially a proportional tax. Businesses were taxed at rates between 28 percent and 36 percent depending on proprietary, monopoly, and residency status.[52] Under the 1991 code, individual taxpayers were taxed differently, depending on the source of income, and taxes from different sources were not aggregated. Moreover, income taxes suffered from the numerous exemptions in the 1991 Investment Law. In 1996 the income tax law was amended, and tax rates for corporations were unified at 35 percent. Single proprietors and partnerships continued to pay a flat rate of 28 percent. Further changes to the income tax law were introduced by presidential decree in early 1999. These amendments reestablished a progressive rate structure for personal income (including income from proprietorships) above YRls 36,000, raised the top tax rate on wages and salaries from 16 percent to 20 percent, included foreign income in the tax base, simplified the depreciation schedule, and clarified the penalty regime.[53] The authorities recognize that further adjustments to the income tax code are desirable to achieve a consistent treatment of income from different sources and restrict exemptions, and are therefore working toward a more comprehensive reform. Of particular importance are the integration of corporate and personal taxes to limit tax avoidance, the taxation of income from agricultural sources and rental income as regular income, the further simplification of the depreciation schedule, the clarification of international tax rules, the simplification of procedures, and the design of an effective penalty regime.

Taxes on Goods and Services

The 1991 law establishing a tax on production, consumption, and services (TPCS) consolidated numerous existing excise taxes. Despite its name, the tax originally covered only about 35 products, including *qat* (see Box 5 in Section VI), and tax rates varied between 5 percent and 40 percent, with imported goods taxed at double the rate of domestic goods. Specific excises were levied on petroleum products and cigarettes. In 1996 the tax base was broadened to about 100 goods and services, and the rate differentiation between domestic and imported goods was eliminated by presidential decree. The decree also established a limited tax credit mechanism to reduce cascading under the TPCS. Moreover, the specific taxes on petroleum products were converted to an ad valorem tax, mostly at a rate of 2 percent, and specific cigarette taxes were converted

[51]See IMF (1997) for a description of the methodology for deriving the trade restrictiveness index.

[52]Tax regimes for oil companies, the major foreign investors, were negotiated separately and individually and were not covered by the income tax laws.

[53]Presidential Decrees No. 12 and 255 of 1999; these also included a provision for the taxation of rental income, but the tax was limited to one month's rent.

to ad valorem taxes at rates of 60 percent for domestic products and 80 percent for imported products.

The amendments introduced by decree were later altered by parliament (Law No. 4 of 1997), which reduced the number of goods and services covered by the TPCS. Additional minor changes in coverage were introduced by decree in January 1999. These related to the list of exempt goods, the tax base for certain imported goods, and confiscation of cigarettes.

Administration of the tax suffers from the multiple rate structure. In addition, the tax has limited revenue potential because of its restricted base. The authorities are therefore committed to replacing the TPCS with a broad-based value-added tax (to be called a General Sales Tax, or GST). A tax law providing for a 10 percent broad-based GST with a strictly limited list of exemptions, a credit mechanism, and zero rating of exports was approved by the government in 1999 and is pending before parliament. The GST would originally apply only to all imports and to domestic sales of the 800 to 1,000 largest taxpayers, depending on turnover. A few excises on petroleum, tobacco products, and qat would remain in place under the cover of the TPCS.

Parliament removed stamp duties on banking and customs transactions in May 1998. Stamp duties had been applied to commercial and government transactions and based on their value. The application of customs and banking stamp duties was complicated, and the lost revenue was largely replaced by taxing services and imports.

Tax Administration

The authorities have taken several steps to improve revenue collection and tax administration. The most important was the introduction of a new taxpayer identification number (TIN) system. Although a TIN system existed before 1997, it suffered from shortcomings due to unnecessary codings. A new, computerized pilot system allowing for online registration of taxpayers at several tax centers was recently introduced, and online registration was initiated in 2000. The new system will allow for a range of tax reports based on information in the taxpayer database. Customs clearance of imports now also depends on the presentation of a valid TIN. In addition, in 1997 the tax authorities introduced cigarette bandrolls to improve identification of untaxed cigarettes. Moreover, through improvements in manual procedures, efficiency gains have been realized in the tax authority. Jointly with the introduction of a GST, the authority plans further reform steps. These include the creation of a large-taxpayer unit, which would handle all taxes, including income taxes and withholding taxes, paid by taxpayers above a certain turnover threshold. Further, the tax authority plans to modernize tax administration through self-assessment procedures, targeted auditing, and enhancement of services provided by the taxpayer services unit established in 1999.

Customs and Customs Administration

As previously noted, the 1990 customs law contained a complicated rate structure, with 15 rates ranging from 5 percent to 200 percent. Most imports were taxed at rates between 20 percent and 30 percent. Although the 1990 law already constituted a major simplification of preunification customs laws, it still gave rise to classification difficulties and disputes. Until the stepwise exchange rate unification in 1995–96, customs revenue was also affected by the application of the highly appreciated customs valuation rate. In 1996, as noted above, the tariff structure was simplified to four bands with rates of 5, 10, 15, and 30 percent; the top rate was reduced to 25 percent in 1997. The customs base also benefited from the stepwise elimination of import bans in 1998 and 1999. Further amendments of the customs law are planned, to bring the regulations and valuation procedures in line with WTO specifications. Two of the import surcharges, the profits tax and the earthquake tax, were abolished by parliament in December 1998. Customs revenue also suffers from broad exemptions introduced through the Investment Law of 1991. That law exempts fixed assets for establishment, expansion, or upgrade of a project licensed by the General Investment Authority from all types of customs duties and taxes. It also provides for simplified customs procedures as soon as a project license is presented at the border.

Customs administration reform focused initially on procedures and regulations. Reforms covered the simplification of clearance procedures and the improvement of the functioning of the customs authority. Control of the authority over the arrival and exit of imports was strengthened, and payment of duties before release of goods was enforced. Further reforms included elimination of the deferment of customs duties, the improvement of controls over temporary admissions, and the development of new customs forms. With support from the United Nations Conference on Trade and Development, the customs authority is now working on introducing the ASYCUDA computerized customs system at three or four points of entry in 2001.

In spite of these reform efforts, enforcement of customs regulations remains difficult. The long coastline and (before the recent signing of the Jeddah border treaty) disputed borders led to major difficulties in controlling points of entry. In addition, the security situation was seen as necessitating a

Table 7. Petroleum Products Prices Compared to World Market Levels (March 2000)
(YRls per liter, unless otherwise stated)

	Domestic Retail Price	Domestic Wholesale Price[1]	International Wholesale Price	International[1] Domestic Price Ratio
Gasoline	35	28.35	32.18	0.88
Diesel	10	6.45	30.72	0.21
Fuel oil	13	10.09	20.23	0.50
Kerosene	16	12.76	31.80	0.40

Sources: International Energy Agency, Oil Market Report (March 2000); Ministry of Finance; and IMF staff estimates.

[1]Domestic wholesale price is calculated by deducting from retail prices appropriate taxes and surcharges imposed for each product. International wholesale prices are actual average prices for February 2000, converted to rials at the current period-average exchange rate. (Gasoline prices are regular northwest Europe prices, while the other products are Mediterranean-based prices; fuel oil corresponds to the 3.5 percent sulfur type.) The International/Domestic Price Ratio is the ratio of the two wholesale prices. For example, the wholesale price for gasoline in Yemen in February 2000 was 88 percent of the level of the international wholesale price.

strong military presence at the border. To the extent that the sharing of responsibilities between the military and customs is ill defined, and because the military has little incentive to prosecute smugglers, border enforcement has been hampered. The declining share of customs revenue in imports likely reflects increasing smuggling and tax evasion.

Public Expenditure Reform

High levels of public expenditure were the root cause of unsustainable public deficits from 1990 to 1995. The major culprits were subsidies for wheat, wheat flour, and petroleum products, as well as the civil service wage bill. In the second half of the 1990s, the government took several steps to contain expenditure, particularly through changes in administered petroleum prices and the removal of subsidies for wheat and wheat flour imports.

Subsidy Reform

Until 1997, wheat and wheat flour subsidies constituted the government's primary social safety net and transfer program. The subsidies were supposed to ensure impoverished families access to basic food items at low prices. However, according to World Bank staff estimates, only one-third of the subsidies reached consumers; the rest was captured by importers, distributors, and smugglers to neighboring countries. Moreover, the poorest groups of the population benefited very little from the subsidies because they spent disproportionately less on wheat and wheat flour than did high-income groups.

Substantial petroleum product subsidies were also instituted to support the rural population. Subsidies for petroleum products other than diesel fuel have been substantially cut over time (Table 7), but diesel prices have remained unchanged since 1997, when an increase of YRl 1 a liter led to political unrest and widespread rioting. Diesel fuel is used for rural transportation as well as agricultural machinery, particularly to pump ground water. But the diesel subsidy has caused large distortions in the Yemeni economy. Car engines designed for regular gasoline have been converted to diesel engines. Diesel-fueled pumps have depleted water tables rapidly, mostly to provide water for *qat* plantations, and richer households as well as many businesses have begun to generate their own power, imposing losses on the electricity company. The company has been losing its best customers, affecting its ability to cross-subsidize its poorest customers.

From 1990 to 1994, subsidies for wheat, wheat flour, and petroleum products were implicit, resulting from the multiple exchange rate regime.[54] Importers of wheat and wheat flour had access to foreign exchange at the official exchange rate, which at the end of 1994 was about one-eighth the parallel rate. Likewise, imports of petroleum products and

[54]In addition to wheat and wheat flour, the Yemeni government subsidized rice, milk, sugar, and medicine. These subsidies were relatively unimportant in magnitude and were eliminated in 1995.

Box 1. Reduction of Subsidies, 1995–99

Domestic prices of wheat, flour, and petroleum products in Yemen have traditionally been set administratively at prices well below market prices, involving large subsidies. After the unification of exchange rates in mid-1996, many of the subsidies that had been implicit, giving importers access to foreign exchange at nonmarket rates, became explicit in the budget.

The subsidies created incentives against domestic wheat production and for the inefficient use of petroleum products (especially diesel fuel). They also encouraged smuggling of subsidized goods to neighboring countries. Moreover, the untargeted subsidies benefited all groups in society regardless of income and gave rise to rent seeking by importers and distributors.

In 1996, the government began to reduce the subsidy bill through several rounds of administered price increases. The wheat and flour subsidies, which by then had reached 7.5 percent of GDP and priced wheat and flour almost 75 percent below their world market prices (see table below), were eliminated entirely by mid-1999.

The decline in the world market price for oil in 1997 and 1998 affected oil and petroleum subsidies, which fell with the increase in administered prices, resulting in violent unrest. However, domestic prices, especially diesel fuel prices, which have been unchanged since 1997, did not keep pace with the increase in oil prices in 1999, and the subsidy rose to about 2 percent of GDP.

Republic of Yemen: Subsidies, 1995–99

	1995	1996	1997	1998	1999
Wheat and flour subsidy					
In percent of market value of consumption[1]	. . .	73.7	65.3	50.5	9.2
In percent of GDP	. . .	7.5	4.7	3.1	0.4
Domestic oil and petroleum subsidy[2]					
In percent of market value of consumption[1]	85.3	48.9	12.0	10.6	27.0
In percent of GDP	10.7	5.5	1.0	0.7	2.1

Sources: Ministry of Finance; and IMF staff estimates.

[1]Evaluated at world market prices and parallel exchange rates.

[2]Calculated as the difference between world market value at parallel exchange rates of domestic crude oil consumption and domestic oil revenue net of explicit budgetary subsidies. This calculation ignores the value-added by refining and the potential additional subsidy or tax implied by selling refined products below or above world market prices.

later sales to domestic refineries took place at exchange rates far removed from market rates. With the move to a unified exchange rate, those subsidies that had been implicit, reducing oil export revenue, have to be recorded explicitly on the expenditure side. Their magnitude became clear in 1996, when the explicit subsidy bill reached 13 percent of GDP after the exchange rates were unified. In addition to the explicit subsidies, there continued to be implicit subsidies through the application of non-market-based transfer prices in the domestic oil sector. In particular, the Aden refinery charged an additional $15 per ton of delivered petroleum products (raised to $17 in 1999) for transport services, part of which likely reflects a production subsidy.

Reduction of subsidies has played an important role in the fiscal adjustment efforts of the government since 1995 (Box 1). Jointly with its move to unify the exchange rate, the government began to raise domestic petroleum retail prices in March 1995. Retail gasoline prices were raised by 100 percent, and fuel oil prices by 74 percent. Despite these increases, domestic wholesale prices (retail prices net of taxes and distribution fees) remained far below world market prices in 1995 (Figure 10). Gasoline prices were closest to world market levels, at about 60 percent, followed by fuel oil at 30 percent and diesel fuel and kerosene at 15 percent. Further substantial administered price increases of 58 percent (for gasoline), 100 percent (diesel fuel), 167 percent (kerosene), and 133 percent (fuel oil) took place from January through March 1996. These brought prices for gasoline close to world market levels but left diesel fuel, kerosene, and fuel oil heavily subsidized. Prices were raised again in 1997, 1998, and 1999, but the price for diesel fuel has remained unchanged since September 1997, as noted previously (Table 8). Owing to these measures, by

Figure 10. Domestic Wholesale Prices of Petroleum Products[1]

(In percent of world market prices)[2]

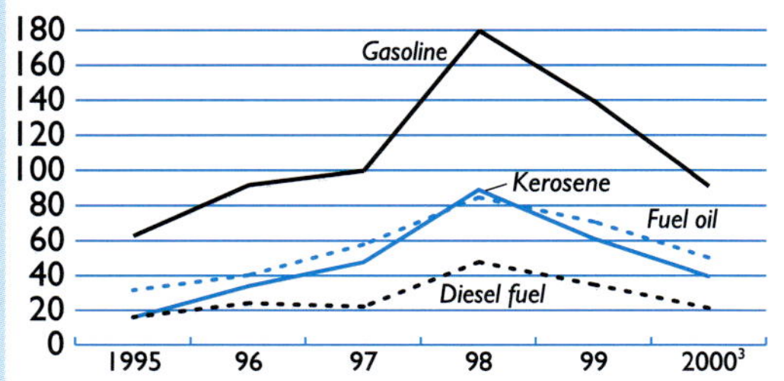

Sources: Data provided by the Yemeni authorities; and International Energy Agency, *Oil Market Report* (March 2000).

[1]Wholesale prices are defined as retail prices net of taxes and distribution fees.

[2]World prices are Mediterranean ex-refinery prices.

[3]First quarter only.

1998 gasoline prices were 80 percent above world market prices and allowed to cross-subsidize diesel fuel and, to a lesser extent, fuel oil and kerosene (Table 8). However, in 1999 rising world oil prices were not matched by equivalent price adjustments, leading to the reappearance of a substantial cash subsidy bill (see Table 5 in Section III). In 1999 the government also changed its transfer pricing system to charge world market prices for crude oil in its transactions with the domestic refineries, as explained in Section II. Sales to refineries are now conducted at export prices. Refineries charge world market prices to the distribution company for petroleum products (the YPC) plus a surcharge (see above). The YPC's losses at the administered retail prices are covered by subsidy payments from the budget.

Progress in removing subsidies in utility tariffs proceeded at a slower pace (Table 8). After a 120 percent increase in water tariffs and a 161 percent average increase in electricity tariffs in January 1996, small increases took place in 1997 and 1998 for the latter. Electricity tariffs have not been changed since then, however, despite the fact that, at the present level, the average tariff covers only about 90 percent of the average cost of production per kilowatt-hour. The previous, opaque system of transfer prices and artificial exchange rates for domestic transactions led to implicit subsidies for consumers and utilities. Higher prices and the new settlement mechanism, combined with the price distortions favoring diesel generation of electricity, led to arrears of the electricity company in its accounts with the petroleum distributor. The government reimbursed these arrears, implying a subsidy to electricity consumption on the order of 0.4 percent of GDP in 1999.

Wheat and wheat flour subsidies were entirely phased out by mid-1999 through increases in administered prices. Small increases, ranging from 10 to 30 percent, took place between the second half of 1996 and January 1999, following a large increase (150 percent) in January 1996.[55] The administration of wheat subsidies was complicated, giving rise to substantial rents for a few privileged import companies and distributors.[56] The government gave importers access to foreign exchange at below-market rates such that the latter were willing to sell at the administered prices.[57] The government also negotiated distribution fees with distributors. Import contracts were distributed through a tendering system, which, however, was not transparent and generally invited bids from the same few companies. There was little competition among distributors.

As a result of the reductions in subsidies, the subsidy bill fell substantially over time, reducing pressure on expenditure. With rising domestic petroleum prices and declining differentials with world market prices, net domestic oil revenue (a measure that tracks domestic oil revenue net of explicit subsidies) rose from 1.8 percent of GDP in 1995 to 5.4 percent in 1999. Wheat and flour subsidies, which peaked at 7.4 percent of GDP in 1996, fell to 3 percent in 1998 and were completely eliminated in 2000.

Civil Service and Wage Reforms

Unification and the political and economic events that followed resulted in a large, partly redundant, and poorly paid civil service. In 1990 the civil services of the YAR and the PDRY were merged, and the pay scale for southern civil service employees was adjusted to the higher levels prevailing in the north. With the return of expatriates and reinstatement of the policy of hiring all university graduates,

[55]The government was still engaged in settling some remaining arrears with wheat importers in early 2000.

[56]Since the removal of the wheat subsidy, the amount of foreign exchange sales by the central bank has not exceeded $200 million a year, compared with the direct provision of $400 million to $600 million annually to wheat importers before wheat imports were liberalized. At the same time, wheat imports have declined by about $100 million a year relative to their preliberalization levels. This suggests that, as a result of the subsidy, between $100 million and $300 million a year was accruing as rents to wheat importers and distributors, probably in the form of overinvoicing and smuggling to neighboring countries, where the price of wheat was higher.

[57]The subsidized exchange rate equalized the administered predistribution price with the actual price of imported wheat at the port of entry.

Table 8. Adjustments in Administered Retail Prices, 1994–99

	Dec.	Jan.	Mar.	Aug.	Jan.	Mar.	Jul.	Sept.	Jul.	Jan.	Jun.
	1994	1995			1996		1997		1998	1999	
	(Percentage change in unit price)										
Gasoline	...	...	100	...	50	7	30	...	40	...	...
Diesel	...	...	...	...	100	...	...	67	...	...	...
Fuel oil[1]	...	...	74	...	133	...	...	57	...	...	18
Fuel oil[2]	...	32	100	...	40	...	...	57	...	...	18
Kerosene	...	...	...	...	167	6	53	...	15	...	7
Aviation fuel	...	67	150	...	8	...	...	...	...	...	85
LPG	...	25	60	50	38	...	...	...	21	...	...
Electricity (average tariff)	...	60	...	...	161	...	...	7	50	...	...
Wheat	...	38	...	...	150	...	15	...	30	25	FL[3]
Flour	...	38	...	...	150	...	11	...	28	17	FL[3]
Rice, milk, sugar, medicine	...	...	FL[3]	...	...	...	...	...	...	...	...
Water	...	...	...	...	120	...	...	...	...	...	...

Sources: Ministry of Oil and Mineral Resources; Ministry of Finance; and World Bank.
[1]For electricity plants.
[2] For cement plants.
[3]FL stands for full liberalization.

the civil service (excluding public enterprises) grew from 168,000 in 1990, to 322,000 in 1995, to 336,000 in 1998. As a share of the total population the civil service rose from 1.3 percent in 1990 to 1.9 percent in 1998, as estimated by the Ministry of Civil Service and Administrative Reform. An estimated additional 83,000 were working in public enterprises in 1998. Most civil servants are employed in the education sector, followed by the health sector and general administration (Table 9). High inflation eroded real civil service wages substantially from 1994 to 1997. Although this helped reduce the wage bill from almost 11 percent of GDP in 1993 to 6 percent in 1997, it also left Yemen with an underqualified, underpaid, and overstaffed civil service that fell short of delivering adequate services to the population.

The government has recently initiated a comprehensive civil service reform program aimed at reducing the size of the civil service through retrenchment and retirement, to allow higher pay increases for the remaining workforce. The program also envisions a restructuring of public administration, beginning with six pilot ministries, the introduction of a new grade structure, and minimum qualifications for each job.

Several steps in the reform program have been implemented. In 1998 a civil service census identified all civil servants by age, occupation, length of service, and other characteristics. The census also identified possible double dippers and overage workers, to prepare the way for future reductions in staff, and it established a database allowing computer-based management of the civil service. The civil service ministry has also begun to issue employee identification numbers. A Civil Service Fund (CSF) was created by presidential decree in January 1999; supported by World Bank financial assistance, the CSF will continue to pay laid-off public workers for a certain period.

Table 9. Distribution of Public Employees by Sector, 1998

Sector	Employees	Total Percent
Education	223,368	53
Health	33,328	8
General administration	33,006	8
Construction	21,751	5
Manufacturing	15,803	4
Other	92,153	22
Total	419,409	100

Source: MOSCAR Employee Database

Despite these preparations, however, no progress was made in reducing staff or containing the wage bill. The retirement of overage workers (estimated at 24,000) was delayed through the end of 2000; however, in February 2001 a total of 14,000 overage workers were retired. Since the CSF was not yet operational in early 2000, the so-called at-home workers, who were supposed to be the first group transferred to the fund, remained on the government payroll. Hiring continued at a level of 20,000 people in 1999; given that there were about 2,000 retirees, this amounts to a net addition of 18,000 civil servants. Average wages continued to rise by more than 20 percent in 1998 and 1999, largely owing to a bill passed by parliament that granted a 100 percent wage increase for teachers and health workers in 1998–2000. As a result, the civil service wage bill rose from 6 percent of GDP in 1997 to 7.5 percent in 1999. Moving ahead with retrenchment and organization will therefore be essential for progress in refocusing government expenditure.

Other Expenditure Reforms

Since 1994 the Yemeni government has reduced its defense spending. At unification, total defense expenditure stood at 8.4 percent of GDP, over 80 percent of which went to pay salaries. During the first years of unification, defense spending remained high, peaking at 9.7 percent of GDP in 1994 during the civil war. Starting in 1995, however, expenditure began to fall, reaching 5.8 percent of GDP in 1999. At the same time, in parallel with the overall decline of the civil service wage bill, military wages declined as a share of total defense spending.

Development expenditure remained volatile because it served as a first resort for expenditure cuts in difficult times. In the years immediately after unification, the government spent more than 8 percent of GDP for development. However, with financial difficulties emerging in 1991, development spending made up less than 4 percent of GDP. This declined further to 2.6 percent of GDP in 1994. With budget pressures easing after the unification of exchange rates and the rise in oil revenue, the government sharply increased development spending to more than 6.5 percent of GDP in 1996 and 1997. However, because development projects are among the few discretionary items in the budget, the drop in oil prices in 1998 and continuing low prices in early 1999 led to cutbacks in spending, to 6.1 percent and 5.6 percent of GDP, respectively.

Between 1990 and 1997, government interest obligations fluctuated between 2 and 3 percent of GDP. Domestic interest payments, which in that period were recorded net of central bank profit transfers, remained between 1 and 2 percent of GDP, with the exception of 1994. External interest obligations remained in the same range. In 1996 obligations were particularly high because the first Paris Club rescheduling agreements required the settlement of some deferred interest payments. In 1998 and 1999, after the Paris Club agreements took full effect, foreign interest obligations were only about 1 percent of GDP. Domestic interest payments have been recorded on a gross basis since 1998 and rose from 2.5 percent in that year to 3 percent in 1999, reflecting rising interest rates in the wake of tight monetary policy.

Social indicators in Yemen point to major deficiencies in human development. For example, Yemen has the highest fertility rate, the highest maternal mortality rate, and the highest infant mortality rate in the Middle East and North Africa region (see Section VI). The public sector is the major provider of basic social services, particularly health services. The Ministry of Public Health (MOPH) administers more than 2,200 public health facilities, including about 100 hospitals, 500 health centers, and 1,600 health units. In addition, two hospitals outside the MOPH structure receive direct allocations from the budget. The MOPH employs more than 30,000 people, including 3,800 physicians and 9,400 nurses. However, health services are distributed unevenly among regions and between rural and urban areas.

Spending on education and health has been on the rise since 1996, the first year in which data on these expenditures were compiled. In that year education expenditure was 3.5 percent of GDP and health expenditure 1 percent of GDP. Seventy percent of education spending and 41 percent of health spending were for wages and salaries. Spending on education rose sharply after 1996 and reached 7.4 percent of GDP in 1999, with 61 percent going to wages and salaries. Thus, although the wage bill has grown more slowly than total allocations to the education sector, the share of wages remains high. In contrast, the share devoted to materials and services fell between 1996 and 1999, from 17 percent to 13 percent. Development expenditure, largely consisting of school construction in rural areas, therefore took an increasing share of education expenditure. Health expenditure increased much less rapidly, to 1.3 percent of GDP in 1999. Wages and salaries continue to take up about 40 percent of this spending.

Yemen appears to spend less on the military than some other countries in the region, but also less on education and health (Table 10). Some of these comparisons should be interpreted cautiously, because of different definitions across countries. Nonetheless, measured as a share of GDP, military and security expenditures in Saudi Arabia, Oman, and Jordan were much higher than in Yemen during the 1990s. Of the countries in the table, only Egypt

Table 10. Regional Comparison of Expenditures on Defense, Education, and Health, 1994–98
(In percent of GDP)

	1994	1995	1996	1997	1998
			Defense		
Yemen	9.7	6.7	5.6	6.0	6.1
Oman[1]	15.6	14.5	12.5	12.4	12.4
Saudi Arabia[2]	9.7	10.0	8.7	9.7	10.3
Jordan	13.4	14.4	15.3	16.0	17.5
Egypt	3.3	3.2	3.1	2.9	2.8
			Education		
Yemen	n.a.	n.a.	3.5	4.6	7.0
Oman	3.1	3.1	2.9	3.0	3.4
Saudi Arabia[3]	8.4	7.8	8.0	8.8	9.9
Jordan[4]	n.a.	n.a.	n.a.	4.4	n.a.
Egypt	2.9	3.4	3.3	3.5	3.9
			Health		
Yemen	n.a.	n.a.	1.0	1.0	1.4
Oman	2.0	2.0	1.9	1.9	2.2
Saudi Arabia[5]	2.6	2.3	2.6	2.9	3.3
Jordan[4]	n.a.	n.a.	n.a.	3.0	n.a.
Egypt	0.6	0.6	0.7	0.7	0.8

Source: Various Recent Economic Development reports.
[1]Includes security expenditures and capital expenditures.
[2]Includes health expenditures.
[3]Manpower expenditures.
[4]The amounts reported for 1997 reflect only direct budgetary spending by the central government and exclude some transfers.
[5]Social development, including health, social welfare, and labor affairs.

shows a considerably lower ratio of military spending to GDP than Yemen. As a result of the sharp rise in education spending since 1996, Yemen now spends a considerably larger percentage of its GDP on education than Oman, but a smaller share than Saudi Arabia spends on educational staffing alone (including vocational training). Health spending remains quite low in Yemen in this regional comparison: Yemen's 1 to 1.4 percent of GDP is lower than spending in Oman (2 percent of GDP) or Saudi Arabia (3 percent of GDP), but higher than that in Egypt.

Budget Management Reform

The budget management reform program attempts to address shortcomings in budget formulation, budget execution, and budget control mechanisms. Budgets were traditionally prepared without regard to a macroeconomic framework or financial limits, leading to a less-than-optimal budget process that failed to address priorities. Indeed, the Ministry of Finance did not follow macroeconomic developments or prepare a macroeconomic framework. Budget execution is cumbersome because each ministry and each independent government agency has three accounts at the central bank: one for current expenditure, one for development expenditure, and one for revenue. Until 2000 the ministry could follow account movements but had no more detailed information about expenditure. Budget control suffers from a clear system of guidelines and procedures as well as weaknesses in independent auditing.

The first phase of an IMF- and UNDP-supported technical assistance program resulted in improvements in budget preparation and accounting procedures. The 2000 budget was prepared with a revised circular and was based on a macroeconomic framework. It also followed the classification of the IMF's *Government Financial Statistics Yearbook*. Budget reports are now regularly requested in standardized format from budgetary units. The accounting software at the central bank, which executes the treasury functions of the Ministry of Finance, was modified to a two-level classification (budget chapter and subchapter) in 1999. Recently, a deputy minister was appointed to head the new macroeconomic studies unit, and its staffing has begun. This unit will track and forecast revenue and expenditure and prepare a basis for a medium-term budget framework.

Reform of the Regulatory Environment

A number of traditional rules and practices in the Yemeni economy effectively sheltered producers from competition and protected monopolies in various sectors. Such obstacles to market entry likely contributed to relatively weak economic growth and job creation outside the oil sector. The government has recently initiated a number of reforms in this area—such as overhauling the Investment Law, the Agencies Law, and the Trade and Supply Law—but is also preparing for the privatization and liberalization of monopolistic activities in the airline and telecommunications industries. The government has also established the Aden Free Zone, where deregulation seems to have taken place at a faster pace, albeit with modest results (Box 2).

The current Investment Law (Law No. 22 of 1991) aims at regulating and promoting the investment of domestic and foreign capital in Yemen. It determines the sectors in which such investment may take place and the procedures to be followed to obtain legal authorization to undertake a business enterprise. It establishes the guarantees and benefits to be accorded

Box 2. The Aden Free Zone

Aden was once one of the world's top ports for ship bunkering and transshipment warehousing. About 7,000 vessels a year used its facilities in the 1950s and 1960s. But the closing of the Suez Canal from 1967 until 1975, the security problems in the region that followed, and changes in international cargo routes led to a sharp decline in business and loss of prosperity. Shortly after reunification, the government decided to initiate a development program for Aden, based on creation of a free zone, to restore some of its former importance.

With Aden's attractive location on the main shipping route between Asia and Europe, the Aden Free Zone and the Aden Container Terminal (ACT) offer a distance advantage over many other ports in the region. The free zone could provide an international gateway to businesses on three continents, provided it can compete with the several other free zones in the region. The development of modern transportation facilities and infrastructure in and around the free zone could spur regional trade, business opportunities, and economic growth.

The Yemen Free Zones Public Authority (YFZPA) was established in 1991 to develop the free zone in Aden and to grant concessions and regulate development. The free zone, covering approximately 31,000 hectares within the Governorate of Aden, was established in 1993. In 1995 Yeminvest, a joint venture between Port of Singapore Authority Corporation Ltd. (PSA) and Yemen Holdings Ltd. (a Saudi-owned company), was awarded exclusive rights to develop the ACT and the industrial estate of the free zone. PSA currently holds 60 percent of the project.

The beginning of operations of the ACT on March 19, 1999, marked the completion of the project's first phase, which gives the port a handling capacity of 500,000 twenty-foot equivalent units (TEUs) annually. This phase included the construction of two berths and a 700-meter quay wall, as well as dredging the harbor channel and berths to 16 meters. The second phase of the project will include the construction of an additional 325 meters of quay with a terminal capacity of up to 1.5 million TEUs annually. Future plans include expansion of the Aden airport and of tourist facilities.

As of mid-1999 the YFZPA had received 653 local, Arab, and international applications to invest in the new free zone, for a total value of $1.5 billion. These applications range across the industrial, storage, commercial, and tourism industries. However, apart from shipping through the ACT, no projects in the free zone have yet started, and even in the ACT activity remains far below the terminal's capacity.

Besides stipulating the formation of a "competent court" in the free zone, in compliance with the judiciary law in force, to settle disputes (in the spirit of commercial law in the United Kingdom), the free zone law provides various investment incentives. These include exemption from taxation on industrial and commercial profits for 15 years (with a possible additional 10 years); the possibility of 100 percent foreign ownership; free transfer of capital and profits outside the zone; and exemptions from income tax on salaries, wages, and bonuses of non-Yemeni employees working on projects in the zone.

to projects, including tax and customs duties and exemptions, and extensively elaborates on the rights and obligations of investors in their foreign exchange transactions. Many features of the law likely deter potential investors. For example, the General Investment Authority (GIA) is granted a high degree of control in approving projects through licensing; in having access to annual balance sheets of projects, which investors are obligated to provide; and in micromanaging aspects of the disposal of property associated with terminated projects, including controls on foreign exchange transactions related to licensed projects. The law limits the kind of commercial activities that may be undertaken within a particular project, and it provides a potential shelter for local production by allowing the imposition of additional customs duties on inputs used in the execution of some projects.

A major reform of the Investment Law was initiated in mid-1999. Amendments, to be considered by parliament shortly, aim at making the law more transparent and at streamlining the procedures for registering investment projects and carrying out related financial transactions. In particular, investment licensing by the GIA is to be eliminated and replaced by a simple registration process; equitable treatment of all investment projects is to be ensured; tax exemptions are to be streamlined and clarified; and controls on foreign exchange transactions related to projects registered under the law are to be liberalized.

Entry restrictions were also implicit in the original Agencies Law (Law No. 36 of 1992), aimed at regulating the establishment of commercial ventures between foreign companies and Yemeni representatives (which must be locally owned companies registered with the Ministry of Supply and Trade). The law made it illegal to act as an agent for a foreign supplier without a license, which must be renewed annually for a fee. Enforcement was in large part achieved through import licensing: licenses were not issued to importers who were not approved agents of foreign companies. In its original form, the law gave discretionary powers to the ministry in the granting of licenses and in allowing import activities without the agent being approved. This led to effective enforcement and protection of import trade monopolies. Amendments to this law decreed in 1997 and 1999 redefined the government's authority and should ensure a more competitive environment for these activities.

Similarly, the original Trade and Supply Law (Law No. 24 of 1990) effectively allowed the government to mandate and enforce prices in the private sector, with the purpose of guaranteeing a stable supply of basic commodities and avoiding overpricing and monopolies. It also aimed at supervising trade activities in the private sector to avoid disruptions in supply, in the spirit of a centrally planned economy. Amendments decreed in 1998 removed the authority of the government to set prices except for a limited number of basic commodities. Moreover, a law to promote competition and prohibit monopolies and commercial fraud was recently issued by presidential decree (Decree No. 19 of 1999). It includes explicit provisions for the market determination of prices of goods and services and for preventing collusion among producers. It calls for the establishment of a Competition Promotion and Anti-Monopoly Authority within the Ministry of Supply and Trade with the purpose of identifying and eliminating monopolistic practices and activities that disrupt the competitive operation of markets.

Transport and Communications

The transportation sector has long remained under the control of various state monopolies (such as the National Shipping Company in the Port of Aden, the Yemen Navigation Line, the General Land Transportation Company, and Yemenia, the state airline) and consequently plagued by inefficiency. The government set tariffs in all areas of transport services and kept the provision of all related services under its control through licensing requirements. Under the economic reform program, privatization and liberalization of land and maritime transport and, to some extent, air transport have been initiated.

In particular, a draft Surface Transportation Law, approved by the cabinet in 1999, calls for establishing a General Land Transport Authority, in charge of granting trucking licenses and posting suggested tariffs, a practice intended to replace administrative tariff setting by the government. By-laws specifically regulating the trucking sector have already been issued, allowing any trucker to obtain a license for operation, valid anywhere in Yemen.[58] Previously, the trucking industry was controlled by the (private) Ferzah cartel, which kept transport costs high through price fixing and preventing free entry, as well as by preventing private sector producers and traders from providing their own transport. Although the regulations recently introduced do not abolish the cartel, the government's intention is to provide a competitive environment by allowing other truckers to enter the market.

Progress in other parts of the transport sector includes the liberalization of stevedoring and the privatization of the National Shipping Company. However, the latter led to the establishment of a cartel of shipping agents at Aden, supported by the government in exchange for the absorption of former public sector employees by these agents. In the air transport industry, privatization of ground handling operations is on hold until the exclusive right of Yemenia to provide these services expires in 2001.

Deregulation of the telecommunications industry is only at an initial stage. The Public Telephone Corporation (PTC) has a monopoly on local services. International services is another monopoly, controlled by TeleYemen, a joint venture between PTC and a U.K. company; its status was renewed for four years in 1999. The only liberalization currently taking place is in the market of mobile services: the government recently tendered two cellular telephone (GSM) licenses, and a few offers were received, but no decision has yet been reached. Although these licenses will break the monopoly enjoyed by TeleYemen in the mobile sector, GSM providers will still have to go through TeleYemen to ensure international communications services to their customers.

Judicial Reform

Reform of the judicial system and, in particular, the functioning of the commercial courts has been initiated. Problems in the way courts were run, records kept, cases processed, and judgments enforced were increasingly recognized as important obstacles to private investment. Moreover, tribal affiliations hindered the administration of court decisions, and lack of adequate staff and judges' absenteeism rendered the process slow and inefficient. To address these issues, the government in recent years has consolidated jurisdiction over the administrative functioning of the courts in one ministry with a view to streamlining the process to reduce the backlog of pending cases. It also created a special unit to monitor the courts, organize the training of judges, and provide technical assistance on legal issues, and in early 2000 it started publication of judgments issued and the reasoning behind them.

The current Land Law also presents obstacles to investment. The system for land registration and proof of ownership is considered ineffective, and in-

[58]The minister of transport has reported that these by-laws are already being implemented; trucking licenses are being granted to all applicants with adequate equipment.

deed, the majority of litigation cases in Yemen are related to land ownership disputes. Yemen uses the registration of deeds system in recording land ownership: a deed, registered by a public officer and with copy held in a registry, testifies to ownership. Land registration is governed by Law No. 12 of 1976, which many experts consider ambiguous and ineffective.[59] Consequently, many land sales are currently transacted without registration, partly to avoid paying the sales tax and the *zakat* tax (a tax funding charitable services by mosques), but also because the parties often have little confidence in the Land Registration Authority, the government body in charge of applying the law. Major problems in certifying ownership arose after unification, leading to the issuance of Decree No. 65 in May 1991 to ensure the return of land in the south to its lawful owners. The decree was not adequately implemented, however, and appears to have led to several instances of land grabbing and corruption. Steps being taken to help remedy the shortcomings in the Land Law include the formation of an interministerial committee, which is currently working to streamline procedures for proving clear title and registration for all properties that will be privatized pending a broad review of the law.

In a step to improve the overall legal environment, the authorities plan, with support from the World Bank, to carry out a diagnostic assessment of the overall legal framework governing economic activity; an awareness campaign on the importance of the law in a democratic society is also being planned. In addition, a steering committee was formed in early 1999, involving both private sector and government institutions, to review the regulatory structure and administrative procedures for trade and investment and assess the obstacles to private sector investment. This committee is expected to make recommendations on further reforms needed to increase efficiency and transparency in the regulation of private sector activity.

Privatization

In early 1995, following the end of the civil war, the government initiated the privatization of public enterprises in various sectors of the economy, including industry, tourism, agriculture, fishing, transportation, oil, trade, and finance. In order to identify the enterprises to be privatized, a census was compiled in mid-1996 listing a total of 192 enterprises, of which more than 110 were located in the formerly socialist south. These public enterprises, employing over 86,500 employees (more than 25 percent of the civil service at the time), inefficiently run and sometimes even shut down, constituted a heavy burden on the budget, as operational losses had to be covered by budget transfers or the accumulation of arrears.

Over 1994–97 nearly 70 small enterprises were privatized; these included 16 tourism enterprises (8 of which were leased to private operators, and 8 privatized by restitution to the former owners) and 53 other properties, most of them agricultural units returned to their original owners. In the absence of a general strategy and a strong institutional framework, these privatization operations were mainly conducted at the discretion of the ministries involved and in an ad hoc manner. Ministries independently established their own internal committees to privatize or liquidate some of the enterprises under their jurisdiction.

The Technical Privatization Office (TPO) was operationally established in 1996. In cases where the TPO was in charge of privatization, the ministerial committees still participated in each step of the process (such as approving the short list of consultants and the report eventually submitted by the chosen consultant). Delays were sometimes encountered in bringing the committee members together and obtaining their inputs. During 1998 and most of 1999, privatization operations were largely put on hold while the government put in place an overall legal framework to conduct these operations in a more systematic and transparent way.

After a long gestation, a Privatization Law was promulgated in November 1999, aimed at organizing and unifying privatization procedures across state-owned economic units. That same month the World Bank approved a project for financial and technical assistance to the privatization program. The Privatization Law called for the establishment of a High Commission to ensure the implementation of standardized, unbiased, and transparent privatization procedures. The High Commission was established in December 1999 and held its first meeting in June 2000. It is chaired by the prime minister; other members include the ministers of planning, finance, legal affairs, and state. It is expected to provide policy oversight of the privatization program, approve transactions and program designs, and appoint temporary executive board members to the state-owned units approved for privatization. A reestablished TPO is expected to act as a secretariat to the commission, coordinating the whole program. Its functions include formulating privatization strategies (mostly by way of carrying out studies and reviewing proposals) and monitoring their implementation. Monitoring operations entail, for example, the provision of advice and assistance to individual ministries

[59] World Bank Country Development Report, Phase I, "Judicial and Legal System Building Block."

in carrying out privatization transactions as well as the preparation of necessary documents and contracts and coordinating with all concerned institutions such as labor unions.

In addition to these two bodies, the law stipulates the establishment of temporary committees representing each concerned ministry and/or its economic unit approved for privatization.[60] Each committee would participate in the privatization of the concerned enterprise, under the supervision of the High Commission and in coordination with the TPO. Although the sector ministries will have responsibility for carrying out the privatization of small and medium-size enterprises in collaboration with the TPO, full authority for approving large privatization transactions remains with the High Commission.

According to the Privatization Law, any person—whether a Yemeni citizen or a foreign national—is eligible to buy or lease the units offered for privatization, and sufficient land will be provided for the investor with the winning bid to conduct the activities of the privatized enterprise, either on a lease or on a sales basis. The terms negotiated between the government and potential investors will also cover the number of employees to be retained, and the conditions offered to these workers (salaries, bonuses, and other benefits) must be at least as good as those they currently enjoy. Those employees that the investors choose to keep would be guaranteed their jobs for a minimum of five years, and the remaining workers would be transferred to the CSF. Although this provision is intended to protect the workers, many observers fear that, as a result, investors will agree to take on only a small number of the existing employees, to avoid being locked into long-term contracts. Privatization proceeds are to be deposited with the central bank, in a special account earmarked to finance economic and social development projects.

Privatization strategies for each of five large enterprises have already been prepared and endorsed by the government, including implementation steps and schedules. For the Aden Refinery Company, new shares would be issued in return for capital contributions by investors, and an internationally recognized refinery operator would be attracted to ensure expert control over the enterprise. The privatization of Airport Ground-Handling Services is also projected to result in a joint shareholding and/or revenue-sharing venture between the government and the private sector. Privatization of the General Land Transport Company is expected to start with strategic restructuring, with the aim of creating a joint-stock limited liability company, partly funded by the government and potentially also by employee stock ownership. The Yemen Corporation for Cement Production and Marketing and the Yemen Drug Company will be privatized through issuing shares to strategic investors and selling government equity.

Quantitative estimates of the impact of the privatization program are available only for the fiscal impact of the large-enterprise component of the project. These estimates indicate that the privatization of these five units would result in net sales proceeds of about $20 million (about 0.3 percent of GDP) and that in the medium term an annual flow of $62 million (0.8 percent of GDP) would accrue to the budget in the form of taxes and dividends from the privatized enterprises. The emergence of new competitors in airport ground-handling services, land transport, and cement production and marketing could generate another $7 million in annual flows to the budget.

In the financial sector, all five state-owned banks are earmarked for liquidation, restructuring, or privatization under the government's reform program. Privatization of the Housing Bank was recently turned over to the TPO.

Financial Sector Reforms

Reforms in the Banking System and in Bank Supervision

In the period between unification and the end of 1994, the authorities' efforts regarding the financial system were focused on unifying the financial structures of the northern and southern parts of the country. (Box 3 describes the current status of the banking system.) Largely reflecting the lack of consensus and coherence in government and the civil service, little progress was made in achieving positive real interest rates and taking steps to stop financial disintermediation. Genuine financial sector reform did not begin until early 1995 as part of the economic reform program. At the start of this process, the authorities tackled interest rate reform and reform in the area of bank supervision, both of which produced quick and quantifiable results.

Interest rate reforms initiated in 1995 entailed the freeing of all lending rates, the elimination of concessional loan rates, and the establishment of minimum benchmark commercial bank savings deposit rates. The benchmark rates were set at high levels in view of the excess liquidity situation and the general reluctance by banks to attract new deposits. These rates were later adjusted in light of macroeconomic conditions, maintaining positive real rates most of the time (Section III).

[60]Such committees have already been established in various ministries (agriculture, supply and trade, and industry), as these have already carried out the privatization of some of the enterprises under their jurisdiction.

Box 3. The Yemeni Banking System

The Yemeni banking system comprises the Central Bank of Yemen, 13 commercial banks, and 3 specialized state-owned development banks. The commercial banking sector is made up of three privately owned domestic banks, four privately owned foreign banks, two state-owned banks, and four Islamic banks. The structure of the banking system has been broadly maintained since unification, with the exception of the Islamic banks, which were established after 1995.

At the end of 1999 the assets of the commercial banks totaled YRls 233 billion ($1.5 billion), equivalent to 22 percent of GDP. The largest bank, with 37 branches and over 20 percent of commercial bank assets, is the Yemen Bank for Reconstruction and Development (YBRD), in which the government has a majority share. The YBRD is heavily undercapitalized and has a large portfolio of nonperforming loans; the bank is being restructured with the objective of bringing it into full compliance with prudential regulations. The government also fully owns the National Bank of Yemen, which was the only commercial bank in the south before unification. This bank will be put up for sale in the near future.

The four privately owned foreign banks are all fully owned branches of banks with headquarters in France, Iraq, Jordan, and Pakistan. Of the three privately owned domestic banks, one is a joint venture with Saudi Arabian banks, with the local owners holding 75 percent. The four Islamic banks began operations between 1995 and 1998, and thus far their share of commercial bank assets is about 8 percent.

The three specialized banks were established to promote agriculture, housing, and industry. All three, but especially the Industrial Bank of Yemen, have been burdened for years with a large portfolio of nonperforming loans. An interministerial committee was recently formed to liquidate this bank.

The banking system as a whole is relatively weak, as reflected at the end of 1999 in a high ratio of nonperforming loans (17 percent of the total), low capitalization (a nonweighted capital adequacy ratio, or Cooke ratio, of 5.2 percent), and significant provisioning shortfalls. These problems are particularly acute for the public sector banks, which hold about one-third of total bank assets.

A number of other problems beset the banking system. Concentration is high: almost 70 percent of both deposits and loans are with the top four banks, and banks are generally located only in a few cities. Cash is the predominant medium of exchange, as reflected in a low ratio of quasi-money to broad money. Banks have generally maintained excess reserves for years, reflecting their reluctance to lend outside of a narrow group of borrowers, in the absence of effective legal recourse for timely recovery of nonperforming loans.

A number of actions by the authorities are aimed at improving the banking environment. The Banking Law of 1998 and subsequent central bank circulars have addressed such problem areas as credit concentration, insider lending, and use of overdraft facilities. Measures have also been taken to improve the operations of the commercial courts, and the central bank is enforcing a notification system under which delinquent borrowers are disqualified from receiving new loans. The new central bank law gives the central bank more independence to perform its role as supervisor of the banking system and to resist open-ended financing of the budget. A recent World Bank assessment revealed that Yemen's banks were either compliant or largely compliant with 10 of the 24 Basle core principles.

In order to improve financial intermediation, reform of bank supervision was also launched in 1995 (Box 3). From early 1996 on, banks were required to report their foreign currency positions, and by the end of 1997 the minimum capital requirement was doubled to YRls 500 million. During 1996–97 the central bank issued a number of circulars related to risk management, loan classification and provisioning, foreign exchange exposure, and external auditing. Provisioning requirements were set at 15 percent for substandard loans (those 90 days past due), 45 percent for doubtful loans (180 days past due), and 100 percent for bad loans (more than 365 days past due). Also, the banks were required to maintain a minimum capital adequacy ratio of 25 percent of total assets, and standards for new audit procedures and terms of reference for external auditors and risk management standards were established. The law governing the operations of moneychangers was amended so that moneychangers had to be licensed by the central bank, and provisions inconsistent with the operation of a free market were eliminated.

Adoption of a new banking law in 1998 established a more solid legal basis for the central bank to address prudential concerns, and in particular to set limits on credit concentration and insider lending. Thus in 1999 the central bank started to lay down clearer operational rules in the areas of credit concentration, insider lending, and use of overdraft facilities. To address the problem of concentration of credit among a small number of companies and groups of companies, a circular was issued limiting total credit to such entities to 15 percent (25 percent under certain circumstances) of total paid-in capital and reserves. If the central bank determines that the interests of two or more groups of persons are so intermingled that they should be considered as one, the liabilities of the two groups are combined and considered as a single liability.

To address the problem of insider lending, the central bank issued a circular that forbids lending to certain insiders and sets limits on lending for others as follows. A member of the board of directors who is not also a senior officer or manager may borrow an aggregate amount that does not exceed one-half of 1 percent of the bank's total paid-in capital and reserves. A shareholder owning 5 percent or more of the common stock or voting power of the bank may borrow an aggregate amount that does not exceed 15 percent of the bank's total paid-in capital and reserves. A senior officer, manager, or employee, including any such person who also is a member of the bank's board of directors, may borrow an aggregate amount that does not exceed that person's total annual wage and salary. The circular also streamlined the process of loan application by insiders.

To deal with the widespread use of overdraft facilities, which account for about 90 percent of bank credits, the central bank first introduced a new category of classification of exposures, called "special attention," to the existing categories of substandard, doubtful, and loss. This category was intended to require banks to identify and remedy potentially weak credit relationships at an early stage. It is to be used to identify and monitor exposures that contain weaknesses or potential weaknesses that, at the time of review, do not jeopardize the repayment of the credit or reflect a potential for loss, but which, if not addressed or corrected, could result in the deterioration of the credit to a substandard or worse classification. Second, to clarify the treatment of bank guarantees, the new regulation allows banks to consider guarantees of other banks as a basis for not classifying an otherwise nonperforming credit exposure. This may be done provided that the banks issuing the guarantees have a capital adequacy ratio of 12 percent or higher, that they are rated A+ or better by a reputable international bank rating agency, and that the guarantees are unrestricted.[61] However, such credits need to be returned to performing status or the guarantee called upon within a reasonable time. Third, the central bank streamlined the process to be used by banks for determining borrower performance for credit lines that are in continuous overdraft for three months or more.

Establishment of the Treasury Bills Market

To develop sources of less inflationary financing of the government budget from the nonbank sector, in December 1995 the authorities initiated central bank auctions of treasury bills to the public. The central bank started its monthly auctions with 30-day treasury bills, but this instrument was discontinued in the following year in favor of three-month and six-month bills. By the end of 1996 the outstanding stock of treasury bills had reached YRls 12 billion (1.7 percent of GDP), over half of which was held by the banking system. During 1997 the authorities introduced a one-year treasury bill and phased out the term deposits facilities in the central bank. The treasury bills issued during 1996–97 were used mainly as monetary policy instruments for liquidity management during that period, reflecting the strengthened fiscal position in each of those years. A sharp increase in the amount of bills issued took place after banks' reserve requirements were lowered from 25 percent to 15 percent in December 1996, in order to mop up the banks' excess liquidity.

With the strengthening of fiscal balances in 1999, issuance of treasury bills slowed down, although in early 2000 the authorities started to convert large amounts of outstanding government overdrafts into treasury bills. Most of these were used to provide additional bills required by banks for their own liquidity management through repurchase operations (repos), initiated in November 1999. Although the central bank offers clearing and settlement facilities, secondary trading of treasury bills has not yet developed. In part, this reflects banks' lack of information on each other and a general mistrust of the information released by individual banks, which to date has also prevented development of an interbank market.

Other Instruments of Monetary Policy

In addition to the changes in the minimum benchmark interest rate and some use of treasury bills for monetary policy purposes, the central bank has relied on reserve requirements on rial deposits and on foreign currency deposits, intervention in the foreign exchange market and credit ceilings, and central bank credit facilities as monetary policy instruments.

Credit facilities were little used, reflecting the excess liquidity situation of the commercial banks. The central bank does not have an overdraft facility, but it can discount treasury bills held by commercial banks (and others) at a rate of 2 percentage points above the highest accepted yield on three-month treasury bills at the latest auction. Throughout 1990–99 the central bank also provided a small amount of credit to public enterprises at market rates and on commercial terms. The central bank has intervened actively in the foreign exchange market, especially in late 1998, to smooth volatility in the exchange rate. Credit ceilings were used in the early

[61] These ratings relate to international banks. This regulation will be modified to include local banks once a local rating system is in place.

Figure 11. Credit and Currency Ratios

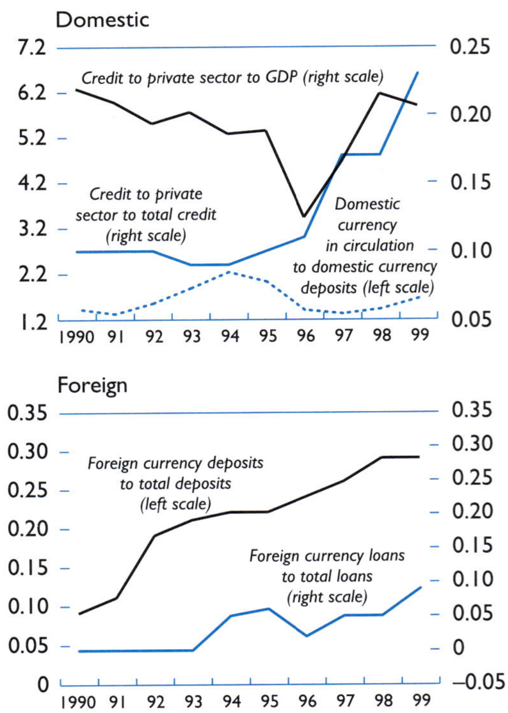

Source: IMF, *International Financial Statistics.*

Figure 12. Money Velocities and Multipliers
(Ratio)

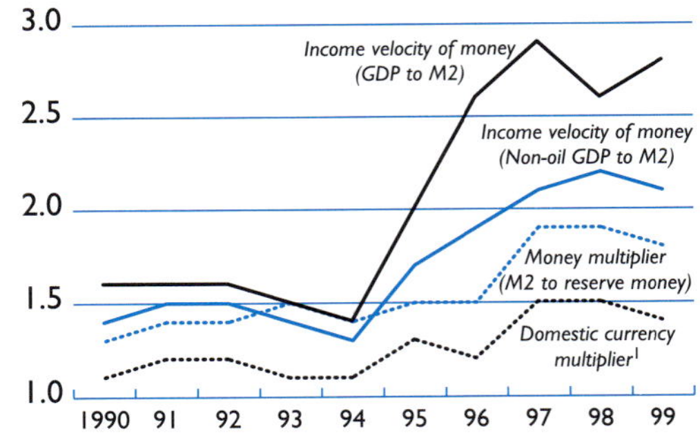

Source: IMF, *International Financial Statistics.*
[1]Ratio of rial money to rial component of reserve money.

postunification period but were hardly ever binding. Since 1997 the central bank has refrained from setting any ceilings.

Financial Deepening and Economic Stabilization

The need for financial deepening has been evident since the early postunification period, as commercial banks maintained excess reserve positions with the central bank, in spite of high legal reserves. This behavior reflected their reluctance to grant loans to the private sector in a regime of fixed interest rates and in the absence of effective legal recourse for the timely recovery of nonperforming loans. Consequently, commercial banks had little interest in mobilizing rial deposits and were content to place a large part of their deposits with the central bank at a rate of 1.5 percent above the banks' average cost of funds. Negative real interest rates were, not surprisingly, accompanied by an increasing trend toward dollarization of the economy. The share of foreign currency deposits in total deposits rose steadily, from 9 percent in 1990 to 29 percent in 1999 (Figure 11), and continued to rise even after real interest rates turned positive in the last three years of the period. This may have reflected, in part, expectations of a depreciation of the rial; indeed, during 1999 holders of dollar deposits earned a real return of only 2 percent, compared with the average minimum saving deposit rate of 10 percent. In addition, Yemeni expatriate workers, reflecting their experience of several years of high inflation and political unrest, traditionally hold part of their remittances in dollar deposits. On the lending side, the growth of foreign currency loans as a percentage of total loans has been much slower, reaching only 9 percent of total loans in 1999. This reflects strict central bank regulations under which borrowers of foreign currency must also be foreign exchange earners.

The economic stabilization program has so far translated into some limited progress in financial deepening. The trend increase in credit to the private sector as a share of total credit is partly the result of the government's repayments to the banking system and the added importance of nonbank financing of the budget deficit. However, it also reflects positive real private credit growth in 1996–99, averaging 2.4 percent a year, compared with an average annual decline of 15.7 percent during 1990–95. A rising multiplier points to increasing efficiency of the banking system (Figure 12), and a rising ratio of credit to non-oil GDP (from 44 percent at the end of 1996 to 78 percent in 1999) indicates that financial deepening is taking place in the non-oil sector. Other indicators point to an opposite trend; for example, the use of currency has grown relative to that of deposits (Fig-

Figure 13. Republic of Yemen and Selected Comparators: Liquidity and Credit Ratios

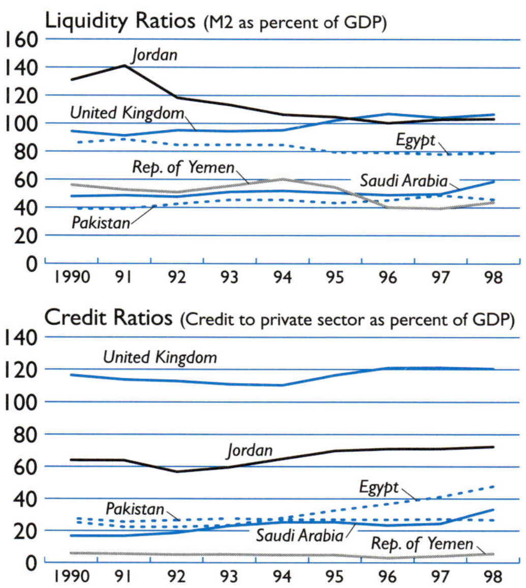

Source: IMF, *International Financial Statistics.*

Figure 14. Republic of Yemen and Selected Comparators: Money Multipliers and Credit Indicators

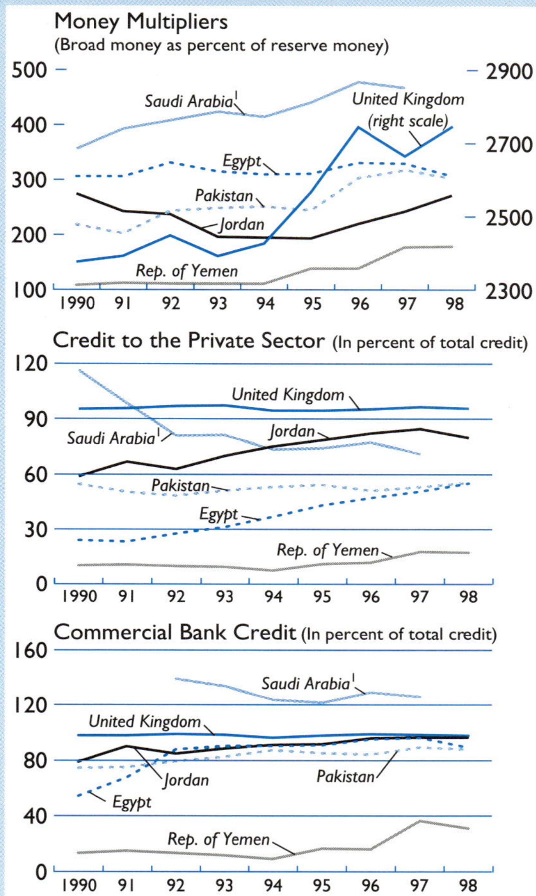

Source: IMF, *International Financial Statistics.*

[1]The high ratios for Saudi Arabia reflect large claims by the government on the banking system.

ure 11). A comparison of various indicators of depth and efficiency of financial markets with a selection of other countries highlights the underdevelopment of Yemen's financial system (Figures 13 and 14).[62] The ratio of broad money (M2) to GDP in Yemen was the lowest among the selected countries in 1998. The same holds for the ratio of private credit to GDP, the share of private sector credit to total credit, and the share of commercial banks' credit as a percentage of total credit; Yemen's money multiplier is much lower than those of the other countries.

Soundness of the Banking System

One of the objectives of the financial reform program was the implementation of legal reforms that would enable the commercial banks to seek effective judicial recourse to deal with nonperforming assets. Such action, together with a more independent central bank implementing stricter supervision over the credit operations of banks, was expected to significantly improve the soundness of the banking system. Despite considerable progress in the central bank's role as bank supervisor, however, implementation of the new legal framework has remained timid. Among the more effective steps was the introduction by the central bank in May 1997 of a notification system for delinquent private sector borrowers, and prohibition of new bank loans to such borrowers until they regularize their relations with their creditor banks. The notification system has yielded some

[62]Saudi Arabia is included as a comparator because it is a neighboring country; Egypt and Jordan were selected because these countries have close relations with Yemen; Pakistan was selected because, like Yemen, it is eligible to borrow from the Poverty Reduction and Growth Facility; and the United Kingdom was selected as a representative industrialized country.

results, as reflected in fewer delinquencies among large borrowers.

Despite wide spreads between lending and deposit rates (Statistical Appendix Table A.26), banks' profitability has remained low, reflecting their large excess reserves (and their lack of interest in granting credit and in mobilizing deposits) as well as large nonperforming portfolios. Wide spreads also reflect the lack of competition from within the banking system and the lack of a nonbank financial system. Low profitability may have also contributed to some erosion of the capital base since the early postunification period, but this was only detected with the strengthening of the provisioning requirements after the reform program was implemented.

Partly reflecting the problems of judicial recourse, commercial banks in Yemen have traditionally been reluctant to lend outside of a core group of customers. The strengthening of the central bank's supervision in these areas is therefore creating considerable friction, as banks resist or try to circumvent enforcement of prudential regulation. Although provisioning against problem loans has improved in recent years, their ratio to total loans has increased (Statistical Appendix Table A.29). Banks' exposure to foreign exchange risk, as measured by the difference between assets and liabilities denominated in foreign exchange, is also a cause for concern, with a large part of total foreign currency exposure relating to two public sector banks. The government began in 1997 to buy back the overdue foreign obligations of one of these banks at a significant discount, and the other is scheduled to be put up for sale shortly. The private commercial banks' exposure to foreign exchange risk is not large. Concentration of credit risk across the sectors of the economy is broadly in line with the structure of GDP, except that lending for construction accounts for only 4 percent of total credit to the nongovernmental sector (Statistical Appendix Table A.27), a much lower percentage than in most economies. This is probably explained by the absence of property guarantees in Yemen, with the consequence that banks extend housing loans only to their best customers. With regard to maturity structure, over 90 percent of all commercial bank loans have maturities of less than one year, reflecting a lack of willingness on the part of banks to lend for investment purposes, and the importance of import and domestic trade financing in the Yemeni economy and the associated prevalence of overdraft facilities.

V Poverty and Social Safety Net Policies

The Yemeni government traditionally offered few social insurance or welfare benefits, leaving the majority of the population to rely on informal safety nets within the family or within the tribal, religious, or other community. The pension system covers only civil servants, the military, security forces, and workers in the tiny formal private sector. Other social assistance is either indirect, through subsidization of food and petroleum products, or through cash transfers, or through transfers with work requirements such as the Social Fund for Development and the public works program. A formal cash transfer program, the Social Welfare Fund, was instituted in 1997. Other budgetary cash transfers include medical grants, benefits for veterans and their families, payments for tribal affairs, and discretionary compensations for emergencies.

Pensions

Yemen has four separate pension schemes. Employees in the public sector are covered by a general scheme for civil servants and public enterprise employees, a military pension plan, and a plan for the internal security forces. The fourth plan covers workers in the formal private sector.

Relatively little public information is available about the plans of the military and security forces; indications are that about 50,000 beneficiaries participate in the military plan and 4,500 in the plan of the security forces. Information for 1993–95 indicates that both funds were running large surpluses. However, the authorities have not undertaken long-term actuarial studies, nor is the financial status of the funds' investment portfolios known.

The public sector plan for civil servants resulted from the merger of the North Yemeni Public Social Security and Pension Agency, created in 1982, with the South Yemeni plan, established in 1967. The South Yemeni plan's surpluses were mostly invested in real estate, which yielded low returns. As a result, the South Yemeni plan added considerable net liabilities to the joint pension system.

Law No. 25 of 1991, as amended by presidential decree in December 1999, governs the public employee pension plan. Participation is mandatory for all public sector employees. Until recently, contributions and benefits were based on the basic wage, which excludes allowances and bonuses and generally amounts to between 50 percent and 60 percent of the full wage. The decree of December 1999 provided that benefits and contributions be based on the full wage. Employees and employers each contribute 6 percent to the public pension plan. An additional contribution of 1 percent is collected for disability and work-related injury insurance. Full public sector pensions of 100 percent of the last wage (until 1999 the last basic wage) are paid after 35 years of service, and the minimum service requirement is 15 years. Standard retirement ages are 55 for women and 60 for men, but early retirement is possible after 20 (women) or 25 years of service (men). Survivor benefits are generous because the pension of the deceased is divided among the extended family, including parents, children, and children of deceased siblings. Benefits can thus continue for a very long time, because a number of survivors may survive the primary beneficiary by many years. A minimum pension, which was doubled to YRls 7,000 a month in December, is paid to those whose benefits would otherwise fall below that threshold.

Retirement of civil servants has not been enforced in part because many overage civil servants would qualify only for the minimum pension. Moreover, as the administrative capacity of the pension authority is weak, while it tries to reconcile individual records for each applicant for benefits, only about 2,000 to 3,000 new pensioners per year have been accepted by the authority. Therefore, as of the end of 1999, more than 20,000 overage civil servants were eligible for retirement. The government started to enforce retirement of these employees in early 2000.

In the near term the public pension plan is expected to remain in a favorable financial position. Between 1995 and 1999 the plan ran surpluses of between 0.5 and 0.8 percent of GDP, reflecting the small ratio of beneficiaries (about 40,000 in 1999) to contributors (more than 400,000). Assets, estimated at YRls 30 billion at the end of 1999, are now mostly invested in treasury bills, with only minor holdings in low-yielding real estate. Because contributions will henceforth be based on the full wage, surpluses are expected to rise in the near future. However, owing to the high replacement rates, the plan is projected to run deficits in the medium and long term, because more and more civil servants will retire and few new employees are expected to be hired. In light of these projections and the necessity to streamline the civil service, the government is committed to a reform of the public pension scheme that will provide for stronger links between benefits and contributions and support the long-run sustainability of the scheme.

The private sector pension plan is based on the North Yemeni institution established in 1987 and is governed by Law No. 26 of 1991. Eligibility and benefit rules are very similar to the public plan, with the exception that there is no minimum pension.[63] Employees contribute 6 percent and employers 9 percent of wages, which, following a 1995 decree of the minister of social insurance, includes the basic salary and other allowances. Disability contributions are 4 percent of wages but are rarely paid or enforced. In 1999 the private fund had about 1,000 beneficiaries, many with small pensions, and 40,000 contributors. The plan ran surpluses between 1995–99 and is expected to continue to do so in the near and medium term. Currently, most assets are held in the form of treasury bills. Actuarial studies show that the private sector's plan benefits are also likely to be unsustainable in the long run.

The Social Welfare Fund and Other Cash Transfers

The Social Welfare Fund (SWF) began operation in 1997. Previously, the Ministry of Social Affairs had paid cash transfers on a discretionary basis to families appealing for assistance. The SWF started with a caseload of 39,000 people. Since then their number has grown rapidly, to about 350,000 cases at the end of 1999. Cash benefits are set at YRls 1,000 per month for a one-family household and rise by YRls 200 for each family member up to YRls 2,000 per family. Payments are made every three months.[64] Beneficiaries must be without fixed income, without assets, and without support of a family member. Targeted groups are the disabled, orphans, women outside a family support network, and the poor. The law stipulates that each case should be reevaluated once a year, but with the rapidly growing caseload the SWF has not been able to keep up with this requirement. Most of the SWF's full-time employees are located in the capital, and its employees who perform evaluations in the governorates are largely part-time. The budget of the SWF has grown with the caseload from YRls 2.4 billion in 1998 to YRls 5.2 billion in 1999 and an estimated YRls 7.7 billion in 2000 (0.7 percent of GDP). Operating costs have remained small, at 4 to 5 percent of total expenditure. However, these low operating expenditures have also resulted in a number of deficiencies of coverage. Spending patterns do not match the geographical distribution of poverty or of the general population, indicating a deficiency in reaching the rural poor. Much of the administration is centralized in the capital, resulting in long delays between application and payment of beneficiaries and difficulties in verifying eligibility.

Other cash transfer programs include benefits for veterans and tribal organizations. These benefits are for fairly narrowly defined subsets of the population. The number of recipients of veteran benefits was estimated at 28,000 to 29,000 in 1999, and about 9,000 people received tribal benefits that year. In addition, the government provides medical grants and cash compensation for emergencies. Detailed breakdowns of transfers were not available before 1997, and the effectiveness of these benefits has not yet been evaluated. Most of these specific transfers have grown little over time and are declining in importance compared with the SWF.

The Social Fund for Development

The Social Fund for Development (SFD) was established by Law No. 10 of 1997 for the purpose of helping alleviate any negative effects of the 1995 economic reform program on the poor. It is headed by a board of directors chaired by the prime minister and with members representing key ministries, nongovernmental organizations, and the private sector. The board decides on the general policies and orientation of the SFD in its annual operation plan and monitors its performance.

Direct management of all aspects of the SFD's operations is the responsibility of the managing director. However, this is undertaken according to a strict and detailed operations manual developed jointly with World Bank consultants.[65] This institutional

[63]Between 1997 and 1999 the operations of the private and the public funds were merged. After expected cost reductions could not be realized and private sector compliance fell, the merger was reversed in 1999.

[64]The poverty line for an individual was estimated at YRls 2,600 per month in 1999.

[65]The managing director is also a member of the board, and the office of the managing director acts as its secretariat.

setup provides a large degree of autonomy within the SFD for quick and efficient decision making and program implementation.

By the end of 1999 the SFD had grown to include over 85 employees and 6 branches. At its inception, a sum exceeding $80 million was earmarked for the first five-year phase of operations, with various donors involved (including the International Development Association, the Arab Fund, and the European Union). The government contributes an annual sum of YRls 98 million. The capital made available to the SFD is deposited in private commercial banks; it is directly accessible to management, which provides for efficient disbursement of funds.

The SFD carries out three major types of programs. First, community development services are aimed at directly improving the living conditions of the poor and the marginalized, and involving, wherever possible, the implementation of labor-intensive subprojects to create employment in the targeted communities. Programs include the provision of basic education, primary health care, water and sewerage facilities, and rural road access. Second, the SFD's small and microenterprise development programs work mainly through the delivery of credit to income-generating activities. Although small enterprise development has not yet taken place, the SFD has undertaken several projects aimed at microenterprise development, through loan packages generally accompanied by participation of beneficiaries in the design of the economic activity that will benefit from the credit. These programs are often implemented through nongovernmental organizations and community-based associations. The third type of program engages in capacity building, to enable local community groups to initiate, operate, and maintain development projects,[66] and to enhance capacity in various nongovernmental organizations, associations, and government institutions.[67]

Programs are usually implemented through committees of beneficiaries, specifically set up for that purpose with SFD support.[68] Projects in education, health, and water and sewerage are also implemented through institutions, such as local councils or nongovernmental organizations, that can provide a legal umbrella (and hence accountability) to ensure the sustainability of operations. There is generally close coordination with the corresponding government institution to avoid duplication of projects and to ensure the supply of employees to work on the projects—in particular, the government supplies the necessary providers to run education and health care facilities.

The SFD follows a two-pronged approach in program development: on one hand, it both responds to demand and targets specific needs; on the other hand, it attempts to cover fairly the Yemeni territory, including remote rural areas and all marginalized groups.[69] Targeting is necessary because most needy communities are often hindered from submitting any demand for various reasons, ranging from helplessness, desperation, and frustration, to illiteracy and physical illness, to domineering by local sheiks. The Planning and Monitoring Unit of the SFD designed a separate measure of poverty based on nine indicators capturing basic sociodemographic and economic characteristics. This measure is regularly updated and refined, and the SFD relies on it in its targeting policy.

The SFD has succeeded in operating efficiently because of a large degree of autonomy and its use of simple decision-making processes, and because of simplified procurement and disbursement procedures.[70] It started operations early in its inception year, contracting 50 projects at a total cost of about $4 million; in 1998 it contracted 337 projects with total investments of $21.2 million and total disbursements of $6.2 million. By September 1999 the SFD had implemented a cumulative total of 785 projects and subprojects covering a large part of the country; total investments were about $47 million, of which about $20 million had been disbursed (Table 11).[71]

The success of the SFD's operations is evident in both the high repayment rate on credits delivered

[66]For example, the SFD provided management and skills training in accountancy for 68 agricultural cooperatives in the governorates of Sana'a and Ibb, in close cooperation with the Federation of Agricultural Cooperatives.

[67]For example, the SFD provided the SWF with technical assistance in developing a new survey to determine eligibility, establishing an electronic database of beneficiaries, and acquiring skills in relevant software to maintain this database.

[68]The SFD insists on a participatory process in most of its projects: local communities participate both in defining the needs and in setting up and running the projects. Sometimes their contribution extends to 50 percent of the project's design and implementation work.

[69]The SFD pays particular attention to females and juveniles; for example, in 1998 a project to improve the living conditions of jailed women was implemented. A school was established in the central jail to provide literacy classes and skills training. The SFD took juveniles out of the central jail and placed them in a hostel. Civil orphan hostels were also established, and there are projects under way to institute seven hostels for boys and girls. Of all the microenterprise development projects implemented so far, more than 50 percent targeted women, and more than 60 percent were in rural areas.

[70]Some SFD projects (in education, for example) are implemented at a third of what it would cost the government to implement, and at a much quicker pace. For the building of schools it now provides efficiency benchmarks for outside government contracts.

[71]This faster-than-expected growth of the SFD's programs forced it to shorten its first operational phase from five years to three and to apply for a larger ($100 million) grant from the World Bank to finance a second five-year phase of operations.

Table 11. Social Fund for Development—Accumulated Investment, Disbursement, Number of Expected Beneficiaries, and Job Opportunities, up to September 30, 1999, According to Sector

Sector	No. of Projects	Committed ($)	Disbursed (4)	Beneficiaries		Job Creation	
				Direct	Indirect	Temporary (Person-day)	Permanent (Person)
Education	490	24,474,98	12,407,008	262,927	40,009	888,057	3,506
Health	101	5,700,093	2,003,775	495,335	38,006	130,951	1,066
Water	85	7,148,680	3,111,320	337,598	8,498	190,217	176
Environmental activities and sewerage	16	2,894,732	338,676	154,575	60,000	104,337	126
Roads	9	855,464	23,255	64,836	55,996	60,709	0
Social services	8	2,859,371	60,929	1,900	0	95,527	138
Capacity building	63	885,498	471,396	7,807	685	13,096	414
Micro enterprise	13	2,220,087	1,582,776	10,995	59,942	2,864	154
Total	785	47,038,913	19,999,135	1,335,973	263,136	1,485,758	5,580

Source: Social Fund for Development Newsletter, Issue No. 8 (October–December, 1999).

and the numbers of beneficiaries served and jobs created by its programs. Although the effective rate of interest charged by the SFD is quite high, often exceeding 20 percent, the repayment rate is well above 90 percent.[72] A cumulative total of 1,335,973 persons were direct beneficiaries of SFD programs by the end of September 1999, and the number of indirect beneficiaries stood at 263,136. During the same period, these projects have allowed the creation of permanent jobs for 5,580 people.

Informal Safety Nets and Development Support Organizations

Besides programs carried out at the central government level, several welfare initiatives were undertaken at the local government and community levels in the 1980s in both North and South Yemen. Local organizations raised contributions within their own communities to undertake development projects such as roads, clinics, schools, and parks. In the early 1980s, as reported in the World Bank's 1996 Poverty Assessment Review (PAR), these organizations completed the construction of 852 kilometers of roads, 783 classrooms, 267 potable water projects, 71 clinic rooms, and 261 parks and mosques. They also undertook a greater number of maintenance projects. Whereas the organizations in North Yemen (known as Local Councils for Cooperative Development) were initially independent but worked with the collaboration of the central government, those in South Yemen were under direct central government control. However, the North Yemeni government increased its control of these units, which discouraged community involvement and commitment and led to a steep decline in financial, labor, and time contributions of local communities.[73]

Although the involvement of Yemeni local communities in welfare operations was on the decline in the first part of the 1990s, mostly for lack of institutional capacity and financing, the role of international and nongovernmental organizations increased. Some 15 reasonably active nongovernmental organizations provide health, education, and other social services to urban areas, and these seem to be relatively successful at targeting low-income groups. However, these organizations have limited capacity and resources available to allow them to grow and improve the efficiency of their services.[74]

Three types of informal safety nets can be identified in Yemen: religious charity, traditional commu-

[72]Most of the SFD programs are based on Islamic banking, for consistency with the tradition and expectations of the concerned communities.

[73]Rural community organizations in North Yemen were first known as Local Development Agencies. They were funded by private donations, *zakat*, and remittances and had a large degree of autonomy. Law No. 12 of 1985 reduced that autonomy by transferring the power and responsibility to provincial governors and reorganizing the cooperatives into the Local Councils for Cooperative Development.

[74]These institutions raise money from the government as well as from individuals and businesses. There are, however, no clear guidelines dictating the extent of government assistance, which is then administered on an apparently ad hoc basis, and bilateral international assistance to these institutions is still limited.

nity-based assistance reinforced by a strong tribal system, and within-family transfers. Religious charity can take the form of *zakat*, which represents the donation of 2 to 5 percent of one's wealth to the poor, or *satqa*, which represents voluntary donations, pecuniary or in kind, to the poor. Community support is provided, for example, through voluntary work or neighbors' labor pooling. In the early 1970s neighborhood groups often grew into organized cooperatives (the Local Councils for Cooperative Development mentioned above). Although hard to estimate, family support must be an important source of assistance, because Yemeni society is very traditional, its structure based more on family network and solidarity than on economic achievement. This is particularly striking in the rural areas, whereas larger cities are being slowly transformed by the transition to a market economy.

Sociologists believe that the informal support systems in Yemen work reasonably well and explain the apparently rare incidence of starvation. However, in the absence of systematic research on the issue, no quantitative assessment of the scope and effects of these safety nets is available.

VI Economic Performance from 1990 to 1999

The performance of Yemen's economy in the 1990s shows clearly the impact of the exogenous shocks it suffered during the period, but it also, in the latter half of the decade, bears witness to the first fruits of the reform process launched in 1995. This section reviews the economic record of the 1990s in terms of the growth of GDP and its components, employment, inflation, poverty and social indicators, saving and investment, and the external accounts.

Growth and Employment

The external shocks to which Yemen was subject in the 1990s had a strong impact on economic growth. Dislocations associated with the Gulf crisis of 1990 and with unification, and again with the civil war in 1994, contributed to sharp economic contractions; however, resumption of economic activity after both episodes was associated with rapid growth (see Table 1 in Section II).[75] These swings in growth rates were exacerbated by a severe drought in 1990–91 and a milder one during the first rainy season of 1999. On the other hand, oil discoveries that brought on stream the large Masila field in mid-1993 compensated for anemic growth in other sectors at the time and helped mitigate the impact of the 1994 civil strife on national income. Indeed, the sectoral composition of GDP shows a growing importance of the oil sector over the decade (Figure 15). Government policies have also played a major role in Yemen's growth performance. As described before, controls imposed in the first part of the decade, laws that either created or protected monopolistic practices, and regulations that inhibited or discouraged private sector activities were important obstacles to economic expansion. On the other hand, the liberalization and reform of the regulatory environment initiated after the end of the civil war were probably important elements in triggering economic growth, although such effects are difficult to quantify.

Figure 15. Composition of Real GDP
(In percent)

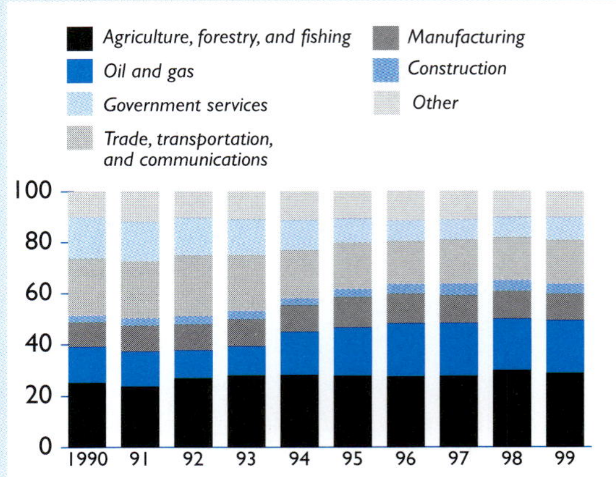

Source: Data provided by the Yemeni authorities.

The improvement in performance is striking when growth is compared over the pre- and post-reform periods (Table 12). Real GDP growth averaged 5.6 percent a year in 1995–99, compared with –0.2 percent in 1991–94. Even if the civil war effect is isolated by eliminating 1994 from the calculations, the difference in average annual growth remains impressive. Although this improvement has its origins in part in the oil sector, average annual non-oil GDP growth also rose, more than doubling in the second half of the decade, even after abstracting from the adverse effect of the civil war. With population growth little changed between these two periods, the faster growth appears to have come

[75]Despite improvements in the methodology underlying the national accounts compiled by the Central Statistics Organization of Yemen (CSO), GDP figures remain unreliable, largely because of a lack of basic underlying data in many areas, as well as a lack of adequate deflators for all components of GDP. Moreover, the existence of a multiple exchange rate system before 1996 probably biases the data for 1990–96 downward, as these may overstate the importance of transactions at the highly overvalued official exchange rate. In the absence of alternative data sources (except for the oil sector), official CSO data are used as the base for assessing broad trends in various sectors of the economy.

Table 12. Macroeconomic Indicators Comparing Pre-Reform and Reform Period, 1991–99

	Annual Average		
	1991–93	1991–94	1995–99
	(Growth rates in percent)		
Real GDP	1.0	–0.2	5.6
Oil GDP	–6.1	4.4	9.8
Non-Oil GDP	2.1	–1.0	4.7
Of which			
Agriculture, forestry, fishing	4.8	2.7	6.1
Manufacturing	4.7	2.1	5.6
Construction	8.3	0.7	13.6
Trade, wholesale, and retail	4.4	–0.3	8.9
Transportation, storage, and communications	–1.7	–6.4	0.0
Financial and real estate services	1.3	2.8	4.6
Government services	–4.0	–7.8	–0.3
Real per capita consumption	–20.3	–26.5	2.9
Inflation	52.6	57.3	25.3
M2-growth (Dec/Dec)	27.1	28.9	13.0
	(In percent of GDP)		
External current account (excluding grants)	–14.1	–9.5	–0.2
Fiscal balance (excluding grants)	–12.0	–13.1	–4.2
Gross national savings	6.4	11.3	21.8
Gross investment	19.7	19.9	21.0

Sources: Yemeni authorities; and IMF staff estimates.

from more rapid capital accumulation and a considerably better performance of total factor productivity (TFP; Box 4). Even so, for the decade as a whole, average TFP growth was negative, pointing to substantial scope for structural reform to improve non-oil growth performance, without necessarily higher levels of investment.

Sectoral Growth in the Non-Oil Economy

Agriculture and Fishing

Agriculture, including forestry and fishing, is the largest sector of the Yemeni economy, accounting in 1998–99 for about 30 percent of GDP and 58 percent of employment (Figure 1 in Section II). Seventy-seven percent of the population derive their income from agriculture and related activities such as trade and transport. However, reliance on irrigation in a country with scarce water resources, coupled with a prevalence of traditional methods of cultivation, constrained agricultural growth over the past decade. Real growth in agriculture averaged a modest 4.5 percent a year between 1990 and 1999, and its contribution to real non-oil growth declined from the first to the second half of the decade (Box 4). The sector is highly vulnerable to variations in rainfall. For instance, following the severe drought in 1990–91, real agricultural activity contracted by 7.6 percent; it recovered impressively in 1992 (20.1 percent real growth), largely because of exceptional rainfall.

Government policies had an important impact on agricultural growth. In the first part of the decade, import subsidies on wheat and flour kept prices artificially low, discouraging local production.[76] More important, the large depreciation of the rial in the parallel market in 1992–94 led to an increase in input costs (seeds, fertilizers, machinery, and parts are imported), which lowered net returns to farmers. At the same time, domestic production was stimulated through import bans on various products, such as fruits, vegetables, fats, and grains, and high import tariff rates on others. The gradual removal of bans and controls in the context of the reform program that started in 1995 nonetheless coincided with an increase in production, partly by reducing the costs of inputs and liberalizing prices, but also because about 50 agricultural units were privatized at

[76]Locally grown wheat is traditionally viewed by Yemenis as having higher quality and better taste than imported wheat, which creates demand for it despite its higher price; this might have mitigated the adverse effect of import subsidies on local production.

Box 4. Accounting for Growth in the Non-Oil Sector

Recent national accounts data indicate that real non-oil growth in the Yemeni economy picked up to an annual average of 4.7 percent in the second half of the 1990s, compared with 2.1 percent in 1991–93. The sectoral composition of the economy remained broadly stable, although the share of agriculture rose by 1.5 percentage points during 1995–99. However, the contribution of agriculture to non-oil growth declined from 70 percent in 1991–93 to 43 percent in 1995–99. This was partly compensated by fishing and by financial institutions and real estate, each of which contributed an additional 3 to 4 percent to non-oil growth in 1995–99 compared with the pre-civil war period. The share of government services in GDP fell slightly over 1995–99. Tourism, although generally perceived as an industry in which Yemen has comparative advantage, did not perform well: its contribution to non-oil growth (proxied by the value added of restaurants and hotels) increased by only 0.3 percent, from a low base of 0.6 percent (see Annex 1).

Sectoral breakdown of Non-Oil GDP

	Sector's Share in Non-Oil GDP		Contribution to Non-Oil GDP Growth	
	1995	1999	1991–93	1995–99
Agriculture and forestry	33.4	35.0	70.5	42.6
Fishing	0.7	1.2	–0.8	3.2
Manufacturing	14.8	13.2	26.0	15.5
Construction	3.9	5.0	13.3	11.6
Transportation, storage, and communications	13.1	11.3	–13.8	0.0
Government services	11.5	10.9	–34.3	–0.9
Wholesale and retail trade	9.1	10.2	17.8	17.3
Restaurants and hotels	0.4	0.5	0.6	0.9
Financial institutions and real estate	7.2	7.6	4.2	7.6
Other	5.4	4.7	16.5	2.2

Sources: Central Statistics Organization of Yemen; and IMF staff estimates.

the onset of the privatization program.[77] Another factor was some improvement in cold storage and transportation facilities for agricultural production. Hence average annual growth in agriculture rose to 6.1 percent a year in 1995–99, compared with 4.8 percent a year in 1991–93 (Table 12).

Two decades of rapid growth under the umbrella of protectionism and subsidies had achieved, by the mid-1990s, near self-sufficiency in both fruits and vegetables. The second half of the 1990s saw a continued rise in the production of these crops, partly underpinned by the spread of irrigation, and despite the gradual removal of import bans imposed on similar products (Statistical Appendix Table A.14). However, production of cereals generally declined over that period, with a sharp drop estimated for 1999 due to the drought that occurred in the first rainy season that year. *Qat* is another important crop in Yemen, capturing more than 7 percent of the total cultivated area (Box 5). However, statistics on *qat* production are inadequate, and its contribution to GDP is difficult to assess. *Qat* does seem highly water intensive; with production largely supported by indirect subsidies on diesel fuel and water pumps, its expansion may have contributed to the decline in cereal production.

Livestock and other noncrop agricultural production increased significantly over the second part of the 1990s (Statistical Appendix Table A.15). Among these products, fish is particularly important. The country is endowed with important resources of surface water fish, as well as deepwater fish, shrimp, and other shellfish. In the first half of the decade, industrial activity related to fishing was protected through a ban on imports of fresh and frozen (but not canned) fish. At the same time, export controls maintained prices of fish at a low level, discouraging fishing. With the removal of trade controls, fishing became more lucrative, and the total catch in-

[77]These were mostly farms that were returned to their past owners after having been nationalized by the socialist regime in the south.

Although poor data quality prevents drawing any precise conclusions, the growth accounting exercise below attempts to shed some light on the roles of factor accumulation and productivity in contributing to growth. For the period 1991–99, growth of non-oil GDP per capita was negative, at –1.3 percent a year on average, even though factor accumulation of both labor and capital was substantial, reflecting relatively rapid population growth and strong investment. Thus total factor productivity was significantly negative, and this result holds for a broad range of reasonable assumptions regarding the share of capital in output and the initial capital stock. Reforms that would enhance factor productivity are therefore a key element in promoting growth. And in fact, factor productivity in the reform years 1996–99 was much higher (by about 50–100 percent, depending on the assumptions) than in the 1991–99 period as a whole.

Growth Decomposition in the Non-Oil Sector, 1991–99[1]
Average Annual Percentage Change

Period	Real Non-Oil GDP	Per Capita	Labor	Capital	TFP (a = 0.2)	TFP (a = 0.4)
1991–99	2.1	–1.3	3.5	10.8	–2.8	–4.2
Of which: 1996–99	4.4	0.3	3.5	9.5	–0.9	–2.1
1991–99	2.1	–1.3	3.5	17.5	–4.1	–6.9
Of which: 1996–99	4.4	0.3	3.5	12.8	–1.6	–3.4
1991–99	2.1	–1.3	3.5	5.6	–1.7	–2.2
Of which: 1996–99	4.4	0.3	3.5	5.9	–0.2	–0.7

[1]Assumes a standard, neo-classical, constant returns to scale, Cobb-Douglas production function: $Y = AK^{a}L^{(1-a)}$, where Y = potential output, A = total factor productivity (TFP), K = capital, L = labor, a = capital/output production share. It is assumed that actual GDP growth equals potential output growth and population growth equals employment growth. Average annual capital stock was calculated as $K(t) = K(t-1)*(1-0.03) + GKF(t)$ where it is assumed that the depreciation rate of capital stock is 3 percent per annum, GKF is real gross capital formation in year t, and K (1990) was set equal to real GDP in the first two rows, to 50 percent of real GDP in the second row, and to 200 percent of GDP in the last two rows.

creased by about 60 percent between 1995 and 1998.

The agriculture and fisheries sector is largely market oriented, with production privately undertaken but encouraged by the government and cooperatives that provide subsidized inputs. The government has traditionally financed the purchase of fertilizers and pesticides at low cost through the Agricultural Credit Bank. Farmers also have long benefited from low prices for diesel fuel and electricity, which encouraged the reliance on pumping water for irrigation and contributed to the depletion of underground water resources. Other bans and controls have practically been eliminated, however, and the government is shifting its focus toward more market-based ways to promote agriculture.

The Ministry of Agriculture is becoming active in the development and maintenance of water resources. In 1999 it undertook preliminary studies for 77 dams, prepared designs for 40 other dams and reservoirs, and prepared an irrigation policy that was approved by the cabinet; the construction of 12 dams was finished, and 17 others are under construction. The ministry also plays an important role in protecting crops from disease through information campaigns, quality control checks on insecticides and pesticides, and assistance to farmers in controlling crop and livestock diseases.[78] It provides funding for various activities such as fertilizing, refrigerated transportation, livestock production, water resource management, and marketing. Although this marks an improvement from earlier neglect of the sector, more needs to be done to encourage cultivation of rain-fed crops, eliminate subsidies (particularly on diesel fuel), and improve the overall quality of public services in agriculture. A strategy for government activity in the sector was recently developed in a broad-based participatory approach in the "Aden Agenda."

[78]For example, the rapid spread of the Newcastle disease among the country's livestock in the last quarter of 1999 was halted by the government, which brought the percentage of livestock infected down from about 26 percent in December 1999 to less than 4 percent in February 2000.

Box 5. The Role of *Qat* in the Yemeni Economy

Chewing of *qat* leaves is a widespread practice in Yemen, usually in the context of social gatherings in the afternoon.[1] The leaves of the hardy and drought-resistant *qat* tree (*Catha edulis*) contain an amphetamine-like substance, and chewing them has a mildly stimulative effect. There are some indications that *qat* chewing was for a long time confined to the wealthy and spread to the wider population only in the 20th century. A study in the 1960s found that, in the city of Ta'iz, about 60 percent of males and 35 percent of females were "habitual" chewers. Since late 1999, *qat* chewing in public buildings and during working hours has been prohibited, and a public campaign to reduce the practice has been launched.

Qat comes in a range of qualities, and prices vary accordingly. Recent household surveys indicate that *qat* absorbs 5 to 10 percent of household expenditure in all regions of Yemen except the desert governorates, and it probably accounts for a similar share of GDP. Consumption is widely thought to have increased in recent years, and the area cultivated with *qat* is believed to have increased by 10 percent between 1995 and 1990 (to 98,000 hectares), roughly in line with total cultivated area. Over the same period, *qat* prices rose faster than the consumer price index.

[1]Statistical information on qat production and use is scarce, in part reflecting official unease with the importance of the stimulant in Yemeni society. This box is based on an unpublished World Bank paper (Ward, 2000) and some information from the authorities.

Qat is appreciated especially by small farmers as a crop with a very high market value that requires relatively little labor. At least in the Sana'a basin, *qat* cultivation depends on irrigation and is highly water intensive. Water is typically pumped with diesel pumps, contributing to the rapid decline in water tables. Although reliable statistics do not exist, production expanded during the 1980s and 1990s, partly displacing other crops such as grapes, coffee, and cereals. Subsidies that kept grain prices low also contributed in the case of cereals (see Box 1).

Qat leaves must be brought fresh to market, to be consumed within 12 hours of harvesting. Accordingly, a highly efficient transport and marketing system has developed, even in the most remote areas. The *qat* trade is probably an important mechanism in transferring wealth from urban to rural areas; it is said to directly benefit 170,000 families, or 1 million people. The import of *qat* is banned. Some exports to neighboring countries and Yemeni communities abroad may occur through informal channels, but no data are available.

Qat retail sales are taxed at 20 percent, but tax collection suffers from logistical and governance problems; in 1999 the *qat* tax yielded YRls 1.6 billion (0.2 percent of GDP). Shifting *qat* tax collection to the local authorities and basing it on acreage rather than sales is under consideration. The Yemeni authorities have recently commissioned a study to better understand the role of *qat* cultivation in the economy, in particular regarding the level of production, water use, profitability and the distribution of revenues, labor requirements, and substitution for other crops.

The Industrial Sector

The industrial sector contributes a meager 16 percent to real GDP, mostly from manufacturing (11 percent in 1999) and construction (4 percent). Manufacturing, limited mainly to the production of consumer goods and construction materials (Statistical Appendix Table A.13) grew steadily at about 4 or 5 percent a year in the first part of the decade. A boom in construction and real estate activities occurred in the early 1990s following the return of some three-quarters of a million expatriate Yemeni workers at the time of the Gulf crisis: the sector registered real growth rates of 6.3 percent in 1991 and 16.1 percent in 1992. This boom may also have been partly due to strong demand for land and property as a hedge against inflation, which was running at 45 to 50 percent annually in 1991–92. The civil strife of 1994 disrupted industrial activity and led to a contraction in both manufacturing (by 5.3 percent) and construction (by 19 percent). Extensive damage to private property and public infrastructure, including the Aden refinery and electric power generating stations, constrained activity mostly in the south but also in the north.

Recovery from the war, coupled with the initiation of the reform program in 1995, led to a strong pickup in industrial activity. A construction boom that began in 1995 extended into 1997. Similarly, a jump in the growth rate of manufacturing took place in 1995 but was not sustained in the following years.

Services

Services today account for about 35 percent of real GDP. Transportation, storage, and communications; government services; and trade each account for 9 percent, and financial institutions and real estate together for 6 percent. Most of these shares were relatively stable throughout the decade except for government services, which declined from 16 percent of GDP in 1990 to 11.5 percent in 1999, and transportation, storage, and communications, which declined from 15 percent of GDP in 1990 to 9 percent in 1996. Although there are considerable doubts about the accuracy of the underlying data, public services may have declined with the privatization of a large number of small-scale public enterprises in 1995–96. The growth pattern in other services also broadly reflects the effects of the Gulf crisis, the civil war, and the reform program of 1995. Trade and financial services jumped in 1991 following the repatriation of Yemeni workers from the Gulf; but whereas trade kept growing at an annual average of 4.2 percent in 1992–93, financial services contracted. The post–civil war period saw another boom in both sectors, with average annual growth reaching 9 percent for wholesale and retail trade and 4.6 percent for financial services. Wholesale and retail trade even grew by 15.5 percent in 1995, probably triggered by the recovery from the civil war, but also influenced by the import and excise tax reforms introduced at the time.

Labor Market Developments

Labor market data in Yemen are scanty and do not go back beyond 1991.[79] Only recently, motivated by the rise in unemployment in the aftermath of the Gulf war, was a more focused monitoring of labor market developments initiated. The Ministry of Labor and Vocational Training was created in 1997. In an effort to consolidate labor market statistics and improve its own effectiveness in vocational training, job matching, and labor force planning, the ministry embarked in 1998 on a major project to develop a Labor Market Information System (LMIS) database. The LMIS will establish links between various concerned government agencies and the labor ministry and its job offices located in different parts of the country. Information will be gathered on the supply and demand of labor according to professional description, based on input provided by various government agencies and periodic market surveys.

The Ministry of Planning estimates that, in early 2000, out of a workforce (defined as the population aged 15 and above) of 9.7 million, the labor force stood at about 4.2 million, for a 43 percent participation rate. Participation rates of the male and female populations differ sharply, at about 72 percent and 15 percent, respectively. By both regional and international standards, this difference is striking. As a result, female labor accounted only for about 18 percent of the total labor force, compared with worldwide averages of 41 percent for low-income countries and 43 percent for high-income countries.

Data on the sectoral distribution of employment (Statistical Appendix Table A.6) indicate a high concentration in sectors where informal employment is the norm, such as agriculture and fisheries (49 percent in 1999), followed by trade, restaurants, and hotels (about 11 percent). Female employment in Yemen is concentrated in these sectors, particularly agriculture and fisheries, which employ about 86 percent of all female workers. Manufacturing and education each account for about 4 percent of female employment. The low female participation rate in general, and in the formal sector in particular, appears to be attributable to a number of factors, such as traditional values, which discourage female employment in nontraditional areas; a tendency toward early marriage for females;[80] relatively low educational attainment among females;[81] and labor legislation, which imposes higher costs on the hiring of female workers (Box 6).

Available unemployment data suggest a growing overall unemployment rate, as the pace of employment creation during the last eight years was insufficient to absorb all new entrants in the labor force. The 1994 population census estimated an unemployment rate of 10.1 percent; preliminary results from the recent labor market survey suggest that unemployment rose to 20 percent in 1999.

There are no reliable data relating unemployment to age, educational level, duration of unemployment, or the causes of unemployment, and data on wages in the private sector are nonexistent. Data available from the 1994 census suggest that the majority of the unemployed (about 60 percent) were below the age of 24, and that unemployment rates fall sharply as age increases (Table 13). The long list of university graduate applicants at the Ministry of Civil Service and Administrative Reform suggests that unemployment is not confined to people with low educational attainment.[82]

---

[79]Available information is based primarily on the 1994 Population Census; other sources include the Household Expenditure Survey of 1998, the Demographic Survey of 1997, and the Educational Survey of 1998–99. All these surveys were not primarily designed to collect detailed information on the labor market. The CSO for the first time conducted a detailed labor market survey in 2000.

[80]Results from the 1998 household survey indicate that the average age at first marriage for women is 20 years.

[81]According to the 1998 household survey, the female illiteracy rate is 71 percent, compared with 24 percent among men.

[82]According to a report by the United Nations Development Programme and the Yemeni Ministry of Planning (UNDP and Ministry of Planning, 1999), registered graduates on the waiting list at the Ministry of Civil Service and Administrative Reform totaled 15,400 at the end of June 1999. Of these, 51.3 percent held degrees in education; 20.5 percent in arts, science, information, religious studies, and law; 9.8 percent in business and economics; 9.6 percent in medicine; and 8.8 percent in engineering, agriculture, computing, and petroleum. In 1999 available government jobs were distributed among education (79.1 percent), health (9.2 percent), other administrative units (6.5 percent), and various positions at other public sector units (5 percent).

Table 13. Distribution of Labor Force by Employment Status, Age Group (+10 Years), and Gender, 1994
(In percent)

Age Group	Unemployed			Total Labor Force		
	Male	Female	Total	Male	Female	Total
10–14	11	39.5	14.7	3.4	14.7	5.7
15–19	23	31.5	23.9	7.7	13.7	8.9
20–24	21	14.7	20.7	11.9	11.1	11.8
25–29	13	6.2	12.1	14.0	12.9	13.8
30–34	8	2.5	6.9	13.2	11.9	12.9
35–39	6	1.5	5.6	13.0	11.6	12.7
40–44	4	1.0	3.9	9.6	8.4	9.4
45–49	3	0.6	3.1	7.6	6.1	7.3
50–54	3	0.7	2.8	6.6	2.2	5.7
55–59	2	0.4	1.7	3.5	2.4	3.3
60–64	2	0.5	1.9	4.3	2.6	4.0
65+	3	0.9	2.6	5.1	2.4	4.5
Unspecified	0	0.1	0.0	0.0	0.0	0.0
Total	100.0	100.0	100.0	100.0	100.0	100.0
Total (thousands)	286	39	325	2,550	659	3,209
Memorandum items:						
Percentage population age 10–24	56	86	59	23	40	26

Sources: Central Statistics Organization; General Population Census 1994.

International Labor Migration Trends

Emigration has a long tradition in Yemen of providing an alternative outlet for new entrants in the labor force and generating much-needed foreign exchange. Migration flows have headed mainly toward three regions of the world: for centuries, many migrants went eastward, particularly to India, Indonesia, and Malaysia; others went to East Africa; and in recent decades migration to the Gulf Cooperation Council (GCC) countries has become dominant. Emigrants to the first two regions have mostly settled permanently and have been assimilated within the local communities, but those in the GCC countries still maintain a strong link with Yemen and remit a sizable portion of their income on a regular basis. The Ministry of Immigrant Affairs estimates the total number of Yemenis abroad at around 6 million to 7 million, of which about 4 million to 5 million are in Indonesia, 0.8 million in the GCC countries, and 0.2 million in African countries, notably Kenya and Ethiopia.

As discussed before, international migration of Yemenis has slowed considerably in the aftermath of the 1990 Gulf crisis. Although in 1997 a resumption of labor migration to the GCC countries appears to have taken place on a small scale, prospects for migration to this region will likely remain limited, since most of the GCC countries are currently facing rising unemployment among their own national labor forces, and Yemeni labor has been replaced by East Asian workers.

Labor Laws and Regulations

The Labor Law was last amended in 1997 and governs employment in the private sector. Among its other features, the law empowers the government to set a minimum wage,[83] provides the right to form labor unions and to conduct strikes, and sets relatively restrictive dismissal rules, working conditions and benefits for women, and maximum working hours (Box 6). In view of the administrative weakness of the implementation agencies, however, the main effect of the law appears to be to add to fiscal and regulatory incentives for firms to remain in the informal sector, contributing to its predominance.

Education and Training

General education in Yemen includes nine years of basic education, three years of secondary schooling, and technical, vocational, and higher education. Technical, vocational, and higher education in Yemen is primarily run by two government bodies:

[83]Since 1981 the minimum wage has been set at YRls 6,000 a month, but apparently this has never been enforced.

Box 6. Provisions of Current Labor Legislation

Yemen's labor legislation, last amended in 1997, deals with private sector employment only. Certain activities such as traditional agriculture and employment of domestic servants, are exempt, as are international organizations. Under the law, every citizen has a right to work; discrimination by sex, age, or race is banned.

Firms must report all vacant jobs to the Ministry of Labor and Vocational Training (MOLVT) first and may hire directly from the market only if the MOLVT does not nominate a candidate within 15 days. Non-Yemeni workers may only be employed in jobs for which no Yemeni expertise is available, and provided they do not exceed 10 percent of the establishment's workforce. Firms hiring foreign workers are required to appoint local counterpart workers with appropriate qualifications and proficiency throughout the tenure of the non-Yemeni employee. Companies in certain sectors, however, may be exempted from these rules.

Unless otherwise specified in the two parties' agreement, contract duration is unlimited for Yemeni employees. After a six-month trial period, a new worker may not be dismissed except for failure to comply with the contract terms, noticeable negligence, or commission of unlawful acts. But the employer may terminate the contract if staff must be reduced for economic or technical reasons. In all cases of contract termination, the employee is eligible for special compensation for resulting damages. The amount of this compensation, determined by a specialized arbitration committee, must not exceed six months' salary.

Special rules apply for employing women and minors. Women may work at most five hours a day in the six months before and after giving birth; they are not to be employed in dangerous jobs, and they are not allowed to work at night except during the holy month of Ramadan and at other times as determined by the MOLVT. A woman worker is entitled to paid leave for 40 days, and to leave without pay for up to 90 days, in the event of her husband's death.

An hour of overtime work earns one hour and a half at the basic wage, and an hour of work at night or on weekends or public holidays earns two hours at the basic wage. The MOLVT may set minimum wages for the economy as a whole or by sector. Wage discrimination based on sex or nationality is prohibited.

Official working hours must not exceed 8 a day, or 48 a week, and each 8-hour period must include at least one break. Employees are entitled to at least 30 days of annual leave (in addition to public holidays), must take at least half of these every year, and may not trade vacation time for financial compensation.

Every establishment of 10 or more employees must formulate, within given guidelines on the obligations and rights of employees, a charter of penalties and the conditions of applying them. These guidelines must be displayed in a conspicuous place.

Employers are required either to provide training directly to their workers or to make annual financial contributions to MOLVT training programs in an amount proportional to the number of employees. The ministry organizes public vocational training programs and supervises the standards of programs offered by the private sector.

Employers are required to adhere to occupational health and safety standards specified by the authorities. The MOLVT's safety and health inspectors are responsible for monitoring workplace conditions and have the authority to conduct unscheduled inspections.

Employers must provide medical care insurance, and larger firms must establish in-house health facilities. At the end of their service, employees are entitled to a monthly pension or a lump-sum reward, determined according to the rules of the social insurance law, and if they are not covered by social insurance or a similar system, they are entitled to severance pay of at least one month's wage for every year of service.

Labor disputes may be resolved through direct MOLVT intermediation, through a specialized arbitration committee set up by the MOLVT, or through a specialized appeals court. Strikes for nonpolitical reasons are permitted only after intermediation efforts have been exhausted and a final court decision has been reached. To be legal, a strike must have been voted for by union members, with a minimum participation of 60 percent and approval by at least 25 percent in a secret ballot. The MOLVT must be notified of the strike three weeks in advance. Some businesses such as hospitals, electricity and telecommunications plants, and banks are required to maintain a minimum level of personnel during strikes.

Both employers and employees have the right to create and join collective organizations to look after their rights. Punitive action against employees participating in union activities is prohibited.

The law describes the penalties and punishments for violations of its various articles. These include a maximum imprisonment of three months and fines ranging between YRls 5,000 and YRls 20,000.

the Ministry of Education, which oversees professional-level education (three-year teachers' training and four-year university education), and the General Authority for Vocational and Technical Training (GAVTT), which falls under the jurisdiction of the Ministry of Labor and Vocational Training. Other ministries that provide specialized education include the health, transport, fisheries, agriculture, tourism, and civil service ministries.

GAVTT operates training institutes at three levels: two-year vocational centers providing semiskilled and skilled training, three-year vocational colleges providing training in crafts, and two- to three-year postsecondary technical colleges offering technician

Table 14. Student Enrollment and Graduation from Colleges and Universities in 1998/99

	Enrollment			Graduation		
	Male	Female	Total	Male	Female	Total
			(Students)			
Technical colleges[1]	3,326	476	3,802	1,015	132	1,147
Teaching colleges	16,190	3,469	19,659	4,293	678	4,971
Universities	117,967	34,128	152,095	15,063	4,433	19,496
Public	109,135	30,687	139,822	13,805	3,940	17,745
Arts and humanities	99,030	26,729	125,759	12,900	3,637	16,537
Science and technical	10,105	3,958	14,063	905	303	1,208
Private	8,832	3,441	12,273	1,258	493	1,751
Arts and humanities	7,110	2,938	10,048	979	438	1,417
Science and technical	1,722	503	2,225	279	55	334
Total	137,483	38,073	175,556	20,371	5,243	25,614
			(In percent)			
Technical colleges	1.9	0.3	2.2	4.0	0.5	4.5
Teaching colleges	9.2	2.0	11.2	16.8	2.6	19.4
Universities	67.2	19.4	86.6	58.8	17.3	76.1
Public	62.2	17.5	79.6	53.9	15.4	69.3
Arts and humanities	56.4	15.2	71.6	50.4	14.2	64.6
Science and technical	5.8	2.3	8.0	3.5	1.2	4.7
Private	5.0	2.0	7.0	4.9	1.9	6.8
Arts and humanities	4.0	1.7	5.7	3.8	1.7	5.5
Science and technical	1.0	0.3	1.3	1.1	0.2	1.3
Total	78.3	21.7	100.0	79.5	20.5	100.0

Sources: Ministry of Planning; UNDP.
[1]Includes training institutes and programs run by GAVTT, Ministries of Health, Communications, Fisheries and Agriculture, Culture, Civil Services, and AWQAF.

diplomas. Currently there are 26 such institutes specializing in such fields as tourism, manufacturing, hotels, agriculture, and veterinary medicine. Funding comes primarily from the budget and from a 1 percent tax on the wages of workers in medium-size and large firms (those with 10 or more workers), plus visa fees for expatriate labor (YRls 5,000).

Enrollment levels and graduation at various colleges and universities are heavily biased toward the arts and humanities colleges; public and private colleges of this type together account for 77 percent of enrollment and 70 percent of graduates. These are followed by teaching colleges (11 percent and 19 percent, respectively) and technical colleges run by GAVTT (Table 14). The education system appears poorly tuned to market needs, and skills mismatch is likely a major cause of unemployment. The current ratio of 1 technical graduate for every 17 university graduates compares with an international standard of about 4 to 1. Among the causes cited for the low enrollment in technical training is the insufficient resources made available to these colleges, the inadequate skills coverage of their programs, and the general preference among the population, particularly among females, for government and administrative jobs.

Inflation

Inflation in Yemen is largely determined by monetary developments, which in turn are driven by domestic budgetary financing needs. As monthly consumer price index (CPI) data prior to 1995 are not available,[84] annual data were used to derive Figure 16, which illustrates that the paths of money growth and

[84]CPI data are compiled by the CSO. In January 1995 a new series was introduced, consisting of a weighted average of the price indices for Sana'a and Aden, where the weights correspond to consumption shares obtained from the 1992 Household Budget Survey. Before that the CPI was based on series from five major cities, using data from the 1977/78 Household Budget Survey, but weighted across cities by population share. Despite the improvement underlying the CPI introduced in 1995, these data remain weak because of poor price collection and absence of monitoring, as well as insufficient coverage. Current efforts are concentrated on producing yet another CPI, covering 20 cities and using new consumption shares derived from the 1998 Household Budget Survey.

Figure 16. Inflation, Money Growth, and Budget Financing
(In percent)

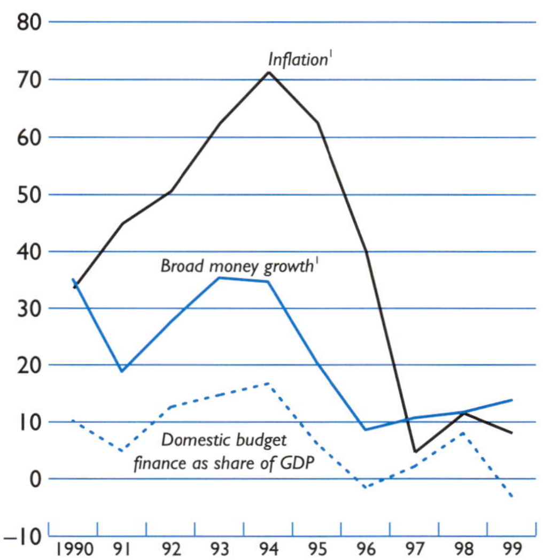

Source: Data provided by the Yemeni authorities.
[1]Change in the average consumer price index or broad money over 12 months.

inflation closely mirror that of domestic deficit financing. Indeed, the correlation coefficient between CPI inflation and domestic fiscal financing (as a percentage of GDP) is 0.66, almost equal to the correlation between CPI inflation and broad money growth. The correlation coefficient between broad money growth and budgetary finance is 0.85.

Price instability was particularly acute in 1990–94. Those years witnessed very high inflation, fueled by large fiscal deficits, which translated into high rates of money growth (see Table 1 in Section II). Inflation accelerated from 34 percent in 1990 to peak at 71 percent in 1994, the year of the civil war, as fiscal deficits and the rate of broad money growth surged.

The structural reform program initiated in early 1995 succeeded at reducing inflation to single-digit levels by the end of 1999. This improvement reflects declining budget deficits (from about 16 percent of GDP in 1994 to near balance in 1999), which allowed money growth to be tightened. Indeed, the average annual rate of expansion of broad money in 1995–99 was half that in the first part of the decade.

Inflation declined only slowly in the beginning of the reform period, however, from 71 percent in 1994 to 63 percent in 1995 and 40 percent in 1996, partly because of significant adjustments in administered prices. Indeed, were it not for the effect of administered price increases,[85] CPI inflation would have reached a much lower 33 percent in 1996. In that year, however, the price of diesel fuel was doubled, wheat and flour prices were raised by 150 percent, and average electricity tariffs were raised by 161 percent. Administrative price increases implemented at different times as part of the reform process (see Table 8 in Section IV) accentuated CPI increases and contributed to inflation at least until the end of 1997. (Throughout that period, inflation excluding administered prices was about 7 to 15 percent lower than overall CPI inflation.)

Figure 17 attempts to isolate the effect of administrative price increases on several CPI components. The transportation price index shows four jumps: in April 1995 following the doubling of gasoline prices; in January 1996 following another 50 percent increase in these prices and a doubling of diesel fuel prices; in September 1997 following another 67 percent increase in diesel fuel prices; and in July 1998 following a 40 percent increase in gasoline prices. The fuel and lighting index shows major jumps in May 1995 following increases in electricity tariffs (60 percent, enacted in January 1995) and fuel oil (74 percent for purchases by the Public Electricity Corporation), and in January 1996 following another 161 percent increase in average electricity tariffs and a 133 percent increase in the fuel oil price. Subsequent increases in the prices of both products (in September 1997, July 1998, and June 1999) were milder and had smaller effects, as shown by the relatively smooth path of the index from February 1996 onward. The price index for cereals also shows an upward effect due to increases in administrative prices of wheat; the two significant responses are registered following the 150 percent increase in wheat prices in January 1996 and the full liberalization in the third quarter of 1999.

Other important factors driving inflation were fluctuations in the prices of vegetables and *qat*. Both products exhibit strong seasonality, with prices affected by rainfall or the lack thereof and by seasonal demand (around holidays for *qat*), and on a trend

[85]It is assumed that the effect of administrative prices is captured by the transportation price index (because it partly accounts for petroleum product prices), the fuel and lighting price index (because it partly accounts for petroleum product prices and electricity tariffs), and the cereals price index (because it includes wheat prices). This might not be a precise measure, given that information on individual items within these categories is not available (and these categories certainly include other items not subject to price setting). Figure 17 indicates, however, that changes in administered prices seem to be reflected in these categories to an extent sufficient to warrant the assumption. Hence in this section the CPI excluding administrative prices refers to the CPI calculated after excluding these items.

Figure 17. Selected Commodity Price Indices
(Index, January 1995 = 100)

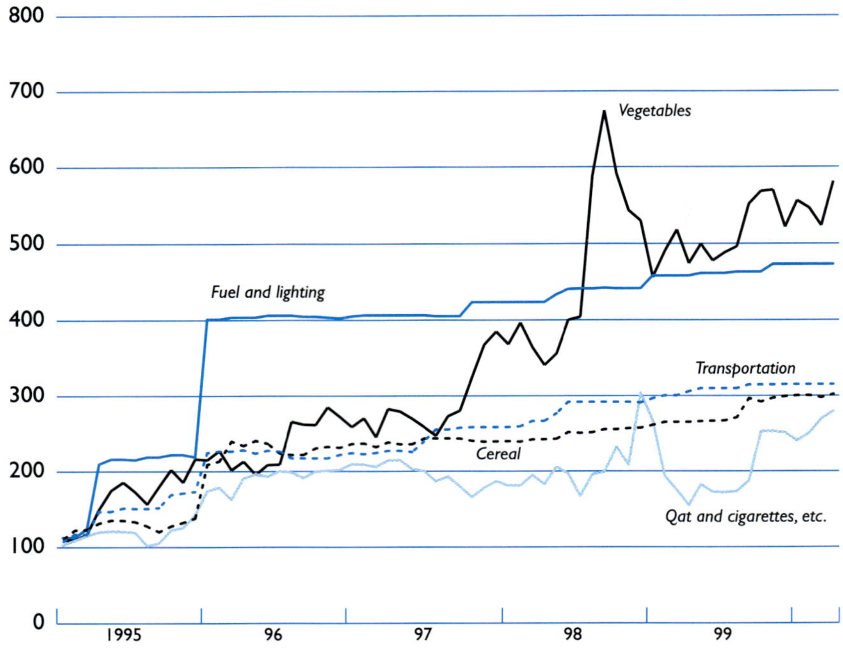

Source: Data provided by the Yemeni authorities.

basis these prices have been rising faster than the overall index. Indeed, CPI inflation has always been lower (by 10 to 25 percent at least) when both products are excluded from its measurement. *Qat* and vegetable prices rose strongly in the first part of 1999 following the severe drought, which contributed more than half of the inflation recorded over the period from April to August 1999. Two additional factors affected the price of vegetables in the reform period: the exchange rate unification in July 1996 led to a rise in the price of imported vegetables, and the gradual phasing out of import bans on vegetables (in March 1998 and in mid-1999) contributed to drops in vegetable prices around these dates (Figure 17).

Poverty and Social Indicators

With an annual average decline in real GDP per capita of about 0.5 percent over the past decade, resulting from both sluggish real growth and a large increase in the population, it is not surprising that poverty seems to have risen. According to a World Bank report (World Bank, 1996), 20 percent of Yemenis lived in conditions of absolute poverty in 1992, with spending below socially acceptable levels, poor health status, and limited access to education. A report by the United Nations Development Programme (UNDP, 1999b) states that by 1998 absolute poverty had spread to cover 30 percent of households, and that 15 percent of families lived below the poverty line.

In its annual *Human Development Report,* the UNDP assigns Yemen a human development index (HDI)[86] based on specific measures of basic human needs, all of which take into consideration a core set of socioeconomic indicators related to levels of income, health, education, and access to basic services

[86]The HDI is an index constructed annually by the UNDP since 1990 to measure average achievement in basic human development. The indicators used in calculating the HDI include life expectancy, educational attainment (measured through literacy and enrollment rates), and income per capita.

Figure 18. Republic of Yemen and Selected Comparators: Dependency Ratios[1]

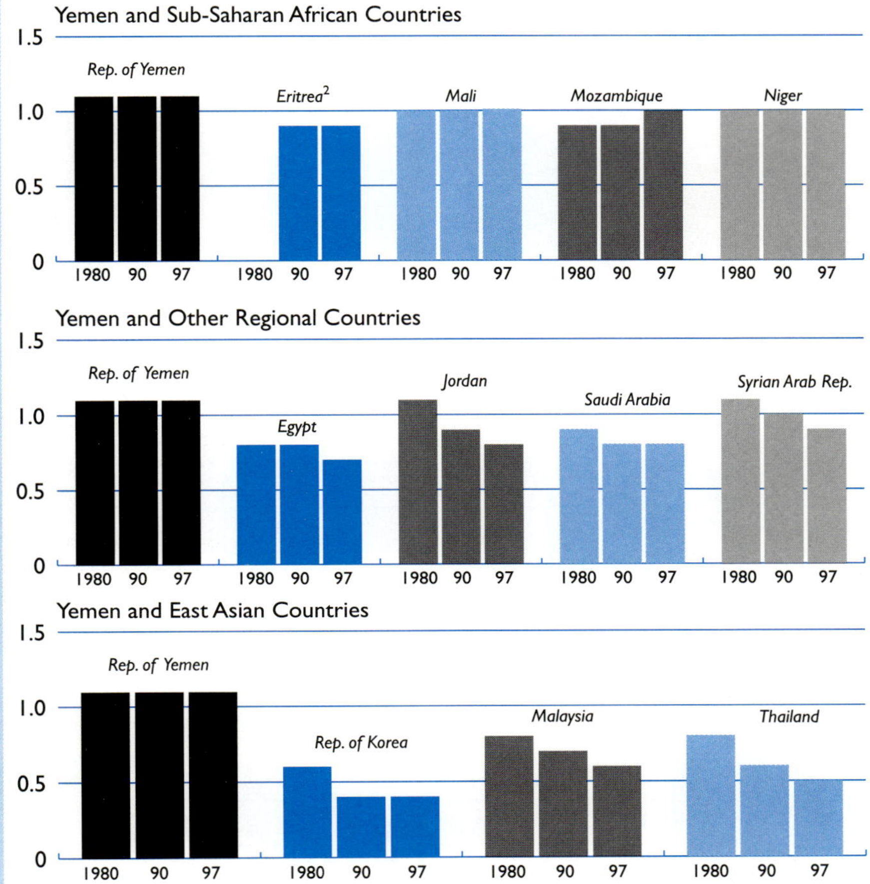

Source: World Bank, *World Development Indicators*.
[1]Ratio of number of dependents to the working-age population.
[2]Data for 1980s are unavailable.

(UNDP, 1999a). In most of these categories, and despite some improvement over the past two decades, Yemen fares poorly relative to the Middle East and North Africa region on average (Figures 18 to 22 compare Yemen's performance with that of several other countries in the region and elsewhere).

Measures of Poverty

The extent of poverty in Yemen can be gauged through sociodemographic variables, which, although showing improvement over the course of the past two decades, look weak compared with those of other countries in the region.[87] Life expectancy at birth, despite having increased by nearly eight years between 1987 and 1998, is about eight years below the average for the Middle East and North Africa. Similarly, although infant and under-five mortality rates in Yemen declined by 15 percent and 31 per-

[87]Sources of the data cited in this section are the 1998 Household Budget Survey of the CSO supplemented by the UNDP Poverty Policy Framework for Yemen, the World Bank 1996 *Poverty Assessment Report* (World Bank, 1996), the IMF *World Economic Outlook* database, the 1998 CSO *Statistical Yearbook,* (CSO, 1998), and the World Bank's *World Development Indicators*.

Figure 19. Republic of Yemen and Selected Comparators: Adult Illiteracy Rate
(In percent of population over the age of 15)

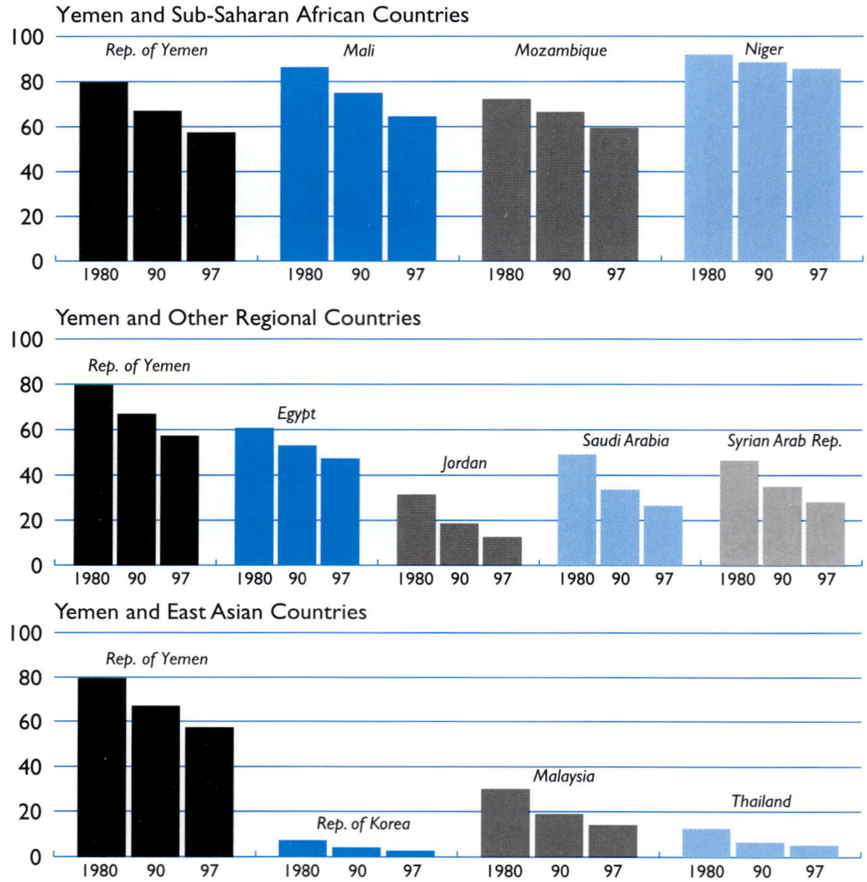

Source: World Bank, *World Development Indicators.*

cent, respectively, within a decade, they remain nearly twice the regional average. The share of the population with access to safe water and sanitation is less than half the regional average. Yemen also trails behind the region as a whole in terms of educational achievement, with a higher illiteracy rate and a widening gender gap in education. At the same time, however, some indicators have improved faster in Yemen over the past two decades than in the rest of the region or than in the average developing country. For example, between 1985 and 1998 the illiteracy rate in Yemen decreased by about 27 percent; the decline over the same period was about 10 percent for the least-developed countries as a group and 15 percent for the Middle East and North Africa region.

Not surprisingly, poverty tends to be correlated directly with family size and inversely with education. The average household size among poor families is 8.5 persons, whereas that for nonpoor households is 6.8. Educational achievement is also significantly worse among the poor: their illiteracy rate of about 66 percent in 1996 compares with only 59 percent for the nonpoor. The difference is even more striking at the household level: 77.3 percent of poor households are headed by illiterates, whereas only 7.7 percent are headed by individuals with secondary education or above. Moreover, the gap between poor

Figure 20. Republic of Yemen and Selected Comparators: Life Expectancy at Birth
(In years)

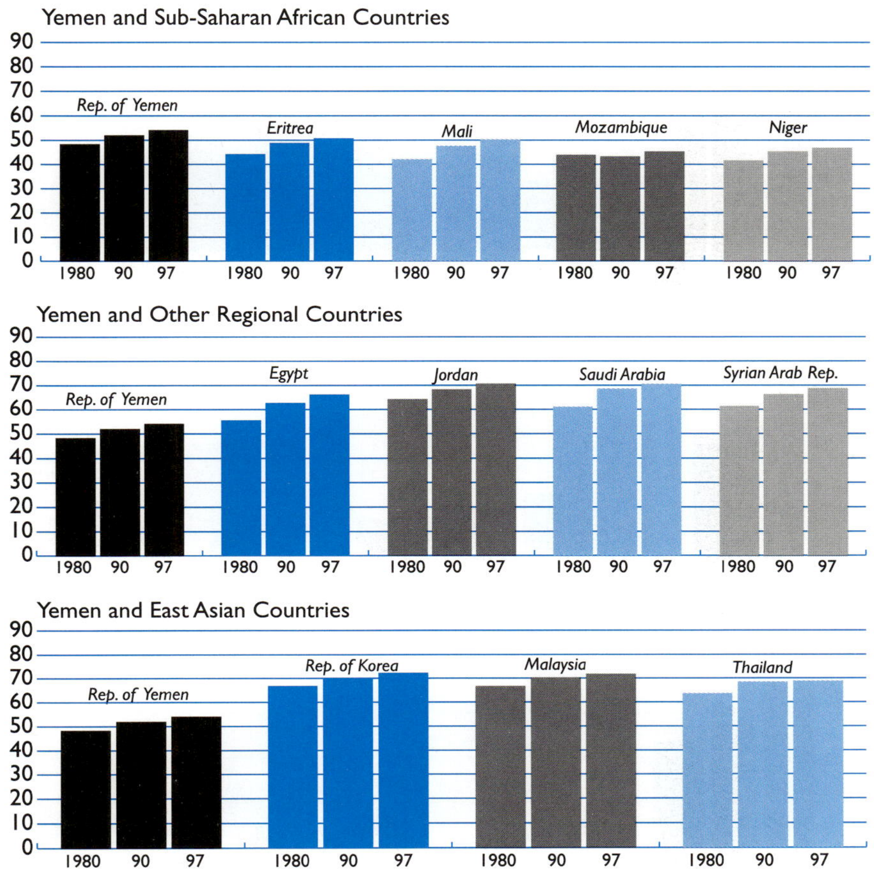

Source: World Bank, *World Development Indicators*.

and nonpoor is wider for females than for males. In 1998, for example, about 80 percent of poor adult females were illiterate, compared with 64 percent of all adult women; the corresponding numbers for males were 44 percent and 31 percent, respectively. Female-headed households are also more likely to be poor: the risk of poverty increases by 20 percent for them compared with male-headed households.

Inequality of expenditure in Yemen reflects poverty patterns. Spending by the poor was only about 6 percent of total private spending in 1992, whereas that of the richest quintile was nearly half of that total. The picture improved a little by 1998: the results of the latest Household Budget Survey indicate that spending in that year by the 30 percent of Yemenis with the lowest level of expenditure (the absolute poor) was about 13 percent of total private spending.[88] However, the richest quintile still captures about 41 percent of that total. Yemen also suffers from growing income inequality: the Gini coefficient for income distribution increased from 0.39 in 1992 to 0.43 in 1998.

As in many poor countries, poverty in Yemen is associated more with low wages than with unem-

[88]The UNDP estimated the food poverty gap—the difference in spending on food between poor and the poverty line (approximated by spending by the nonpoor)—at $160 million a year, or 2 percent of GDP, in 1998.

Figure 21. Republic of Yemen and Selected Comparators: Infant Mortality Rate
(In deaths per thousand live births)

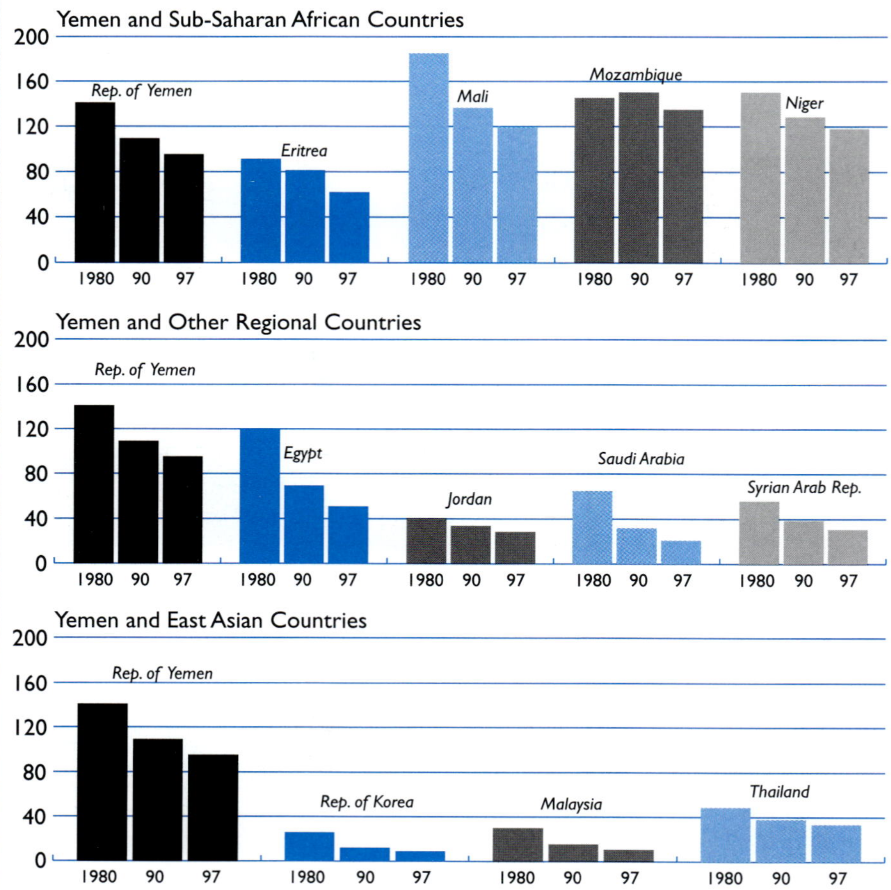

Source: World Bank, *World Development Indicators.*

ployment. Indeed, 80 percent of the poor are employed; given that the labor force is about 25 percent of the population, this suggests that the percentage of nonpoor employed is lower. Although the poor tend to enter the labor force earlier than the nonpoor and remain employed until later in life, both groups have the same labor force participation rate, which indicates that poor people do not suffer from a higher incidence of unemployment than the nonpoor. The percentage of the poor employed in the private sector (about 80 percent) is somewhat higher than that of the nonpoor (about 73 percent).

Poverty in Yemen is mainly a rural phenomenon: in 1995 only 3.8 percent of urban families lived in poverty, compared with 16.7 percent of the rural population. This is not surprising given anecdotal evidence that living conditions, in terms of access to education, health services, and sanitation, seem much worse in rural than in urban areas.[89] In particular, there seem to be more schools and health facili-

[89]Hashem (1996) reports that 13 percent of the population moved from rural to urban areas between 1992 and 1994. This heavy migration may be due not only to job hunting but also to a search for better living conditions.

Figure 22. Republic of Yemen and Selected Comparators: Access to Safe Water
(In percent of population with access)

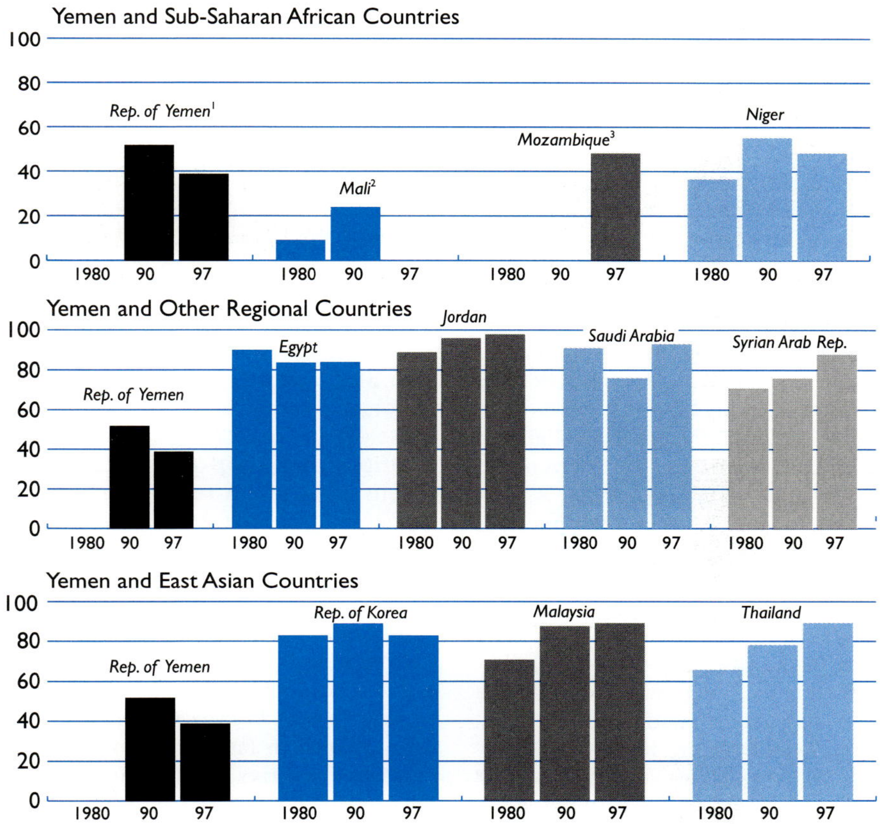

Source: World Bank, *World Development Indicators.*
[1]Data for 1980 are unavailable.
[2]Data for 1997 are unavailable.
[3]Data for 1980 and 1990 are unavailable.

ties per capita in larger agglomerations than in small villages. Only 19 percent of the rural population have access to safe water, compared with 74 percent in urban areas. This difference is far smaller in developing countries as a group (50 percent and 61 percent, respectively, in 1993) and for the Middle East and North Africa region (70 percent and 98 percent, respectively, in 1990).

Another striking characteristic of poverty in Yemen, emphasized by UNDP and World Bank assessments, is its unbalanced distribution across parts of the country. About 43 percent of the poor live in three of the country's 17 governorates—Sana'a, Ta'iz, and Ibb—and an additional 28 percent live in Dhamar, Hodeidah, and Hadramout. Four population groups in particular are distinguished as suffering from high poverty levels: Somali refugees of Yemeni descent, foreign refugees living in refugee camps, dispossessed farmers in the south who were not compensated after the government returned the land to its original owners, and the Akhdam, an ethnic group constituting the lowest social class in Yemen.[90]

[90]The 1996 World Bank *Poverty Assessment Report* (World Bank, 1996) estimated the numbers of the first three groups at 100,000, 10,000, and 100,000, respectively.

Main Causes of Poverty

A number of characteristics specific to Yemen contribute to the country's poverty. The harsh, desert-like climate in certain parts of the country and the general scarcity of water prevent the use of much of the land for agricultural production and severely limit the productivity of the agricultural land that exists. Another factor is rapid population growth, which exceeded 3 percent a year for most of the 1990s, partly due to a high fertility rate, which contributes to large household size and high dependency ratios. Coupled with a low labor force participation rate, rapid growth of the population prohibits the achievement of satisfactory productivity levels and keeps income per capita depressed.

Two major shocks contributed to economic decline, and thus to increasing poverty, in the 1990s. First, the war in the Gulf led to the repatriation of about three-quarters of a million Yemenis, who left most of their possessions behind. For a society geared toward migration and dependent on workers abroad for the provision of essential financial transfers, the return of the workers had a two-pronged negative effect. A substantial cut in national income resulted from the loss of remittances, and the closure of regional labor markets to Yemeni workers led to a significant increase in unemployment at home; both factors reduced income per capita and worsened dependency ratios. The costly civil war that broke out in 1994 was another contributor to the decline in living standards, and the resulting economic losses accentuated poverty.

However, as discussed elsewhere in this paper, inadequate economic policies also played an important role in keeping poverty high. Many distortions in the Yemeni economy have been addressed only since the adjustment program was implemented in 1995. High rates of inflation, a multiple exchange rate system, and extensive protectionist policies depressed real income, distorted the rural-urban terms of trade by creating a bias against promotion of exports in agriculture, and led to inadequate access to credit in the early 1990s.

The inadequate design and composition of government expenditure accentuated the inefficiencies that contribute to the persistence of poverty in Yemen. Unification in 1990 resulted in a bloated and inefficient civil service, with wages and benefits absorbing a large share of public expenditure. Current expenses are large relative to spending on core activities such as infrastructure creation and social programs. Moreover, as explained elsewhere, the government spends large amounts on generalized subsidies, intensifying economic distortions while not necessarily benefiting the most needy.[91] Even more-direct transfer policies such as the provision of cash to the most deprived face difficulties because of problems beneficiaries face in asserting their claims; this causes benefits to leak to the nonpoor.

Poor implementation of government antipoverty programs adds to the negative effects of inadequate budgeting. For example, the World Bank *Poverty Assessment Report* highlights the mismatch between the distribution of the population (or the incidence of poverty) across regions and the shares of the education budget that regions receive; some remote poor areas are virtually ignored by such programs, which end up being implemented in areas with relatively less needy people. A second important problem is the low quality of services offered by these programs, which translates into low success rates. For example, although health expenditure per capita was comparable in Yemen and Egypt in the mid-1990s ($39 in Yemen in 1994, versus $38 in Egypt in 1995), Egypt reported seven years longer life expectancy, 47 percent lower infant mortality, and 65 to 80 percent higher immunization rates. In education, low program quality takes the form of unsatisfactory facilities (lacking water, electricity, and sanitation) and poor-quality teaching. This translates into high grade repetition rates. Although public spending on education in the mid-1990s was higher in Yemen (as a share of GDP) than the average for the Middle East and North Africa (6.1 percent versus 5.2 percent), the adult illiteracy rate in Yemen is higher, at 47.3 percent compared with 37.8 percent. Yemen's high illiteracy rate is in large part due to very low female literacy; the World Bank *Poverty Assessment Report* states that female education is hampered in large measure by the absence of adequate facilities in schools to host female students (such as suitable toilets, separate classrooms, or flexible hours to accommodate female child labor within families).

Saving, Investment, and External Vulnerability

Data on private investment are highly unreliable and based mostly on estimation rather than recorded observations; saving is estimated as a residual using GDP and external sector estimates. Accordingly, any analysis of saving and investment can at best hope to highlight broad trends. On this basis, over the period 1990–99 gross fixed capital formation rose from 12.3 percent of GDP in 1990 to 18.6 percent in 1999 (Table 15). There was some shift in the composition of investment (Figure 23): as a share of

[91]The World Bank *Poverty Assessment Report* mentions that less than 17 percent of government subsidies benefited the poorest 20 percent of the population in 1995.

Table 15. Republic of Yemen: Phasing of Macroeconomic Adjustment, 1990–99[1]

	1990	1991	1992	1993	1994	1995	1996	1997	1998	1999
					(Change in percent)					
Real GDP at market prices[1]	. . .	–2.1	4.8	0.4	–3.6	7.9	2.9	8.1	5.3	3.8
Real non-oil GDP[1]	. . .	–1.5	8.0	–0.1	–9.6	5.5	0.5	8.2	5.9	3.2
Inflation	. . .	44.9	50.6	54.8	71.3	62.5	40.0	4.6	11.5	8.0
					(In percent of GDP)					
Consumption	96.3	98.9	97.2	103.3	82.1	85.8	85.3	85.3	96.6	88.2
Public sector	19.5	21.1	21.3	20.7	21.2	16.0	15.0	15.8	17.2	16.9
Private sector	76.9	77.8	75.9	82.6	60.9	69.9	70.4	69.5	79.5	71.4
Gross investment	14.6	16.8	22.4	20.0	20.5	20.7	20.8	23.7	21.1	18.6
Change in stock	2.3	2.6	2.0	2.1	1.0	0.4	0.4	0.4	0.0	0.0
Gross fixed capital formation	12.3	14.2	20.4	17.9	19.4	20.3	20.4	23.3	21.1	18.6
Public sector	8.7	4.0	3.4	3.5	2.6	3.1	6.6	6.8	6.1	5.6
Private sector	3.6	10.2	17.0	14.4	16.9	17.2	13.8	16.5	15.0	13.0
Domestic absorption	110.9	115.7	119.5	123.4	102.6	106.5	106.1	109.0	117.8	106.8
Net exports of goods and nonfactor services[1]	–10.9	–15.7	–19.5	–23.4	–2.6	–6.5	–6.1	–9.0	–17.8	–6.8
Gross domestic product	100.0	100.0	100.0	100.0	100.0	100.0	100.0	100.0	100.0	100.0
Net factor income[1]	–4.8	–7.1	–6.2	–6.2	–8.9	–7.7	–10.6	–9.6	–5.7	–9.6
Net current transfers[1]	12.7	12.1	12.5	13.4	17.1	17.0	18.4	19.0	19.9	19.2
Gross national disposable income	107.8	105.0	106.3	107.3	108.2	109.3	107.8	109.5	114.2	109.7
Gross national savings	11.5	6.1	9.1	4.0	26.1	23.5	22.5	24.2	17.6	21.5
Public sector	–3.7	–3.0	–9.4	–11.1	–13.6	–3.0	2.7	4.9	–0.2	5.3
Private sector	15.2	9.1	18.5	15.1	39.7	26.5	19.8	19.3	17.7	16.1
Total fiscal revenue and grants	19.8	23.1	16.1	14.9	12.8	19.5	35.9	32.8	26.4	31.8
Fiscal revenue	18.7	22.0	15.8	14.7	12.6	19.2	35.6	32.2	26.0	30.9
Oil revenue and payment for past excess cost recovery	7.5	9.4	4.7	4.2	3.7	9.3	25.1	22.1	13.8	19.8
Non-oil revenue	11.2	12.6	11.1	10.5	8.9	9.8	10.5	10.1	12.2	11.1
Grants	1.1	1.0	0.3	0.1	0.3	0.3	0.3	0.6	0.4	0.9
					(In percent of GDP)					
Total fiscal expenditures	32.3	30.1	28.9	29.5	29.0	25.6	39.8	34.7	32.7	32.1
Current expenditure	23.6	26.1	25.5	26.0	26.4	22.5	33.2	27.9	26.6	26.5
Development expenditure	8.7	4.0	3.4	3.5	2.6	3.1	6.6	6.8	6.1	5.6
Overall fiscal balance (cash basis)	–11.7	–5.6	–11.7	–13.9	–15.7	–5.2	0.6	–1.8	–7.9	–0.4
Foreign financing (net)	2.7	1.6	0.2	0.2	0.1	–0.2	0.4	0.3	1.2	2.3
Domestic financing (net)	8.8	4.4	11.8	19.7	15.7	5.3	–1.1	1.5	6.7	–2.3
External trade balance	–3.6	–8.8	–9.7	–11.9	4.6	–0.2	–0.5	–2.0	–11.5	0.4
Exports, f.o.b.	14.8	15.0	13.3	15.1	28.0	29.9	35.2	34.5	23.8	36.1
Oil and oil products	13.9	14.4	11.7	13.1	26.0	28.9	34.0	32.5	21.7	34.0
Non-oil	0.8	0.6	1.6	2.0	2.0	1.1	1.2	2.0	2.1	2.0
Imports	–18.4	–23.8	–22.9	–26.9	–23.4	–30.1	–35.7	–36.5	–35.4	–35.7
Total current account balance	–3.1	–10.7	–13.2	–16.1	5.6	2.8	1.7	0.3	–3.7	2.9
Memorandum items:										
Debt service (as share of exports of goods and services, obligation basis)	46.7	91.3	89.1	80.8	46.8	42.1	31.9	12.6	17.0	10.5
Gross official reserves (in months of imports)	2.8	4.2	2.2	0.9	2.9	3.1	4.6	5.3	4.2	6.0
Total subsidies (implicit and explicit in percent of GDP)	20.2	10.0	15.2	17.6	18.4	8.9	13.5	7.7	2.2	2.5
Real per capita consumption (1996=100)	335.4	271.8	217.1	169.8	97.6	104.9	100.0	112.4	110.8	112.7
Real per capita private consumption (1996=100)	438.7	350.6	278.0	222.5	87.9	103.6	100.0	111.1	110.6	110.6
Real per capita GNDI (1996=100)	297.2	228.4	188.0	139.5	101.8	105.8	100.0	114.1	103.1	110.9
Incremental capital output ratio (ICOR)	. . .	–8.0	4.6	50.1	–5.6	2.6	7.1	2.9	4.0	4.9
Terms of trade	122.3	113.0	107.4	91.8	85.5	85.3	100.0	100.7	69.5	114.1
Real effective exchange rate	. . .	. . .	. . .	. . .	. . .	76.2	100.0	109.7	119.5	107.1

Sources: Yemeni authorities; and IMF staff estimates.

[1]For 1990–96, a weighted exchange rate based on the official and parallel rates was used to convert external transactions into Yemeni rials, following the methodology set out in SNA 1993. This allows adjustment for the implicit taxes (subsidies) involved in export transactions undertaken at the more appreciated (depreciated) rate and in import transactions undertaken at the more depreciated (appreciated) rate.

Figure 23. Saving and Investment
(In percent of GDP)

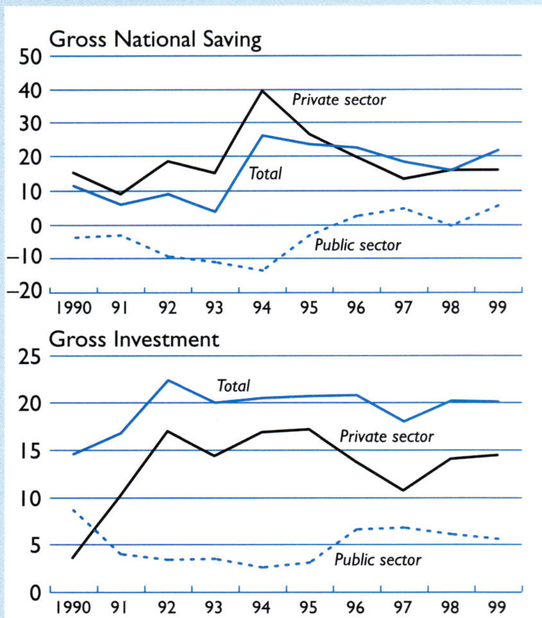

Sources: Data provided by the Yemeni authorities; IMF staff estimates.

GDP, private sector investment remained unchanged on average from the first to the second half of the decade, while government investment rose. The latter reflected the improving fiscal situation, efforts at reconstruction after the 1994 civil war, and a growing focus on the state as provider of infrastructure and social services.

During 1991–94 the relatively low level of private investment likely reflected macroeconomic instability and the uncertainty associated with very high rates of inflation, large fiscal deficits crowding out bank credit to the private sector, multiple exchange rates, external shocks, political instability, and deep-rooted weaknesses in the investment environment.[92] Private investment in 1990 was particularly low, probably because of measurement problems associated with the first year of unification. However, the stagnation in private investment around 15 percent of GDP on average in the pre- and postreform periods is somewhat difficult to explain. Macroeconomic stabilization, price liberalization, the removal of trade and exchange restrictions, and other structural reforms aimed at facilitating and encouraging private investment should have significantly improved the investment climate after 1995 and should have led to a significant increase in the share of private investment in GDP. Yet the more deep-rooted obstacles to investment were hardly addressed, and high real interest rates stifled investment projects. In addition, major investments in the oil sector had been completed by the mid-1990s. Although the data do not permit oil-related investments to be separated out, it may well be that non-oil investment ratios rose in the reform period.

Private saving averaged 19.9 percent of GDP during 1995–99, compared with an annual average of 20.6 percent of GDP during 1991–94. During the earlier period, high inflation was disruptive to saving, producing negative real interest rates and increasing the difficulty in anticipating real future returns and interest rates. Yet it is striking that the relatively low and stable inflation during 1995–99 appears to have been insufficient to stimulate higher private saving. Given the drastic improvement in public saving between the two periods (as detailed in Section IV), this may in part reflect a measure of Ricardian equivalence (in which agents increase their saving during periods of high fiscal deficits in anticipation of higher future taxes). But it may also reflect the presence of liquidity constraints that forced the population to reduce saving in order to meet consumption needs. Indeed, the path of consumption seems to confirm the strong effect of liquidity constraints: real consumption per capita declined dramatically during 1990–95 and improved only marginally during 1996–99; in 1999 real consumption per capita was still below its 1993 level. This decline mainly mirrored the decline in real income per capita in the first half of the 1990s, and the weak growth in more recent years, which is also consistent with the observed rise in poverty. Finally, with oil revenue accruing largely to the government, private saving had to come out of non-oil income (including workers' remittances); as a share of non-oil GDP, private saving attained a respectable 23.2 percent during 1997–99, considerably higher than during 1991–93, when it averaged 15.4 percent.

As a result mainly of the sharp improvement in government saving, the external current account improved dramatically in the second half of the 1990s, from an average deficit of 9.5 percent of GDP during 1991–94 to near balance on average during 1995–99 (Table 15). When the civil war period is excluded, the difference is even more striking: the deficit narrowed by 14 percentage points on average. Like the movements in the fiscal balance, these developments

[92]Weaknesses in the investment environment include ineffective commercial courts, poor enforcement of contracts and land ownership rights, lack of understanding and familiarity with commercial law, poor infrastructure, lack of skilled labor, and governance problems in the public administration.

Table 16. Vulnerability Indicators
(In percent, unless otherwise indicated)

	1990	1991	1992	1993	1994	1995	1996	1997	1998	1999
External solvency indicators										
Real effective exchange rate (average period, percent change)	. . .	39.2	42.0	67.7	62.3	–41.0	–42.6	–33.6	8.9	–10.4
Total external debt (in millions of US$)	9,915.2	10,323.5	10,540.7	10,734.7	10,876.2	11,017.4	11,134.7	5,359.2	5,373.4	5,490.1
(in percent of GDP)	105.7	129.5	127.9	138.5	167.1	170.1	173.2	81.2	85.3	80.4
Short-term external debt (in millions of US$)[1]	586.0	975.6	922.4	916.4	766.7	747.2	659.0	218.2	225.4	204.5
Debt service ratio (obligations basis, in percent of GNFS exports)	46.7	91.3	89.1	80.8	46.8	42.1	31.9	12.6	17.0	10.5
External liquidity indicators										
Total official own gross foreign reserves (in millions of US$)	424.0	679.6	322.6	147.4	357.0	525.5	937.4	1,152.2	853.2	1,350.7
In months of imports	2.8	4.2	2.2	0.9	2.9	3.1	4.6	5.3	4.2	6.0
In percent of short-term external debt	72.4	69.7	35.0	16.1	46.6	70.3	142.3	528.1	378.5	660.5
In percent of M0	18.6	44.7	24.8	12.6	32.5	51.7	98.8	118.4	86.5	129.3
In percent of M2	9.9	22.8	12.2	6.5	17.5	26.9	44.1	50.4	36.3	56.9
Public sector solvency indicators	11.7	12.0	12.0	12.0	12.0	50.0	126.9	130.5	141.7	159.7
Government's net domestic debt/GDP	60.7	55.1	54.5	63.4	67.9	46.2	30.9	25.3	32.3	24.2
Government's external debt/GDP	105.7	129.5	127.9	138.5	167.1	170.1	173.2	81.2	85.3	80.4
Total debt service/total revenue[1,2]	40.3	47.6	49.0	50.2	47.1	39.4	39.2	17.3	27.5	22.1
Interest payments/total revenue[1,2]	12.0	12.6	11.6	17.7	22.6	7.6	9.3	7.2	14.0	12.7
Oil revenue/total revenue[3]	37.8	40.8	29.1	28.1	28.7	47.9	69.9	67.4	52.1	62.7
Financial sector indicators										
Net domestic credit (percent change)[4]	18.9	10.1	21.9	40.7	40.7	16.6	–11.7	–5.5	37.5	–13.8
Private sector credit (percent change)	33.1	14.9	15.3	26.0	39.2	35.4	–6.3	53.8	57.7	15.2
Net domestic credit/GDP[4]	63.5	58.9	56.5	64.2	70.4	49.1	30.2	23.5	32.2	22.3
Of which										
Nongovernment credit/GDP	8.8	9.0	7.6	7.1	9.3	7.1	3.5	4.2	6.5	6.0
Nonperforming loans/GDP	. . .	. . .	. . .	. . .	. . .	. . .	21.0	10.2	15.2	17.0
Average maturity of public domestic debt (months)	. . .	. . .	. . .	. . .	. . .	1.0	4.7	6.0	7.9	7.2
Treasury bill spread (over U.S. T-bills)	. . .	. . .	. . .	. . .	. . .	18.1	19.7	7.8	7.1	7.2
Private credit/total assets of banks	14.7	13.5	12.1	11.3	11.1	13.4	12.5	18.0	25.6	25.8
Share of crude oil exports in total exports	80.7	77.2	65.2	62.0	81.9	82.0	80.7	78.4	71.3	80.8

Source: The Yemeni authorities.
[1] Defined as amortization obligations with maturity of less than one year.
[2] Domestic interest payments are recorded net of central bank profits until 1998.
[3] Includes domestic oil and gas revenue.
[4] Net domestic credit refers to the sum of net credit to government and nongovernment sectors, and excludes other items net.

reflect mostly the rise in oil revenue. The surging share of exports in GDP is virtually all due to oil, although non-oil exports also doubled (from extremely low levels) as a share of GDP, from 1 percent in the early 1990s to 2 percent in recent years. Coffee and fish still account for most non-oil exports, but exports of these items are stagnating or declining, and non-oil export growth was largely driven by fruits and vegetables for the regional market. The weak development of non-oil exports is consistent with the observed trend of a real appreciation of the Yemeni rial against the currencies of partner countries in recent years and may be a symptom of Dutch disease in Yemen. (In Dutch disease, demand for a dominant export, typically a natural resource export, causes an appreciation of the domestic currency that makes other exports uncompetitive.) In the same vein, imports grew strongly throughout the decade, nearly doubling their share of GDP from 20 percent in 1990 to 36 percent in 1999. Other components of the current account have been rather stable over the decade. Workers' remittances have been broadly stable after the secular decline in the early 1990s. The performance of the tourism industry, meanwhile, has been disappointing: security problems and inadequate infrastructure have hindered development of this industry despite its obvious potential to create jobs and generate foreign exchange earnings (see Annex I).

Growing dependency on oil underlies the improvement in the external account but also engenders a growing vulnerability to oil price and production volatility. Even so, recent years have witnessed a reduction in Yemen's external financial vulnerability (Table 16). In particular, thanks to substantial debt relief and a prudent borrowing policy, the external debt has declined dramatically as a share of GDP. This decline masks an even larger fall in the net present value of the debt, as new borrowing has been largely on concessional terms, and debt rescheduling has similarly stretched the maturities of existing debt (see Section II for details). Accordingly, debt service on a commitment basis fell, as a ratio to goods and nonfactor services, to 11 percent in 1999, from eight to nine times that level in the early 1990s. The elimination of the external debt overhang was not, however, bought at the expense of domestic indebtedness. The government's domestic debt was cut, if less dramatically, from more than half of GDP in the early 1990s to a quarter in 1999, even though interest payments as a share of government income remained at about 10 percent, reflecting the phasing out of financial repression as the government has increasingly paid market rates for its borrowing. At the same time, the maturity of public domestic debt increased steadily during the reform period. By any measure, the reserve position has also greatly strengthened. Since 1996, gross official reserves (net of reserves needed to cover foreign exchange deposits of commercial banks with the central bank) roughly covered high-powered money, and by the end of 1999 they also covered more than half of broad money. Since 1995, reserves have exceeded the equivalent of three months of imports, a level often taken as a benchmark of sufficiency.

The limited role of financial intermediation also limits the potential risks emanating from the financial sector. The ratio of credit to GDP has been declining, reaching 22 percent in 1999 compared with over 50 percent in the mid-1990s. This decline, however, is mostly due to the strong fiscal situation, as private sector credit remains about 6 to 7 percent of GDP. However, as discussed elsewhere in this report, recorded vulnerabilities in the banking sector have been rising in recent years (although this likely reflects better reporting and enforcement of prudential regulations rather than a genuine deterioration of portfolios). The size of nonperforming loans (17 percent of GDP in 1999), although still manageable, points to the importance of the planned reforms in the banking sector. Yemen has no private credit ratings, and in the absence of a secondary treasury bill market, interest rates may not fully reflect market forces. However, the declining yield spread of Yemeni government paper over U.S. Treasury bills indicates that, in the view of investors inside (and outside) Yemen, progress in macroeconomic stabilization is appreciated and has substantially improved Yemen's creditworthiness.

Annex I Tourism Sector in Yemen: Problems and Prospects

The tourism sector is widely seen as a potential source of growth in the non-oil sector. It is also widely recognized that a number of structural impediments—such as security concerns, first and foremost, and lack of infrastructure—constrain this potential and would need to be fundamentally addressed before the tourism industry could start making a major contribution to future economic growth and employment.

Sector Potential

Yemen has abundant tourism resources and potential for further growth and development. Yemen's long history, reflected in its rich and unique culture, has left a wealth of significant archaeological sites and a unique vernacular architecture. Yemen has a mixture of scenery—ranging from desert through verdant valleys to mountain ranges—some 2,000 kilometers of coastline, fringing the Red Sea and the Gulf of Aden, and more than hundred islands. Finally, after centuries of isolation from the rest of the world, Yemen remains one of the last unknown destinations.

In addition to the traditional tourism potential of its existing historic and scenic attractions, Yemen has significant opportunities for the development of other forms of tourism that are still largely unknown there, but which possess increasing market potential. These include trekking and mountain hiking, mountain biking, beach resort tourism, scuba diving, and eco-tourism, both terrestrial and marine.

Figure 24. Visitor Arrivals
(In thousands)

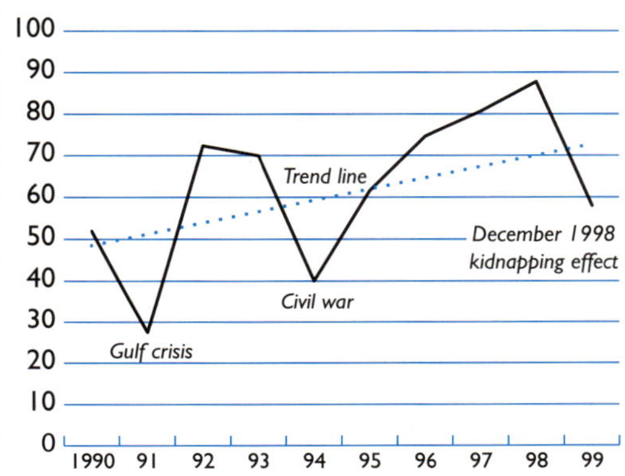

Source: Data provided by the Yemeni authorities.

Size and Trends

In general, since unification in 1990, international tourism in Yemen has been on an upward, trend, with visitor arrivals growing on average by about 5 percent a year (Table 17 and Figure 24). The tourism sector suffered major setbacks in 1991, after the Gulf crisis erupted; in 1994, the year of the civil war in Yemen; and in 1999, after a fatal kidnapping incident in December 1998.

Table 17. Visitor Arrivals and Tourism Revenues

	1990	1991	1992	1993	1994	1995	1996	1997	1998	1999
Visitor arrivals, thousands	51.8	27.3	72.2	69.8	39.9	61.4	74.5	80.5	87.6	57.8
Revenue, US$ million	40.0	21.0	46.9	54.0	35.0	50.0	55.0	69.0	84.0	48.4

Source: General Tourism Authority.

Table 18. Average Tourism Statistics Since Unification

	Yearly Arrivals, Thousands	Duration of Stay, Nights	Revenue per Stay, US dollars
	63.9	5.4	805
	(Of which: By Region)		
	Percent Share	Nights	
Europe	65.2	6.1	. . .
Middle East	17.4	5.4	. . .
Asia	7.2	5.6	. . .
The Americas	6.7	6.4	. . .
Africa	2.4	7.7	. . .
Australia	1.1	5.1	. . .

Source: General Tourism Authority.

Yemen's principal tourism source market is Western Europe (Table 18), in particular, Germany, France, Italy, and Britain, which to a large extent reflects the contacts established by the existing tour operators. The peak tourist season in Yemen is between October and March. International tourism is mainly concentrated in the governorates of Sana'a, Hadhramout, Al-Jouf, Al-Hodeidah, Marib, and Shabwa.

In 1998, the tourism sector provided jobs, either directly or indirectly, to an estimated 23,000 workers, including those in the hotel industry and related sectors. As tourism extends to remote regions, it helps provide employment opportunities and increases incomes among the local population. Total foreign exchange revenues from tourism are still relatively small—at about 3 percent of total exports of goods and services, or 18 percent of non-oil exports in recent years—but have been growing on average by 8 percent a year.

The Yemeni government believes that developing tourism will help enhance long-term economic growth and improve the living standards of the Yemeni people, as well as protect and preserve Yemen's cultural heritage and natural environment.

Structural Impediments

Concerns over peace and security, and inadequate infrastructure, are the two largest immediate obstacles to the successful development of the tourism industry in Yemen, while the danger of losing the historic and cultural heritage and environmental degradation are longer-term problems.

Security Concerns

At present, the image of Yemen in the Western world is relatively poor and, prompted by continuous security-related incidents, the country is often characterized in the Western media as "kidnapping and bombing prone."[93]

Although Yemen was unified in 1990, civil unrest lasted and a 70-day civil war erupted in 1994. There are areas, especially in the North, which are still not under the full control of the central government. Reportedly, there are large numbers of firearms in the country, almost four per head.[94] Illicit weapons, including assault rifles, are openly carried. Politically motivated violence persists and security violations occasionally occur in rural areas.[95] Tribal disputes, kidnappings, and shootouts between sheikhs' armed entourages and government security forces are frequent, including in major cities and public places such as Sana'a International Airport.

More than 100 kidnappings have occurred throughout Yemen since 1991, mainly conducted by armed tribesmen with specific grievances against the government.[96] These kidnappings are normally resolved peacefully, but tribesmen have held some foreigners for extended periods, and the December 1998 incident—when four tourists were executed by a group of Islamic militants—gave Yemen front page international news coverage and dealt a severe blow to the nascent tourism industry.

Since then, many countries, including the United States, the United Kingdom, and Japan, have advised their nationals against traveling to Yemen;[97] Germany has reduced the number of accredited Yemeni tourist agencies to two; and KLM Airlines has suspended its service to Yemen.[98]

Inadequate Infrastructure

Addressing security concerns is necessary, but not enough for the successful development of the tourism sector in Yemen. The lack of adequate infra-

[93]See *The Economist*, April 10, 1999, page 61.

[94]See *Yemen—A Travel Survival Kit*, Lonely Planet Publications, January 1996, page 87.

[95]See *Business Middle East*, January 1, 2000, The Economist Intelligence Unit, page 11.

[96]See *Yemen—Consular Information Sheet*, September 14, 1999, U.S. Department of State website, *http://travel.state.gov/yemen.html*, and *Business Middle East*, February 1, 1999; The Economist Intelligence Unit, page 10.

[97]See *Yemen—Travel Warning*, November 5, 1999, U.S. Department of State website, *http://travel.state.gov/yemen warning.html*.

[98]Preliminary estimates suggest that, as a result, tourist arrivals in 1999 declined by about 35 percent relative to 1998 and tourism foreign exchange receipts stood at less than 60 percent of their 1998 level. The two largest hotels in Sana'a have seen their occupancy rates drop below 50 percent, and Yemenia Airlines was reported to have lost more than US$2 million in revenues.

structure—such as hotels, roads, catering, and airport services—is another major factor constraining the growth of the tourism sector.

Only a third of roads in Yemen are paved. Poor roads and lack of easy access to tourist attractions entail long and uncomfortable journeys by four-wheel drive vehicles, which means that visits to places of interest have to be of relatively short duration.

Existing hotel stock is heavily concentrated in the urban areas of Sana'a, Aden, Hadhramout, and Taiz, with more than 50 percent of first class rooms located in Sana'a. Despite a significant increase in hotel construction since unification, the number of hotel rooms suitable for international tourists who prefer to stay in high-grade properties has remained unchanged and is currently only about 1,100, or less than 15 percent of the total room stock.[99] Consequently, tour operators have reported problems getting enough rooms of a suitable standard during the high season and have often had to reject big tour group reservations because of accommodation and transportation constraints.[100]

The development of tourism is also constrained by the absence of basic services—such as eating and toilet facilities—and a shortage of potable water both at places of interest and at possible stopover points. Furthermore, there are no tourist information or interpretation centers outside Sana'a, while those available in Sana'a are not up to international standards, lacking appropriately trained or licensed tour guides.

The situation is compounded by the shortage of trained and experienced local personnel and the absence of facilities providing professional training in the services sector. As a result, expatriates often have to be hired, especially in the hotel industry, thus further hindering the development of a local tourism sector.

Finally, airport facilities have limited baggage and passenger handling capacity, partly reflecting Yemenia's monopoly in this area, and could become congested if more than one aircraft is being served.

Threat to Historic Heritage and Natural Environment

At present, regulations to prevent the destruction of buildings of historic and cultural significance or protect the natural environment are limited and poorly enforced. As a result, there is a real threat to the historic heritage of Yemen, the very feature that constitutes the principal tourist attraction. According to anecdotal evidence, some 30 percent of "physical" heritage in the countryside has been lost in the past 10 years to unregulated commercial development, and parts of the coastline with significant beach resort potential are being lost to industrial development.[101] Furthermore, the potential for ecotourism, especially in the coastal areas, is being destroyed as various species—such as sea turtles—are driven to extinction because of poor enforcement of seasonal hunting and fishing restrictions.

Policy Implications

Given the undoubted potential of tourism in Yemen, the foregoing discussion suggests that the following are critical to the successful development of the tourism sector in Yemen:

- Guaranteeing of security and maintaining a stable political and economic environment as preconditions for investment, both domestic and foreign, in the tourism sector, given the long-term, and hence high-risk, nature of such investment;
- Investing in essential infrastructure and tourism-related services and facilities;
- Providing training and licensing for both public and private sector tourism personnel to ensure that tourists receive a standard of service consistent with internationally accepted norms; and
- Protecting and conserving the historic and cultural heritage and natural environment of the country.

The formation of a public sector institutional structure, with well-defined functional responsibilities that would readily facilitate planning, development, marketing, and regulation, is critical to the attainment of policy objectives for the tourism sector in Yemen. This would require structural changes and training initiatives in order to make the public sector more effective in carrying out its statutory functions, and would include collaboration with the private sector.

Government Efforts to Date

After the kidnapping incident in December 1998, the government stepped up its effort to address the

[99]Currently, there are about 250 hotel establishments offering some 7,700 rooms.

[100]The potential absorptive capacity of the tourism sector in Yemen is rather limited. According to local businessmen, existing historic and scenic attractions can potentially accommodate no more than 150,000 visitors a year. This requires the tourism sector to be oriented towards low volumes and high yields, attracting the more affluent category of international tourists. These are mostly senior citizens in the middle and higher income groups, who require more comfortable accommodation than younger and more adventurous backpackers.

[101]The most recent examples of the latter include the proposed construction of Burum Port, 20 km southwest of Mukalla, and a gas pipeline through a white sand beach at Bir Ali.

security problem and shore up the tourism industry. Special courts were set up to try kidnappers, and the death penalty was introduced for the offence.[102] Weapons were banned in the capital, and a Special Forces unit was formed in November 1999 to combat terrorism.

A new Tourism Law was issued in August 1999, and three new government entities were established—the Tourism Promotion Board, the High Council on Tourism, and the Environmental Council—in addition to the existing government structures in charge of tourism affairs, such as the Ministry of Tourism and Culture and the General Tourism Authority.[103]

The Tourism Promotion Board was set up under the umbrella of the Ministry of Tourism and Culture and consists of representatives of the government, the private sector, and the media. It is charged with improving the image of Yemen in the Western media as well as increasing the general awareness abroad and at home of tourism in Yemen. It is chaired by the Minister of Tourism and holds weekly meetings to discuss the sector's promotion and development strategy, but has no decision-making authority. In addition, the Board has undertaken to study the experience of Egypt in limiting the fall-out from terrorism on the tourism industry.

The High Council on Tourism is chaired by the Prime Minister and comprises seven other ministers, including the Ministers of Tourism, Information, Industry, Planning, Interior, and Defense. It meets to discuss key policy, investment, and security issues in the area of tourism and has decision-making powers.

The authorities, led in their efforts by the General Tourism Authority, have recently been actively seeking technical assistance and external financing for project implementation, including updating the Master Plan for Tourism Development in Yemen which was sponsored in 1991 by the European Community.

[102]Three kidnappers in the 1998 case, including the group leader, were sentenced to death by the court and have been executed.

[103]According to a local observer, there is currently a lot of duplication and a lack of coordination the various government and public entities involved in the tourism sector, some of which also appear to be overstaffed and lack the technical capability to carry out their statutory obligations satisfactorily.

Annex II Summary of the Tax System as of End-June 2000

Summary of the Tax System as of End-June 2000

Tax	Nature of Tax	Exemptions and Deductions	Rates
1. Taxes on business income			
1.1 Domestic corporations	Levied on net profits. Assessment base encompasses most forms of income, including interest, dividends, and foreign income	Deductions: Operating costs; depreciation allowance; charitable contributions up to 5 percent of net income; and Zakat. Exemptions: Income of cooperatives, and agricultural and humanitarian societies, provided trade is limited to members; and income from agriculture, livestock, poultry, fishing, and beekeeping, subject to regulations. Corporations may be granted an exemption if they qualify under the Investment Law (IL); this entails a five-year exemption, but Council of Ministers may grant an additional five years	35 percent flat rate Penalties are levied for late payment
1.2 Foreign corporations	Same as above	Same as above	35 percent flat rate
1.3 Proprietorships	Same as above	Deductions: Same as above Exemption: YRls 36,000	Personal tax rates, 10 percent–35 percent
2. Taxes on personal income			
2.1 Tax on wages and salaries	Levied on total wage income (wages, salaries, bonuses, etc.,) including gratuities in cash or kind. Monthly withholding by the employer from wages of both residents and nonresidents and paid to tax authorities during the first 10 days of the following month. Companies with eight or more workers must keep tax records for their employees	Deductions: Pension contributions, and work-related costs Exemptions: Monthly exemption: YRls 3,000. Exemption not granted for nonresidents Fully exempted: diplomats; UN experts; pension and severance payments; wages paid to Yemeni agricultural and fishing workers; domestic servants; and income of day laborers	Personal tax rates with a ceiling of 20 percent.
2.2 Tax on professional income	Levied on noncommercial and nonindustrial income.	Deductions: Costs deducted according to specified list	Personal tax rates, 10 percent–35 percent.
3. Social security and retirement contributions			
3.1 Civil service and public enterprise employees	Paid to General Authority for Insurance and Pensions (GAIP)		12 percent with equal contributions from employees and Government; Government also pays 1 percent for accident insurance.

3.2 Police employees	Paid to separate pension fund		12 percent with equal contributions from employees and Government
3.3 Defense employees	Paid to separate pension fund		12 percent with equal contributions from employees and Government
3.4 Private sector employees	Paid to separate pension fund		6 percent employee, 9 percent employer
4. Taxes on property			
4.1 Real estate income tax	Levied on all net income from leased buildings and land	Exemptions: Government; religious organizations; local councils; diplomatic housing; and hospitals	One month's rent (8.33 percent)
4.2 Real estate sales tax	Levied on sales proceeds from land and buildings	Deductions: None allowed. Exemptions: Transfers through inheritance; donations to religious or charitable organizations; religious organizations; and agricultural land	3 percent of sales value
5. Taxes on goods and services			
5.1 General excise taxes	Harmonized taxes are levied on certain domestic and imported goods. The tax applies to the import costs (before the tariff) or at the domestic manufacturer level. For mineral water and soft drinks, tax applies to retail price paid by consumer		5, 7, 11, 15 percent; 25 percent applies to certain specified transportation vehicles and luxury items
5.2 Selected excise taxes	Items taxable at manufacture level		
5.2.2 Tobacco	Levied on domestically produced and domestically trademarked or foreign trademarked cigarettes; imported tobacco, and tobacco products		For domestically produced cigarettes: 60 percent on domestically-trademarked and 65 percent on foreign-trademarked; 80 percent on imported cigarettes; 60 percent for cigars; 25 percent for imported tobacco
5.2.3 Taxes on petroleum products	Levied on retail sales price		Percent Gasoline: 2 Kerosene: 2 Turpentine: 2 Oils: 2 Diesel oil: 2 Liquid gas: 0.5 per cylinder Lubricants: 1
5.3 Qat tax	Levied on assessed market value		25 percent

Summary of the Tax System *(concluded)*

Tax	Nature of Tax	Exemptions and Deductions	Rates
6. Customs tariff	Applied to all imports not specifically exempted	Exemptions may be provided to corporations that qualify under the IL	Four-band structure with rates of 5, 10, 15, and 30 percent. A single exemption of 70 percent applied to cigarettes and other tobacco products
7. Other taxes			
7.1 Motor vehicle taxes	Levied on all motorized vehicles operating in Yemen with gasoline or diesel powered engines; levied on purchases of fuel (domestic or imported)	Exemptions: Government vehicles, diplomatic and embassy cars, and emergency vehicles	YRls 0.25 per litre of gasoline; YRls 0.15 per litre of diesel
7.3 Counselor fees	For Yemeni visas		According to a specific schedule
7.4 Passport fee			Fee varies with the type of passport
7.5 Compulsory military service fee	Levied on Yemenis for exemption from or postponement of compulsory national military service		Yrls 86,000 for exemption

References

Alier, Max, and Martin Kaufman, "Nonrenewable Resources: A Case for Persistent Fiscal Surpluses," IMF Working Paper 99/44 (Washington: International Monetary Fund).

Arab Oil and Gas Directory, 1999 (Beirut : Arab Petroleum Research Center).

Backus and Crucini, 2000, "Oil Prices and the Terms of Trade," *Journal of International Economics*, Vol. 50, pp. 185–213.

Bassett, Sheila, Alejandro Garcia, and Claire Liuksila, "Fiscal-Policy Sustainability in Oil-Producing Countries," IMF Working Paper 94/137 (Washington: International Monetary Fund).

Burrowes, Robert D., 1989, "Oil Strike and Leadership Struggle in South Yemen: 1986 and Beyond," *Middle East Journal*, Vol. 43, No. 3, pp. 437–454.

Cashin, Paul, Hong Liang, and C. John McDermott, "How Persistent are Shocks to World Commodity Prices?" IMF Working Paper 99/80 (Washington: International Monetary Fund).

Chalk, Nigel, "Fiscal Sustainability with Non-Renewable Resources," IMF Working Paper 98/26 (Washington: International Monetary Fund).

Colton, Nora Ann, 1993, "Homeward Bound: Yemeni Return Migration," *International Migration Review*, Vol. 27 (Winter).

Conge, Patrick, and Guem Okruhlik, 1997, "National Autonomy, Labor Migration and Political Crisis: Yemen and Saudi Arabia," *Middle East Journal*, Vol. 51, No. 4, pp. 554–565.

Dunbar, Charles, 1992, "The Unification of Yemen," *Middle East Journal*, Vol. 46, No. 3, pp. 456–476.

Easterly, William, and Stanley Fischer, 1990, "The Economics of the Government Budget Constraint," *The World Bank Research Observer*, Vol. 5, (July) No. 2, pp. 127–142.

Engel, Eduardo, and Rodrigo Valdes, 2000, "Optimal Fiscal Strategy for Oil Exporting Countries: A User's Manual," Paper prepared for the MED Seminar Series (unpublished; Washington: Middle Eastern Department, International Monetary Fund).

Hashem, Mouna, 1996, *Goals for Social Integration and Realities of Social Exclusion in the Republic of Yemen*, (Geneva: International Institute for Labour Studies).

Household Budget Survey 1998, 1999, (Sana'a, Yemen: Central Statistical Office).

International Bank for Reconstruction and Development, 1996, *Poverty Assessment Report*, March, (Washington).

Kostiner, Joseph, 1996, "Yemen—The Tortuous Quest for Unity, 1990–94," *Royal Institute for International Affairs*.

Pindyck, Robert, 1999, "The Long-Run Evolution of Energy Prices," *Energy Journal*, Vol. 20, No. 2, pp. 1–27.

Tersman, Gunnar, "Oil, National Wealth, and Current and Future Consumption Possibilities," IMF Working Paper 91/69 (Washington: International Monetary Fund).

United Nations, Development Program, 1999a, *Poverty Policy Framework for Yemen*, Strategic paper prepared by Mohammed Al-Saqour, April (Sana'a).

———, Development Program, 1999b, *Human Development Report* (New York: Oxford University Press).

Ward, Christopher, 2000, "Qat in Yemen" World Bank, unpublished.

Statistical Appendix

Table A.1. Social and Demographic Indicators, 1995 and 1997

	1995	1997	Selected MENA[1,2]
Sociodemographic indicators			
GNP per capita (in U.S. dollars)	260	270	2,070
GNP per capita (PPP, current international dollar)	730	720	4,630
Total population (in millions)	15.3	16.1	280
Population growth rate (in percent)[3]	3.2	3.5	2.1
Total fertility rate	6.7	6.4	3.6
Age dependency ratio (dependents to working-age population)	1.2	1.1	0.7
Urban population (in percent)	33.6	34.4	58.4
Labor participation rate (in percent of population aged 14–64)	69.3	67.0	57.2
Female labor participation rate (in percent of total population)	27.8	27.9	26.5
Health			
Life expectancy at birth (in years)[3]	53	59	67
Infant mortality rate (per 1,000 live births)[3]	100	98	49
Under five mortality rate (per 1,000 live births)	145	137	63
Maternal mortality rate (per 100,000 live births)	1,471	...	205
Immunized: DPT, under 12 months (in percent of age group)	53	57	90
Child malnutrition, under 5 years (in percent of age group)	30	29	14
Access to safe water (percent of population)	39	...	85
Access to sanitation (percent of population)	19	...	62
Education			
Adult literacy rate	40	42	62

Sources: Central Statistics Organization, Statistical Year Book; and IBRD, World Development Indicators database.

[1]Algeria, Bahrain, Djibouti, Egypt, Iran, Iraq, Jordan, Lebanon, Libya, Malta, Morocco, Oman, Saudi Arabia, Syria, and Tunisia.

[2]Data for the nearest year to 1997.

[3]Second column data are for 1998.

Table A.2. Selected Economic and Financial Indicators, 1994–99

	1994	1995	1996	1997	1998	1999
			(Change in percent)			
Production and prices						
Nominal GDP at market prices	28.4	67.1	43.7	21.5	0.4	24.3
Real GDP at market prices	–3.6	7.9	2.9	8.1	5.3	3.8
Real non-oil GDP	–9.6	5.5	0.5	8.2	5.9	3.2
Real oil GDP	43.7	20.0	13.5	7.5	2.7	6.2
Consumer price index (annual average)	71.3	62.5	40.0	4.6	11.5	8.0
Crude export oil price						
(weighted average, U.S. dollar per barrel)	15.4	16.9	20.3	18.5	11.6	18.7
			(In percent of GDP)			
Government finance						
Total revenue and grants	12.8	19.5	35.9	32.8	26.4	31.8
Oil revenue	3.7	9.3	25.1	22.1	13.8	19.8
Non-oil revenue	8.9	9.8	10.5	10.1	12.2	11.1
Grants	0.3	0.3	0.3	0.6	0.4	0.9
Total expenditure	29.0	25.6	39.8	34.7	32.7	32.1
Current	26.4	22.5	33.2	27.9	26.6	26.5
Development	2.6	3.1	6.6	6.8	6.1	5.6
Overall balance (commitment basis)	–16.3	–16.3	–16.3	–16.3	–16.3	–16.3
Overall balance including grants (cash basis)	–15.7	–5.2	0.6	–1.8	–7.9	–0.4
			(12-month change in percent of initial broad money)			
Monetary data						
Broad money	34.7	20.4	8.6	10.7	11.7	13.8
Credit to nongovernment sector	69.0	28.0	–29.4	46.6	54.2	15.0
Benchmark deposit interest rate (percent p.a.)	6.5	20.0	25.0	11.0	15.0	18.0
Velocity (Non-oil GDP/M2)	1.2	1.7	1.9	2.0	2.2	2.1
			(In millions of U.S. dollars)			
External sector						
Exports, f.o.b.	1,824	1,937	2,263	2,274	1,501	2,466
Of which						
Crude oil	1,615	1,735	1,976	1,945	1,229	2,131
Imports, f.o.b.	–1,522	–1,948	–2,294	–2,407	–2,228	–2,440
Services (net)	–475	–411	–370	–470	–398	–489
Private remittances and transfers (net)	1,117	1,104	1,188	1,256	1,254	1,314
Capital account (net)	–641	–876	–397	34	–154	11
Overall balance	–779	–38	–625	116	–463	320
Central bank own gross foreign reserves	357	525	937	1,152	853	1,351
In months of imports[1]	2.9	3.1	4.6	5.3	4.2	6.0
Current account, including grants (in percent of GDP)	5.6	2.8	1.7	0.3	–3.7	2.9
Debt service ratios[2]						
Obligation basis	46.8	42.1	31.9	12.6	17.0	10.5
Actual	3.3	6.6	8.7	10.3	14.0	8.3
Official external debt	10,876	11,017	11,135	5,359	5,373	5,490
(In percent of GDP)	167	170	173	81	85	80
Terms of trade (1996=100)	85.5	85.3	100.0	100.7	69.5	114.1
Exchange rate (free market, eop) (YRls/US$)	101.0	127.1	126.9	130.5	141.7	159.7
Real effective exchange rate (1996=100)[3]	. . .	76.2	100.0	109.7	119.5	107.1

Sources: Yemeni authorities; and IMF staff estimates.

[1]Gross reserves minus commercial bank foreign exchange deposits held with the central bank. Imports are for the current year and exclude oil and gas sector imports.

[2]Public and publicly guaranteed debt, including central bank foreign liabilities. In percent of exports of goods and services.

[3]INS, based on free market rate.

Table A.3. Sectoral Origin of Gross Domestic Product at Current Prices, 1994–99

	1994	1995	1996	1997	1998	1999
			(In millions of Yemeni rials)			
Agriculture and forestry	63,342	90,330	108,526	124,750	158,397	167,441
Fishing	5,814	8,832	10,700	13,256	16,110	18,610
Mining and quarrying	858	1,640	2,449	2,506	2,524	2,705
Oil and gas[1]	17,790	69,116	191,273	244,915	137,758	263,309
Manufacturing	39,300	64,287	57,065	65,605	77,191	83,829
Oil refining	2,438	8,645	23,207	26,600	27,769	30,433
Electricity, gas, and water	2,034	3,111	5,334	6,718	7,912	8,401
Construction	10,423	16,867	25,713	37,442	41,977	41,867
Wholesale and retail trade	30,077	49,634	58,918	72,877	87,910	99,807
Restaurants and hotels	2,065	3,375	4,047	5,101	6,152	6,983
Transportation, storage, and communications	44,625	64,618	83,056	104,337	113,219	127,814
Financial institutions	13,868	18,828	16,856	17,437	31,467	33,602
Real estate and business services	7,831	12,149	16,840	21,007	25,045	28,827
Community, social, and personal services	6,933	11,000	12,784	14,536	16,728	18,625
Government services	48,609	65,777	73,963	82,175	96,479	121,982
Private, nonprofit services	196	140	270	304	342	384
Import duties	7,440	16,804	25,997	29,034	29,653	30,994
Less: Imputed bank services charges	–11,364	–16,644	–14,886	–15,703	–20,688	–22,056
Total GDP	292,279	488,509	702,112	852,897	855,945	1,063,557
Of which:						
Non-oil GDP	274,489	419,393	510,839	607,982	718,187	800,247
			(In percent of GDP)			
Agriculture and forestry	21.7	18.5	15.5	14.6	18.5	15.7
Fishing	2.0	1.8	1.5	1.6	1.9	1.7
Mining and quarrying	0.3	0.3	0.3	0.3	0.3	0.3
Oil and gas	6.1	14.1	27.2	28.7	16.1	24.8
Manufacturing	13.4	13.2	8.1	7.7	9.0	7.9
Oil refining	0.8	1.8	3.3	3.1	3.2	2.9
Electricity, gas, and water	0.7	0.6	0.8	0.8	0.9	0.8
Construction	3.6	3.5	3.7	4.4	4.9	3.9
Wholesale and retail trade	10.3	10.2	8.4	8.5	10.3	9.4
Restaurants and hotels	0.7	0.7	0.6	0.6	0.7	0.7
Transportation, storage, and communications	15.3	13.2	11.8	12.2	13.2	12.0
Financial institutions	4.7	3.9	2.4	2.0	3.7	3.2
Real estate and business services	2.7	2.5	2.4	2.5	2.9	2.7
Community, social, and personal services	2.4	2.3	1.8	1.7	2.0	1.8
Government services	16.6	13.5	10.5	9.6	11.3	11.5
Non-oil GDP	93.9	85.9	72.8	71.3	83.9	75.2

Source: Central Statistics Organization.

[1]The large increases in oil and gas GDP in 1995 and 1996 are in large part due to exchange rate effects. The official exchange rate increased from YRls 12/US$ in 1994 to YRls 40.5/US$ in 1995 and YRls 114 /US$ in 1996.

Table A.4. Use of Resources at Current Prices, 1994–99

(In million of Yemeni rials)

	1994	1995	1996	1997	1998	1999
Consumption	240,105	419,296	599,098	727,558	827,233	938,112
Public sector[1]	61,976	78,033	105,161	134,623	146,820	179,257
Private sector	178,129	341,263	493,937	592,935	680,413	758,855
Gross investment	59,785	101,057	146,155	202,029	180,976	197,758
Gross fixed capital formation	56,773	99,025	143,207	198,543	180,976	197,758
Public sector	7,498	15,048	46,529	57,815	52,584	59,496
Private sector	49,275	83,977	96,678	140,728	128,392	138,262
Of which:						
Oil companies	14,678	15,307	18,598	20,106	16,850	23,246
Change in stocks	3,012	2,032	2,948	3,486	0	0
Domestic absorption	299,890	520,352	745,253	929,587	1,008,209	1,135,870
Net exports of goods and nonfactor services	–7,611	–31,843	–43,141	–76,690	–152,264	–72,318
GDP at market prices	292,279	488,509	702,112	852,897	855,945	1,063,557
Net factor income[2]	–25,994	–37,682	–74,414	–81,535	–48,813	–101,968
Gross national product	266,285	450,827	627,698	771,362	807,132	961,589
Net current transfers[2,3]	50,019	83,278	129,212	162,350	170,340	204,675
Gross national disposable income	316,304	534,105	756,909	933,712	977,473	1,166,264
Gross domestic saving	52,174	69,213	103,014	125,339	28,712	125,445
Gross national savings from disposable income	76,199	114,810	157,812	206,154	150,239	228,152
Public sector national savings[4]	–39,706	–14,696	18,834	41,391	–1,537	56,877
Private sector national savings[4]	115,905	129,506	138,977	164,763	151,776	171,275
			(In percent of GDP)			
Consumption	82.1	85.8	85.3	85.3	96.6	88.2
Public sector	21.2	16.0	15.0	15.8	17.2	16.9
Private sector	60.9	69.9	70.4	69.5	79.5	71.4
Gross investment	20.5	20.7	20.8	23.7	21.1	18.6
Gross fixed capital formation	19.4	20.3	20.4	23.3	21.1	18.6
Public sector	2.6	3.1	6.6	6.8	6.1	5.6
Private sector	16.9	17.2	13.8	16.5	15.0	13.0
Change in stocks	1.0	0.4	0.4	0.4	0.0	0.0
Domestic absorption	102.6	106.5	106.1	109.0	117.8	106.8
Net exports of goods and nonfactor services	–2.6	–6.5	–6.1	–9.0	–17.8	–6.8
Net factor income	–8.9	–7.7	–10.6	–9.6	–5.7	–9.6
Gross national product	91.1	92.3	89.4	90.4	94.3	90.4
Net current transfers	17.1	17.0	18.4	19.0	19.9	19.2
Gross national disposable income	108.2	109.3	107.8	109.5	114.2	109.7
Gross domestic saving	17.9	14.2	14.7	14.7	3.4	11.8
Gross national savings from disposable income	26.1	23.5	22.5	24.2	17.6	21.5
Public sector national savings[4]	–13.6	–3.0	2.7	4.9	–0.2	5.3
Private sector national savings[4]	39.7	26.5	19.8	19.3	17.7	16.1

Sources: Yemeni authorities; and IMF staff estimates.

[1]Uses data from the fiscal accounts.

[2]Uses balance of payments data.

[3]Includes workers' remittances.

[4]The large increases in public sector savings and declines in private sector savings in 1995–96 are attributable largely to the effects of exchange rate depreciations and world prices increases.

Table A.5. Sectoral Origin of Gross Domestic Product at Constant Prices, 1994–99

	1994	1995	1996	1997	1998	1999
			(In millions of 1990 Yemeni rials)			
Agriculture and forestry	33,365	35,688	36,158	39,075	44,497	44,375
Fishing	688	722	930	1,267	1,381	1,505
Mining and quarrying	312	345	396	403	364	368
Oil and gas	20,156	24,197	27,469	29,542	30,326	32,217
Manufacturing	10,449	13,334	13,524	13,682	14,438	14,518
Oil refining	2,322	2,470	2,376	2,385	2,233	2,266
Electricity, gas, and water	1,552	1,763	1,979	2,018	2,066	2,215
Construction	3,373	4,206	5,092	6,734	6,771	6,371
Wholesale and retail trade	8,452	9,764	10,563	11,263	12,185	12,929
Restaurants and hotels	408	467	506	563	609	646
Transportation, storage, and communications	14,379	13,973	12,016	13,998	13,623	14,373
Financial institutions	3,616	3,289	2,495	2,469	3,996	3,988
Real estate and business services	4,117	4,404	4,598	4,953	5,296	5,697
Community, social, and personal services	2,364	2,395	2,573	2,771	2,860	2,976
Government services	14,135	12,249	10,588	11,157	11,748	13,893
Private, nonprofit services	57	65	69	73	67	76
Import duties	4,831	4,681	5,450	5,387	4,378	4,237
Less: imputed bank services charges	–3,303	–3,100	–2,028	–2,088	–3,496	–3,490
Total GDP at market prices,	121,273	130,912	134,754	145,652	153,342	159,160
Of which:						
Non-oil GDP	101,117	106,715	107,285	116,110	123,016	126,943
			(Changes in percent)			
Agriculture and forestry	–3.3	7.0	1.3	8.1	13.9	–0.3
Fishing	–7.3	4.9	28.8	36.2	9.0	9.0
Mining and quarrying	–3.1	10.6	14.8	1.8	–9.7	1.1
Oil and gas	43.7	20.0	13.5	7.5	2.7	6.2
Manufacturing	–4.4	27.6	1.4	1.2	5.5	0.6
Oil refining	–9.5	6.4	–3.8	0.4	–6.4	1.5
Electricity, gas, and water	–10.3	13.6	12.3	2.0	2.4	7.2
Construction	–18.9	24.7	21.1	32.2	0.5	–5.9
Wholesale and retail trade	–13.2	15.5	8.2	6.6	8.2	6.1
Restaurants and hotels	–13.6	14.5	8.4	11.3	8.2	6.1
Transportation, storage, and communications	–19.2	–2.8	–14.0	16.5	–2.7	5.5
Financial institutions	8.6	–9.0	–24.1	–1.0	61.8	–0.2
Real estate and business services	6.2	7.0	4.4	7.7	6.9	7.6
Community, social, and personal services	4.5	1.3	7.4	7.7	3.2	4.1
Government services	–18.4	–13.3	–13.6	5.4	5.3	18.3
GDP	–3.6	7.9	2.9	8.1	5.3	3.8
Non-oil GDP	–9.6	5.5	0.5	8.2	5.9	3.2

Sources: Central Statistics Organization; and Central Bank of Yemen.

Table A.6. Distribution of Employment (Age 15 Years and Over) by Economic Activity[1]

Activity	1994 Thousand	1994 Percent of Total Employed	1998 Thousand	1998 Percent of Total Employed	1999 Thousand	1999 Percent of Total Employed
Private sector						
Agriculture, forestry, and fishing	1,667	52.3	1,928	49.2	1,996	48.5
Mining and quarrying	10	0.3	13	0.3	13	0.3
Manufacturing	131	4.1	188	4.8	206	5.0
Electricity, gas, and water	14	0.4	21	0.5	21	0.5
Construction	217	6.8	341	8.7	382	9.3
Trade, restaurants, and hotels	332	10.4	415	10.6	440	10.7
Transport, storage, and communication	150	4.7	196	5.0	210	5.1
Finance, insurance, and real estate	35	1.1	47	1.2	49	1.2
Social and community services	224	7.0	365	9.3	412	10.0
Public administration	410	12.9	405	10.3	389	9.5
Total employment	3,188	100.0	3,919	100.0	4,119	100.0

Source: Ministry of Planning.
[1]Data for 1994 are based on the general population census of that year; 1998 and 1999 data based on Ministry of Planning estimates.

Table A.7. Distribution of Employment (Age 10 Years and Over) by Sectors in Urban and Rural Areas, 1998

(In percent; unless otherwise specified)

Sector	Urban Male	Urban Female	Urban Total	Rural Male	Rural Female	Rural Total	Total Employment Male	Total Employment Female	Total Employment Total
Government	38.7	58.3	41.2	14.5	1.3	10.9	19.7	6.8	16.5
Administration	29.9	49.3	32.4	12.6	1.2	9.4	16.3	5.8	13.7
Other	8.8	9.0	8.8	2.0	0.2	1.5	3.5	1.0	2.9
Private sector	59.5	39.7	57.0	84.4	97.7	88.0	79.0	92.1	82.3
National	58.8	38.3	56.2	83.9	97.6	87.7	78.6	91.9	81.9
Foreign	0.7	1.4	0.8	0.4	0.1	0.3	0.5	0.2	0.4
Mixed	0.6	0.7	0.6	0.2	0.0	0.2	0.3	0.1	0.2
Cooperative	0.4	0.4	0.4	0.1	0.2	0.2	0.2	0.2	0.2
Other	0.9	1.0	0.9	0.8	0.7	0.8	0.8	0.8	0.8
Total	100.0	100.0	100.0	100.0	100.0	100.0	100.0	100.0	100.0
Total (thousand)	669.4	99.3	768.7	2,453.7	931.0	3,384.7	3,123.1	1,030.3	4,153.4

Source: Central Statistics Organization, 1998 Household Expenditure Survey.

Table A.8. Household Income and Expenditure, 1998
(Yemeni Rials, unless otherwise specified)

	Urban	Rural	Total
Average household income	36,988	26,654	29,035
Average household member income	5,024	3,763	4,096
Average household expenditure on food	20,727	19,818	20,026
Average household expenditure on nonfood	17,624	9,562	11,421
Ratio of household income to expenditure (in percent)	96.4	90.7	92.3
Memorandum items:			
Average household size (persons)	7.11	7.08	7.09
Illiteracy rate (in percent)	27.47	56.57	49.47
Median age of population (in years)	15.9	14.2	14.6

Source: Central Statistics Organization, 1998 Household Expenditure Survey.

Table A.9. Distribution of Population (10 Years and Over) by Education Level, Region, and Gender, 1994, 1998
(In percent of total)

	1994					1998				
	Urban	Rural	Male	Female	Total	Urban	Rural	Male	Female	Total
Illiterate	34.2	63.5	36.7	76.3	56.0	27.5	56.6	28.2	70.9	49.5
Read and write	33.4	24.5	36.9	16.1	26.8	38.2	30.3	44.4	20.0	32.2
Primary	9.2	5.4	9.4	3.1	6.3	5.4	2.8	4.5	2.3	3.4
Combined level	2.5	0.8	1.6	0.8	1.2	1.5	0.9	1.2	0.9	1.0
Preparatory	8.2	3.5	7.4	1.8	4.7	10.9	5.2	10.2	3.0	6.6
Pre-secondary diploma	0.9	0.3	0.8	0.1	0.5	1.1	0.4	1.0	0.2	0.6
Secondary	7.7	1.6	4.9	1.3	3.2	10.3	2.8	7.2	2.0	4.6
Post-high school diploma	0.8	0.2	0.6	0.1	0.4	1.4	0.6	1.3	0.2	0.8
University and above	3.1	0.4	1.7	0.4	1.1	3.8	0.5	2.0	0.6	1.3
Total	100	100	100	100	100	100	100	100	100	100
Total (thousand)	2,417	7,040	4,853	4,604	9,457	2,581	8,009	5,303	5,287	10,590

Sources: Central Statistics Organization; General Population Census 1994; and Household Expenditure Survey 1998.

Table A.10. Crude Oil Summary, 1994–99

(In thousands of barrels per day)

	1994	1995	1996	1997	1998	1999
A Total net output[1]	334	342	344	360	367	389
Marib	185	168	162	149	129	116
Masila	149	174	177	190	201	207
Jannah	...	...	4	20	19	48
East Shabwa	...	...	...	...	16	17
Ayad	...	...	...	1	1	1
B. Companies' exports	154	155	137	137	177	158
Marib	69	57	53	49	52	47
Masila	85	98	82	79	104	77
Jannah[2]	...	...	2	8	8	20
East Shabwa	...	...	...	...	13	13
Ayad	...	...	...	1	1	1
1. Companies' net output share	107	110	117	118	100	112
Marib	82	81	81	75	61	56
Masila	25	28	35	41	35	47
Jannah[2]	...	...	1	2	3	7
East Shabwa	...	...	...	...	1	2
Ayad	...	...	...	0	0	0
2. Cost recovery	88	85	60	56	107	75
Marib	28	16	12	12	21	18
Masila	60	69	47	38	69	31
Jannah	...	...	1	6	5	13
East Shabwa	...	...	...	...	11	12
Ayad	...	...	...	1	1	1
3. Income tax	41	41	40	37	30	28
Marib	41	41	40	37	30	28
Masila	0	0	0	0	0	0
Jannah	...	...	0	0	0	0
East Shabwa	...	...	...	...	0	0
Ayad	...	...	...	0	0	0
C. Government exports	135	123	129	150	112	146
D. Government sales to refineries	45	64	78	73	77	85
Average oil export price (US$/bbl)	15	17	20	18	12	19
Export revenue (million US$)	1,615	1,735	1,976	1,945	1,229	2,131
Companies	862	957	1,018	933	758	1,138
Government	753	778	958	1,012	471	993

Source: Ministry of Oil and Mineral Resources.
[1]Net of miscellaneous oil field uses.
[2]Including YICOM share.

Table A.11. Oil Exploration Blocks Awarded in 1996–99

Block Number	Company Licensed	Year Awarded	Selected Terms of Contract
13	Bakrie	1996	
R2	Bakrie	1996	
S1	Vintage/TransGlobe	1997	150 km^2 of 3-d seismic data to be acquired and three wells to be drilled over the first 2½-year phase, at estimated minimum cost US$11 million.
S2	Preussag	1997	Block had just been relinquished by consortium of Oxy/Amerada Hess/Mol.
9	Cal Valley Petroleum	1997	US$8 million to be spent during the initial three-year exploration period.
31	Oil and Gas Mine Co.	1997	US$20 million to be spent on the two blocks (31 and 41) including the acquisition of 800 km of 2-d seismic data and the drilling of two exploration wells.
41	Oil and Gas Mine Co.	1997	
49	MOL	1997	Minimum expenditure of US$8 million, including 300 km of seismic acquisition and two exploration wells over three years.
50	Kerr-McGee/CanadianOxy/ YGCOG	1997	Current stakes are 47.5 percent, 47.5 percent, and 5 percent, respectively.
51	Kerr-McGee/CanadianOxy/ YGCOG	1997	Current stakes are 47.5 percent, 47.5 percent, and 5 percent, respectively.
53	Dove/YGCOG	1997	Stakes: 75 percent and 25 percent respectively.
11	CanadianOxy	1998	At least US$11.5 million to be spent over seven years.
12	CanadianOxy	1998	At least US$11.5 million to be spent over seven years.
36	CanadianOxy	1998	At least US$11.5 million to be spent over seven years.
43	First Calgary Petroleum/ Ocean Energy	1998	Expenditure set at US$7.5 million for each of the two 2½-year periods
48	MOL	1998	A minimum of US$15 million to be spent over three years; work program to include acquisition of 500 km of 2-d seismic data and the drilling of two exploration wells.
54	CanadianOxy	1998	At least US$11.5 million to be spent over seven years.
15	Oil Search/Muhammad Al-Otaiba Group	1999	A minimum US$10 million to be invested in the first phase, two exploration wells to be drilled, and geological studies to be conducted.
2	Agip/Sonatrach	1999	The Algerian Sonatrach has a 40 percent interest in the block.
20	Adair International Oil and Gas Inc./PIE	1999	Seismic operations to have begun in 2000; two exploratory wells and a minimum of US$16.8 million to be spent in two exploratory periods.

Sources: Arab Oil Directory; and Ministry of Oil and Mineral resources.

Table A.12. Domestic Consumption of Petroleum Products, 1994–99

	1994	1995	1996	1997	1998	1999
			(Millions of liters)			
Total petroleum products	3,653	3,927	4,033	4,155	4,043	3,911
Gasoline	1,332	1,458	1,391	1,420	1,322	1,107
Diesel	1,023	1,083	1,175	1,273	1,215	1,302
Kerosene	147	172	169	163	150	140
Aviation fuel	93	102	93	93	99	111
Fuel oil	589	808	909	909	938	898
LPG	468	303	297	297	318	353
			(Percent change)			
Total petroleum products	–7.6	7.5	2.7	3.0	–2.7	–3.3
Gasoline	0.2	9.5	–4.6	2.1	–6.9	–16.2
Diesel	–1.4	5.9	8.4	8.4	–4.6	7.1
Kerosene	–9.0	17.0	–1.7	–3.4	–8.0	–6.7
Aviation fuel	–11.0	8.7	–8.0	–0.5	6.2	12.6
Fuel oil	–27.6	37.2	12.4	0.0	3.2	–4.3
LPG	–28.5	–35.2	–2.2	0.0	7.2	10.8

Source: Ministry of Finance.

Table A.13. Output of Industrial Products, 1994–99[1]

	1994	1995	1996	1997	1998	1999
Electricity (million kwh)	2,159	2,369	2,457	2,482	2,557	2,633
Extractive industries						
Salt (thousand tons)	118	71	135	136	147	149
Quarried stone (thousand cubic meters)	...	2,823	2,397	2,437	2,497	2,547
Gypsum (thousand tons)	99	100	97	99	102	103
Food, beverage, and tobacco industries						
Bread (thousand tons)	7	178	159	162	170	179
Biscuits and confectioneries (thousand tons)	69	68	64	65	43	44
Ghee and edible oils (thousand tons)	99	97	106	108	108	109
Soft drinks (million liters)	67	51	34	35	45	46
Mineral water (thousand cubic meters)	114	81	76	77	56	57
Vimto drink (thousand of liters)	1,602	2,963	2,718	2,491	...	...
Ice (thousand tons)	36	54	58	59	61	61
Milk and products (million liters)	68	66	47	48	54	55
Ice cream (tons)	144	2,054	1,632	1,665	1,715	1,749
Cigarettes (million units)	5,423	6,540	6,740	6,800	6,040	5,859
Textile industries						
Underwear (thousand pieces)	360	278	287	293	...	...
Woolen pullover (thousand pieces)	...	0	28	0	...	...
Weaving (million meters)	7	5	5	5	5	...
Ginning (thousand tons)	1	1	2	2	...	...
Metallic industries						
Household utensils (tons)	747	604	2,434	1,740	1,775	1,793
Barrels (thousands)	4	3	3	...	723	730
Doors and windows (thousand square meters)	...	604	690	703	...	...
Metallic scrubbers (tons)	123	110	52	53	...	...
Stationary engines (thousands)	...	28	31	32	...	...
Metal suitcases (thousands)	50	...	10	...	...	...
Beds (thousands)	...	...	1	...	...	...
Nonmetallic industries						
Cement (thousand tons)	898	1,100	1,070	1,038	1,207	1,231
Red bricks (thousands)	...	14,033	14,319	14,605	14,897	15,120
Cement bricks (thousands)	...	81,118	85,315	87,021	89,000	90,780
Tiles (millions)	9	34	81	83	73	72
Marble (thousand square meters)	11	75	82	83	86	88
Chemical industries						
Plastic footwear (thousand pairs)	5	9	7	7	7	7
Foam rubber (tons)	1,642	1,918	1,556	1,572	...	...
Household utensils (tons)	985	4,730	3,830	3,873	...	...
Buckets (tons)	1,387	1,532	1,804	1,840	...	...
Water tubes (tons)	813	5,917	3,721	3,759	...	...
Plastic sheets (tons)	4,786	5,673	10,151	10,354	...	...
Plastic tubes (tons)	4,307	7,640	7,264	7,409	...	...
Paint (thousand liters)	7,752	9,882	8,331	8,247	7,137	...
Soap (thousand tons)	30	32	24	23	20	...
Perfume (thousand ounces)	1,049	900	901	919	...	...
Oxygen gas (thousand cubic meters)	110	117	0	...	...	...
Heat insulation (tons)	...	12	13	...	...	...
Fuel gas (thousand tons)	233	313	298	325	...	...
Paper and printing						
Paper tissues (tons)	455	1,082	1,917	1,936	1,948	1,967
School books (tons)	...	6,807	6,944	4,014	7,063	7,204
Cartons (thousand tons)	12	12	11	11	13	14

Source: Central Statistics Organization.

[1]Data for 1998–99 are provisional, as compilation of the underlying data is not yet completed.

Table A.14. Production, Area, and Yield of Major Crops, 1994–99[1]

(Production in thousand metric tons; area in thousand hectares; and yield in tons per hectare)

	1994	1995	1996	1997	1998	1999
Cereals (total)						
Production	802.0	810.2	663.9	646.2	833.3	687.0
Area	734.7	733.2	704.2	720.2	770.4	770.4
Sorghum and millet						
Production	567.9	575.5	461.4	469.8	609.8	479.2
Area	585.5	582.2	552.6	567.8	609.7	609.7
Yield	1.0	1.0	0.8	0.8	1.0	0.8
Wheat						
Production	171.0	170.9	148.9	129.2	167.4	154.4
Area	100.4	101.6	102.8	103.6	111.3	111.3
Yield	1.7	1.7	1.4	1.2	1.5	1.4
Barley						
Production	63.1	63.8	53.6	47.2	56.2	53.4
Area	48.8	49.5	48.8	48.8	49.4	49.4
Yield	1.3	1.3	1.1	1.0	1.1	1.1
Legumes						
Production	68.3	70.4	67.3	66.1	78.0	73.1
Area	54.2	54.2	53.9	57.1	62.5	62.5
Yield	1.3	1.3	1.2	1.2	1.2	1.2
Potatoes						
Production	181.0	184.5	182.8	195.6	196.5	198.8
Area	13.2	13.6	14.2	15.4	15.6	15.6
Yield	13.7	13.6	12.9	12.7	12.6	12.7
Vegetables						
Production	464.8	484.3	520.4	522.0	550.7	567.0
Area	38.1	39.9	43.1	43.9	46.2	46.2
Yield	12.2	12.1	12.1	11.9	11.9	12.3
Grapes, dates, and other fruits						
Production	360.7	402.2	391.3	469.4	554.8	588.0
Area	70.4	74.9	78.9	80.9	84.1	84.1
Grapes						
Production	146.4	150.6	98.0	150.2	154.9	159.1
Area	20.7	21.1	21.2	21.2	22.1	22.1
Yield	7.1	7.1	4.6	7.1	7.0	7.2
Dates						
Production	20.6	23.2	24.2	26.2	26.9	29.1
Area	16.6	18.6	19.4	20.1	20.6	20.6
Yield	1.2	1.2	1.2	1.3	1.3	1.4
Other fruits						
Production	193.7	228.4	269.1	293.0	373.0	399.8
Area	33.1	35.2	38.3	39.6	41.4	41.4
Yield	5.9	6.5	7.0	7.4	9.0	9.7
Coffee						
Production	8.5	9.0	10.6	10.3	11.3	11.3
Area	25.1	27.3	29.2	31.6	32.0	32.0
Yield	0.3	0.3	0.4	0.3	0.4	0.4
Tobacco						
Production	7.2	8.1	8.6	10.2	11.5	11.5
Area	3.6	4.0	4.2	5.0	5.4	5.4
Yield	2.0	2.0	2.0	2.0	2.1	2.1
Sesame						
Production	12.1	14.0	15.0	16.4	17.5	17.5
Area	20.4	23.1	26.0	29.5	30.3	30.3
Yield	0.6	0.6	0.6	0.6	0.6	0.6
Alfalfa						
Production	158.6	166.0	177.1	192.5	222.9	222.9
Area	20.4	21.4	22.5	23.7	24.5	24.5
Yield	7.8	7.8	7.9	8.1	9.1	9.1

Sources: Ministry of Agriculture; and Central Statistics Organization.

[1]Data for 1999 are preliminary.

Table A.15. Noncrop Primary Production, 1994–99
(In thousands of metric tons)

	1994	1995	1996	1997	1998	1999
Total meat and milk	220.4	241.3	253.0	261.1	274.9	280.4
Meat	39.8	40.6	41.6	43.1	45.3	46.2
Poultry	30.1	47.2	55.5	56.3	61.4	62.6
Milk	150.5	153.5	155.8	161.7	168.2	171.6
Eggs (millions)	351.0	358.0	367.0	495.0	600.0	612.0
Total fish catch	81.9	85.9	103.7	115.6	127.6	137.3
Surface water fish	80.3	84.3	94.3	93.5	104.9	111.2
Deep water fish	0.1	0.1	6.7	12.4	12.1	14.5
Other aquatic catch	1.5	1.5	2.7	9.7	10.6	11.6

Sources: Central Statistics Organization and Ministry of Agriculture.

Table A.16. Consumer Price Index for Urban Areas, 1994–99[1]

	December					
	1994	1995	1996	1997	1998	1999
			(December 1994 = 100)			
Overall index	100.0	157.2	200.0	214.1	239.6	264.0
Foodstuff	100.0	146.8	187.4	199.6	231.6	257.3
Housing	100.0	169.7	232.2	248.1	269.2	296.4
Clothing	100.0	207.8	250.4	280.3	248.7	258.2
Others	100.0	180.1	197.9	212.7	236.0	254.4
			(Changes in percent)			
Overall index	n.a.	57.2	27.2	7.1	11.9	10.2
Foodstuff	n.a.	46.8	27.7	6.5	16.1	11.1
Housing	n.a.	69.7	36.8	6.8	8.5	10.1
Clothing	n.a.	107.8	20.5	11.9	–11.3	3.8
Others	n.a.	80.1	9.9	7.5	11.0	7.8

Sources: Central Statistics Organization; and IMF staff estimates.

[1]The CPI is based on consumption shares from the 1992 Household Budget Survey and consists of a weighted average of the price indices for Sana'a and Aden. The numbers are end-of-period.

Table A.17. Domestic Retail Prices for Petroleum Products and Electricity, 1995–2000

	Jan. 1995	Aug. 1995	Apr. 1996	Jul. 1997	Sep. 1997	Jul. 1998	Jun. 1999	Apr. 2000
				(In Yemeni rials per liter, unless otherwise indicated)				
Gasoline	6.0	12.0	19.3	25.0	25.0	35.0	35.0	35.0
Diesel	3.0	3.0	6.0	6.0	10.0	10.0	10.0	10.0
Fuel oil[1]	1.7	3.0	7.0	7.0	11.0	11.0	13.0	13.0
Fuel oil[2]	2.5	5.0	7.0	7.0	11.0	11.0	13.0	13.0
Kerosene	3.0	3.0	8.5	13.0	13.0	15.0	16.0	16.0
Aviation fuel[3]	5.0	12.5	13.5	13.5	13.5	13.5	25.0	35.0
LPG (12.5 kg cylinder)	50.0	120.0	165.0	165.0	165.0	200.0	200.0	200.0
Electricity (per kWh)	2.07	2.07	5.40	5.40	5.80	8.70	8.70	8.70
				(In U.S. dollars per liter, unless otherwise indicated)				
Gasoline	0.05	0.16	0.15	0.19	0.19	0.26	0.22	0.22
Diesel	0.02	0.04	0.05	0.05	0.08	0.07	0.06	0.06
Fuel oil[1]	0.01	0.04	0.05	0.05	0.08	0.08	0.08	0.08
Fuel oil[2]	0.02	0.07	0.05	0.05	0.08	0.08	0.08	0.08
Kerosene	0.02	0.04	0.07	0.10	0.10	0.11	0.10	0.10
Aviation fuel	0.04	0.16	0.10	0.10	0.10	0.10	0.16	0.22
LPG (12.5 kg cylinder)	0.41	1.58	1.28	1.27	1.25	1.46	1.25	1.24
Electricity (per kWh)	0.02	0.03	0.04	0.04	0.04	0.06	0.05	0.05
Memorandum item:								
Exchange rate (YRls/US$)[4]	120.5	76.0	129.0	130.2	132.5	137.0	160.5	161.0

Sources: Ministry of Oil and Mineral Resources; and IMF staff estimates.

[1]For electricity plants.

[2]For cement plants.

[3]In May 1999, aviation fuel prices were increased above world market levels and were to be maintained at levels exceeding international prices, which explains the increase implemented in April 2000.

[4]End-period free market exchange rate for the relevant month.

Table A.18. Summary of Central Government Finances, 1994–99

	1994	1995	1996	1997	1998	1999
			(In millions of rials)			
Total revenue and grants	37,538	95,296	251,899	279,459	225,959	338,253
Total revenue	36,681	93,676	250,029	274,659	222,620	328,394
Oil and gas revenue	10,786	45,621	176,192	188,415	117,772	210,598
Crude oil exports	9,194	31,559	98,824	128,999	73,002	134,854
Domestic oil and gas	1,592	14,062	77,368	59,416	44,770	75,744
Nonoil revenue	25,895	48,055	73,837	86,243	104,848	117,796
Tax	20,267	39,006	58,834	69,570	78,852	85,419
Nontax	5,628	9,050	15,003	16,673	25,996	32,377
Grants (cash)	856	1,620	1,870	4,800	3,339	9,859
Total expenditure and net lending	84,741	125,040	279,594	295,882	280,080	340,872
Current expenditure	77,243	109,992	233,065	238,067	227,496	281,376
Civilian wages and salaries	28,435	35,754	47,664	52,390	64,287	78,341
Materials and services	5,278	7,507	16,241	24,872	25,632	32,527
Defense (wage and nonwage)	28,263	32,912	39,170	51,334	52,247	61,548
Interest obligations	8,471	7,287	23,510	20,018	31,562	43,570
Domestic (net)	6,584	1,459	9,615	7,882	22,459	32,260
External	1,887	5,828	13,895	12,136	9,103	11,310
Explicit subsidies	0	16,497	91,244	65,504	25,702	26,116
Wheat and flour	0	11,465	51,964	38,592	25,702	4,329
Petroleum products	0	5,032	37,300	24,751	0	21,787
Electricity: transfer to PEC	0	0	1,980	2,161	0	0
Current transfers	6,796	7,446	11,280	13,541	18,680	28,278
Of which:						
Public enterprises	1,906	1,781	2,470	4,025	4,970	6,455
Civil service pension fund	0	0	300	2,230	2,736	. . .
Social welfare fund	0	0	500	1,700	4,388	5,946
Development operation and maintenance fund	0	0	0	2,000	2,000	2,300
Other[1]	0	2,589	3,956	8,408	7,386	8,696
Development expenditure	7,498	15,048	46,529	57,815	52,584	59,496
Ministry of Planning	5,526	10,381	37,675	44,443	36,813	. . .
Capital transfers	1,972	4,667	8,854	11,872	15,135	. . .
Public works	0	0	0	1,500	636	. . .
Net lending	0	0	0	0	0	0
Overall balance (commitment)	–47,203	–29,744	–27,695	–16,424	–54,121	–2,619
Rescheduled and pending interest obligations	1,439	4,456	9,721	9,285	4,004	1,317
Domestic arrears	0	0	22,341	–8,573	–17,705	–3,000
Overall balance (cash)	–45,764	–25,288	4,367	–15,712	–67,822	–4,302
Financing	46,293	25,342	–4,837	15,647	67,865	441
External (net)	416	–735	2,851	2,740	10,089	24,668
Bilateral and multilateral loans (net)	–8,222	–28,111	–59,446	–8,597	–8,654	4,211
Disbursements	986	2,151	15,790	19,615	21,980	36,060
Amortization obligations	–9,208	–30,262	–75,236	–28,212	–30,634	–31,850
Amortization arrears	8,638	27,376	62,297	–698	–553	0
Rescheduled amortization	0	0	0	19,897	19,297	20,458
Payment of late interest and short-term arrears (Paris Club and other)	0	0	0	–2,237	0	0
Domestic (net)	45,878	26,078	–7,688	12,907	57,776	–24,228
Bank	45,878	24,914	–10,747	–1,158	28,280	–46,888
Central bank	46,949	22,412	–17,371	–28,764	26,464	–50,616
Commercial banks	–1,071	2,502	6,624	27,606	1,816	3,727
Nonbank	0	1,164	3,060	14,065	29,496	22,660
Discrepancy	529	55	–470	–65	43	–3,861

Table A.18 (*concluded*)

	1994	1995	1996	1997	1998	1999
			(In percent of GDP)			
Overall balance (commitment)	–17.4	–6.6	–3.9	–1.9	–6.3	–0.2
Overall balance (cash)	–16.9	–5.6	0.6	–1.8	–7.9	–0.4
Primary cash balance[2]	–14.3	–5.0	2.6	–0.6	–4.7	3.9
Public sector savings	–15.0	–3.6	2.4	4.3	–0.6	4..4
Total revenue and grants	13.9	21.1	35.9	32.8	26.4	31.8
Total revenue	13.5	20.7	35.6	32.2	26.0	30.9
Oil and gas revenue	4.0	10.1	25.1	22.1	13.8	19.8
Crude oil exports	3.4	7.0	14.1	15.1	8.5	12.7
Domestic oil and gas	0.6	3.1	11.0	7.0	5.2	7.1
Nonoil revenue	9.6	10.6	10.5	10.1	12.2	11.1
Tax revenue	7.5	8.6	8.4	8.2	9.2	8.0
Nontax revenue	2.1	2.0	2.1	2.0	3.0	3.0
Grants	0.3	0.4	0.3	0.6	0.4	0.9
Total expenditure and net lending	31.3	27.7	39.8	34.7	32.7	32.1
Current expenditure	28.5	24.4	33.2	27.9	26.6	26.5
Civilian wages and salaries	10.5	7.9	6.8	6.1	7.5	7.4
Materials and services	1.9	1.7	2.3	2.9	3.0	3.1
Defense	10.4	7.3	5.6	6.0	6.1	5.8
Of which:						
Wages and salaries	8.5	5.1	3.8	3.5	3.8	3.6
Interest obligations	3.1	1.6	3.3	2.3	3.7	4.1
Domestic (net)	2.4	0.3	1.4	0.9	2.6	3.0
External	0.7	1.3	2.0	1.4	1.1	1.1
Explicit subsidies	0.0	3.7	13.0	7.7	3.0	2.5
Wheat and flour	0.0	2.5	7.4	4.5	3.0	0.4
Petroleum	0.0	1.1	5.3	2.9	0.0	2.0
Electricity	0.0	0.0	0.3	0.3	0.0	0.0
Current transfers	2.5	1.6	1.6	1.6	2.2	2.7
Public enterprises	0.7	0.4	0.4	0.5	0.6	...
Civil service pension fund	0.0	0.0	0.0	0.3	0.3	...
Social welfare fund	0.0	0.0	0.1	0.2	0.5	0.6
Development expenditure	2.8	3.3	6.6	6.8	6.1	5.6
Ministry of Planning	2.0	2.3	5.4	5.2	4.3	...
Capital transfers	0.7	1.0	1.3	1.4	1.8	...
Public works	0.0	0.0	0.0	0.2	0.1	...
Net lending	0.0	0.0	0.0	0.0	0.0	0.0
Financing	17.1	5.6	–0.7	1.8	7.9	0.0
External (net)	0.2	–0.2	0.4	0.3	1.2	2.3
Domestic (net)	16.9	5.8	–1.1	1.5	6.7	–2.3
Bank	16.9	5.5	–1.5	–0.1	3.3	–4.4
Central bank	17.3	5.0	–2.5	–3.4	3.1	–4.8
Commercial banks	–0.4	0.6	0.9	3.2	0.2	0.4
Nonbank	0.0	0.3	0.4	1.6	3.4	2.1
Discrepancy	0.2	0.0	–0.1	0.0	0.0	–0.4

Sources: Ministry of Finance; Central Bank of Yemen; and IMF staff estimates.

[1]Allocations to the Agriculture and Roads Maintenance Funds, development operation and maintenance, and other items.

[2] Overall balance, excluding interest obligations.

Table A.19. Composition of Central Government Revenues, 1994–99

	1994	1995	1996	1997	1998	1999
			(In millions of Yemeni rials)			
Total revenue	36,681	93,676	250,029	274,659	222,620	328,394
Oil revenue	10,786	45,621	176,192	188,415	117,772	210,598
Crude oil export receipts	9,194	31,559	98,824	128,999	73,002	134,854
Domestic oil and gas revenues	1,592	14,062	77,368	59,416	44,770	75,744
Of which:						
Payment for past excess cost recovery	0	0	16,290	0	0	0
Non-oil revenue	25,895	48,055	73,837	86,243	104,848	117,796
Tax revenue	20,267	39,006	58,834	69,570	78,852	85,419
Customs duties	7,440	16,804	26,294	25,814	24,121	25,703
Taxes on goods and services	4,394	9,996	15,180	21,226	24,974	24,419
Taxes on income	3,786	5,553	8,765	10,685	13,093	16,389
Corporate profits tax	3,128	4,262	5,804	8,318	13,156	14,498
Stamp taxes[1]	1,101	1,858	973	1,177	797	. . .
Zakat	0	0	1,316	1,489	1,906	2,255
Zakat equivalent on foreign companies	0	0	42	85	48	. . .
Real estate transfer tax	418	533	460	776	757	943
Nontax revenue	5,628	9,050	15,003	16,673	25,996	32,377
Profit transfers	2,514	5,471	6,772	8,712	16,677	19,376
CBY	. . .	. . .	. . .	. . .	13,000	13,750
Commercial banks	109	103	138	227	12	53
Aden refinery	200	651	1,180	255	200	10
YPC	1,402	388	140	386	753	1,499
Non-oil nonfinancial public enterprises	803	4,329	5,314	7,844	2,712	4,064
Cement	. . .	2,964	3,471	5,397	1,079	1,329
Post and telecommunications	. . .	200	300	789	574	700
Ports	. . .	370	685	875	635	946
Airlines	. . .	50	0	5	3	0
Other	. . .	746	858	778	422	1,089
Fees and charges	1,248	2,978	4,481	4,349	6,695	. . .
Construction	268	690	277	282	357	. . .
Security	263	188	1,316	678	2,019	. . .
Educational	207	414	233	129	228	. . .
Foreign oil company exploration fees	0	0	252	130	169	. . .
Vehicle fees	0	0	427	443	530	596
Consular fees	0	0	778	382	187	210
Delayed military service fee	0	0	230	305	453	510
Other[2]	510	1,686	968	2,000	2,752	. . .
Other nontax revenue	1,866	600	3,750	3,612	2,624	. . .
Fines and forfeitures	231	236	350	. . .	. . .	. . .
Asset sales	115	43	2,580	. . .	814	. . .
Foreign oil company signature bonuses	36	0	500	1,211	882	. . .
Other	1,484	321	320	. . .	928	. . .
			(In percent of GDP)			
Total revenue	13.5	20.7	35.6	32.2	26.0	30.9
Oil revenue	4.0	10.1	25.1	22.1	13.8	19.8
Crude oil exports	3.4	7.0	14.1	15.1	8.5	12.7
Domestic oil and gas revenues	0.6	3.1	11.0	7.0	5.2	7.1
Payment for past excess cost recovery	0.0	0.0	2.3	0.0	0.0	0.0
Non-oil revenue	9.6	10.6	10.5	10.1	12.2	11.1
Tax revenue	7.5	8.6	8.4	8.2	9.2	8.0
Customs duties	2.7	3.7	3.7	3.0	2.8	2.4
Taxes on goods and services	1.6	2.2	2.2	2.5	2.9	2.3
Taxes on income	1.4	1.2	1.2	1.3	1.5	1.5
Corporate profits tax	1.2	0.9	0.8	1.0	1.5	1.4
Nontax revenue	2.1	2.0	2.1	2.0	3.0	3.0
Profit transfers	0.9	1.2	1.0	1.0	1.9	1.8
Non-oil public enterprises	0.3	1.0	0.8	0.9	0.3	0.4
Fees and charges	0.5	0.7	0.6	0.5	0.8	. . .
Other nontax revenue	0.7	0.1	0.5	0.4	0.3	. . .
Memorandum item						
GDP at market prices (in millions YRls)	270,900	451,530	702,112	852,897	855,945	1,063,557

Sources: Ministry of Finance; Central Bank of Yemen; and IMF staff estimates.
[1]Includes Zakat for 1993–95.
[2]For 1994–96, includes fees not attributed to entries specified above.

Table A.20. Composition of Central Government Expenditure, 1994–99

	1994	1995	1996	1997	1998	Prel. 1999
			(In millions of Yemeni rials)			
Total expenditure and net lending	84,741	125,040	279,594	295,882	280,080	340,872
Current expenditures	77,243	109,992	233,065	238,067	227,496	281,376
Civilian wages and salaries	28,435	35,754	47,664	52,390	64,287	78,341
Materials and services	5,278	7,507	16,241	24,872	25,632	32,527
Agricultural and road maintenance funds	0	729	1,870	2,381	2,732	1,856
Defense	28,263	32,912	39,170	51,334	52,247	61,548
Salaries	23,000	23,123	26,419	29,803	32,464	38,659
Nonsalary	5,263	9,790	12,751	21,531	19,783	22,889
Interest obligations	8,471	7,287	23,510	20,018	31,562	43,570
Domestic (net)	6,584	1,459	9,615	7,882	22,459	32,260
External	1,887	5,828	13,895	12,136	9,103	11,310
Of which:						
Parliamentary and judiciary expenses	0	1,860	2,086	2,968	4,023	5,945
Accounting and audit authority	0	0	0	474	538	746
Election committee	0	0	0	2,585	93	150
Explicit subsidies	0	16,497	91,244	65,504	25,702	26,116
Wheat and flour	0	11,465	51,964	38,592	25,702	4,329
Petroleum products	0	5,032	37,300	24,751	0	21,787
Consumer subsidy	0	530	32,295	19,067	0	21,787
Unsettled claims	0	4,502	5,005	5,684	0	0
Electricity; transfer to PEC	0	0	1,980	2,161	0	0
Current transfers	6,796	7,446	11,280	13,541	18,680	28,278
Public enterprises	1,906	1,781	2,470	4,025	4,970	6,455
Social welfare	1,954	2,780	2,821	4,021	6,709	. . .
Of which:						
Social welfare fund	0	0	500	1,700	4,388	5,946
Regular pension contributions	527	737	0	2,230	2,736	. . .
Pension supplements	0	0	0	0	0	. . .
Transfers to civil service pension fund	0	0	300	0	0	. . .
Medical grants	133	320	302	650	604	. . .
Social and sports activities	1,026	1,270	1,300	1,078	. . .	. . .
Other	1,250	559	4,087	1,536	. . .	. . .
Development operation and maintenance fund	0	0	0	2,000	2,000	2,300
Development expenditure	7,498	15,048	46,529	57,815	52,584	59,496
Ministry of Planning	5,526	10,381	37,675	44,443	36,813	. . .
Capital transfers	1,972	4,667	8,854	11,872	15,135	. . .
Public works[1]	0	0	0	1,500	636	. . .
Net lending	0	0	0	0	0	0
Memorandum item: GDP	292,279	488,509	702,112	852,897	855,945	1,063,557
			(In percent of GDP)			
Total expenditure and net lending	29.0	25.6	39.8	34.7	32.7	32.1
Current expenditure	26.4	22.5	33.2	27.9	26.6	26.5
Civilian wages and salaries	9.7	7.3	6.8	6.1	7.5	7.4
Materials and services	1.8	1.5	2.3	2.9	3.0	3.1
Defense	9.7	6.7	5.6	6.0	6.1	5.8
Of which:						
Salaries	7.9	4.7	3.8	3.5	3.8	3.6
Interest obligations	2.9	1.5	3.3	2.3	3.7	4.1
Domestic	2.3	0.3	1.4	0.9	2.6	3.0
External	0.6	1.2	2.0	1.4	1.1	1.1
Explicit subsidies	0.0	3.4	13.0	7.7	3.0	2.5
Wheat and flour	0.0	2.3	7.4	4.5	3.0	0.4
Petroleum products	0.0	1.0	5.3	2.9	0.0	2.0
Electricity	0.0	0.0	0.3	0.3	0.0	0.0
Current transfers	2.3	1.5	1.6	1.6	2.2	2.7
Development expenditure	2.6	3.1	6.6	6.8	6.1	5.6
Ministry of Planning	1.9	2.1	5.4	5.2	4.3	. . .

Sources: Ministry of Finance; Central Bank of Yemen; and IMF staff estimates.

[1]Related to the IDA public works project.

Table A.21. Current and Capital Transfers to Public Enterprises, 1994–98
(In millions of Yemeni rials)

	1994	1995	1996[1]	1997	1998
Current transfers	1,906	1,780	2,900	3,984	4,967
Broadcasting and Television Corporation	313	372	1,017	1,260	1,599
Mineral Exploration Organization	79	78	153	163	191
Oil Exploration Corporation	96	107	145	237	253
Organization for Agricultural Research	140	148	202	233	318
Rural Development Organization	52	51	72	102	140
Al-Thawra Hospital	237	331	430	883	781
Touhama Development Organization	90	96	157	157	198
Yemen News Agency	52	57	68	107	145
Other agricultural and industrial enterprises	162	180	109	155	333
Others	685	360	547	280	697
Financial support for troubled enterprises	0	0	0	407	312
Capital transfers	1,972	5,084	. . .	11,950	15,135
Broadcasting and Television Corporation	28	936	. . .	486	338
Civil Aviation and Meteorology Authority	60	84	. . .	323	622
National Water and Sewerage Corporation	198	0	. . .	1,406	3,009
Postal Service Organization	75	26	. . .	64	60
Public Authority for Rural Electricity and Water	369	0	. . .	3,130	2,587
Public Electricity Corporation	256	3,935	. . .	5,521	7,201
Rural Areas Development Organization	93	0	. . .	150	115
Al-Thawra Hospital	26	103	. . .	80	139
Yemen Company for Oil Investment in Jannah	0	0	. . .	400	400
Aden Free Zone Authority	0	0	. . .	91	107
Other	867	0	. . .	299	557
Total	3,878	6,864	2,900	15,934	20,102

Source: Ministry of Finance.
[1]The data for 1996 predate the data presented in Tables 13 and 15. No detailed data are available for the updated aggregate figures in Tables 13 and 15.

Table A.22. Monetary Survey, 1994–99
(In millions of Yemeni rials; end of period)

	1994	1995	1996	1997	1998	1999
Broad money	206,190	248,265	269,551	298,388	333,350	379,294
Money	139,709	164,135	156,698	166,384	179,927	207,197
Currency	111,006	129,114	120,477	126,904	139,668	166,924
Demand deposits	28,703	35,021	36,221	39,480	40,259	40,273
Quasi-money	20,847	28,530	48,979	55,594	57,431	60,430
Foreign currency deposits	45,635	55,599	63,875	76,410	95,992	111,668
Foreign assets (net)	22,953	38,899	103,344	145,177	112,532	200,029
Central bank (net)	1,624	19,784	87,514	93,637	54,789	136,286
Assets	4,288	31,107	131,445	160,249	138,927	237,687
Liabilities	2,664	11,323	43,931	66,613	84,138	101,401
Commercial banks (net)	21,329	19,115	15,830	51,540	57,743	63,743
Assets	49,151	43,088	42,453	59,472	64,857	70,991
Liabilities	27,822	23,973	26,624	7,932	7,114	7,248
Domestic assets (net)	183,237	209,366	166,208	153,212	220,818	179,266
Claims on government (net)	178,447	205,003	187,310	164,156	219,768	173,468
Central bank (net)	195,274	222,309	204,901	158,304	185,160	135,181
Claims	199,074	231,842	221,520	175,864	201,724	159,621
Budget financing	181,197	209,342	199,057	171,234	196,702	153,962
Counterpart to YBRD claims on CBY	17,877	22,500	22,463	4,630	5,022	5,659
Deposits	3,800	9,533	16,620	17,560	16,564	24,440
Commercial banks (net)	–2,333	169	6,793	34,398	36,215	39,942
Claims	390	1,295	6,963	34,873	36,267	39,972
Deposits	2,723	1,127	171	474	52	30
Total budget financing (net) excluding YBRD	175,064	199,977	189,230	188,072	216,352	169,464
Pension fund term deposits at CBY	14,494	17,475	24,383	28,546	1,607	1,655
Claims on nongovernment sector	27,246	34,875	24,605	36,071	55,630	63,970
Private sector	17,619	23,865	22,358	34,380	54,205	62,426
Rials	13,684	18,840	17,212	24,631	40,212	42,948
Foreign currency	3,935	5,025	5,146	9,749	13,993	19,478
Public enterprises	9,433	10,826	2,066	1,503	1,120	895
Rials	2,449	2,052	1,921	1,308	1,120	895
Foreign currency	6,984	8,774	145	196	0	0
Mixed enterprises	194	185	181	188	305	649
Valuation adjustment	–25,374	–17,207	–11,856	–14,900	–14,399	–10,430
Other items (net)	2,917	–13,305	–33,851	–32,116	–40,181	–47,742
Capital and reserves	–3,429	–5,201	–7,269	–11,362	–23,729	–28,762
Other (net)	6,346	–8,104	–26,582	–20,754	–16,452	–18,980
Memorandum items:						
Rial broad money	160,555	192,666	205,676	221,978	237,358	267,627
			(In millions of U.S. dollars)			
Total net foreign currency position	197.4	388.8	578.1	663.3	356.6	832.6
Central bank	–28.2	244.9	535.2	585.0	269.6	740.0
Of which:						
Net foreign assets	135.2	395.4	689.6	717.7	386.7	853.3
Foreign currency deposits	–153.2	–252.9	–263.6	–223.9	–266.5	–303.1
Commercial banks	225.7	143.9	43.0	78.3	87.0	92.6
Of which:						
Net foreign assets	211.2	150.4	124.7	395.1	407.5	399.1
Foreign currency deposits	–437.3	–395.0	–390.1	–491.8	–600.7	–625.3
YBRD claims on Central Bank of Yemen	177.0	177.0	177.0	35.5	35.4	35.4
Official exchange rate (end-period)	12.0	50.0	126.9	130.5	141.7	159.7
Free market exchange rate (end-period)	101.0	127.1	126.9	130.5	141.7	159.7

Source: Central Bank of Yemen.

Table A.23. Factors Affecting Domestic Liquidity, 1994–99

	1994	1995	1996	1997	1998	1999
	(Changes in end-year stocks, in millions of Yemeni rials)					
Broad money	53,068	42,075	21,286	28,837	34,962	45,944
Money	36,354	24,427	–7,437	9,686	13,543	27,269
Currency	31,987	18,109	–8,638	6,427	12,765	27,255
Demand deposits	4,368	6,318	1,200	3,259	779	14
Quasi-money	3,439	7,683	20,448	6,616	1,836	3,000
Foreign currency deposits	13,274	9,965	8,275	12,535	19,582	15,676
Net foreign assets	11,212	15,946	64,445	41,833	–32,645	87,496
Central bank (net)	1,785	18,160	67,730	6,123	–38,848	81,497
Commercial banks (net)	9,427	–2,214	–3,285	35,711	6,203	6,000
Net domestic assets	41,856	26,129	–43,158	–12,996	67,606	–41,552
Claims on government (net)	48,361	26,555	–17,693	–23,154	55,611	–46,300
Of which:						
Central bank (net)	52,835	27,035	–17,408	–46,597	26,856	–49,979
Total budget financing (net)	46,949	22,412	–17,371	–28,764	26,464	–50,616
Counterpart to Yemen Bank for Reconstruction and Development claims on the Central Bank of Yemen	5,886	4,623	–37	–17,833	393	637
Commercial banks (net)	–1,071	2,502	6,624	27,606	1,816	3,727
Claims on nongovernment sector	11,121	7,629	–10,271	11,467	19,559	8,340
Private sector	4,966	6,246	–1,507	12,022	19,825	8,221
Public enterprises	6,107	1,393	–8,760	–563	–383	–225
Mixed enterprises	48	–9	–5	8	117	344
Valuation adjustments	–19,521	8,167	5,351	–3,045	0	0
Other items (net)	1,896	–16,222	–20,547	1,736	–7,564	–3,592
Capital and reserves	–832	–1,772	–2,068	–4,093	501	3,969
Other	2,728	–14,450	–18,479	5,828	–8,065	–7,561
(Changes in percent of broad money)	*(Changes in percent)*					
Broad money	34.7	20.4	8.6	10.7	11.7	13.8
Money	23.7	11.8	–3.0	3.6	4.5	8.2
Currency	20.9	8.8	–3.5	2.4	4.3	8.2
Demand deposits	2.9	3.1	0.5	1.2	0.3	0.0
Quasi-money	2.2	3.7	8.2	2.5	0.6	0.9
Foreign currency deposits	8.7	4.8	3.3	4.7	6.6	4.7
Net foreign assets	7.3	7.7	26.0	15.5	–10.9	26.2
Central bank (net)	1.2	8.8	27.3	2.3	–13.0	24.4
Commercial banks (net)	6.2	–1.1	–1.3	13.2	2.1	1.8
Net domestic assets	27.3	12.7	–17.4	–4.8	22.7	–12.5
Claims on government (net)	31.6	12.9	–7.1	–8.6	18.6	–13.9
Of which:						
Total budget financing (net)	30.7	10.9	–7.0	–10.7	8.9	–15.2
Claims on nongovernment sector	7.3	3.7	–4.1	4.3	6.6	2.5
Private sector	3.2	3.0	–0.6	4.5	6.6	2.5
Public enterprises	4.0	0.7	–3.5	–0.2	–0.1	–0.1
Mixed enterprises	0.0	0.0	0.0	0.0	0.0	0.1
Valuation adjustments	–12.7	4.0	2.2	–1.1	0.2	0.0
Other items (net)	1.2	–7.9	–8.3	0.6	–2.5	–1.1
Capital and reserves	–0.5	–0.9	–0.8	–1.5	0.2	1.2
Other	1.8	–7.0	–7.4	2.2	–2.7	–2.3
Memorandum items:						
Rial broad money	33.0	20.0	6.8	7.9	6.9	12.8
Currency	40.5	16.3	–6.7	5.3	10.1	19.5
Rial demand deposits	17.9	22.0	3.4	9.0	2.0	0.0
Rial quasi-money	19.8	36.9	71.7	13.5	3.3	5.2
Claims on private sector	39.2	35.4	–6.3	53.8	57.7	15.2
Rials	. . .	37.7	–8.6	43.1	63.3	6.8
Foreign currency	. . .	27.7	2.4	89.5	43.5	39.2
U.S. dollar equivalent	. . .	1.5	2.6	84.3	32.1	23.5
	(Ratios to rial broad money)					
Currency	0.69	0.67	0.59	0.57	0.59	0.62
Rial demand deposits	0.18	0.18	0.18	0.18	0.17	0.15
Rial quasi-money	0.13	0.15	0.24	0.25	0.24	0.23

Source: Central Bank of Yemen.

Table A.24. Balance Sheet of the Central Bank, 1994–99

	1994	1995	1996	1997	1998	1999
			(In Yemeni Rials)			
Foreign assets	4,288	31,107	131,445	160,249	138,927	237,687
Gold, silver, and foreign currency	280	1,767	6,391	5,359	5,946	6,945
Foreign exchange held abroad	3,425	26,586	106,524	132,240	107,635	192,319
Foreign securities	0	0	12,459	151	3,436	10,180
SDR holdings	583	2,753	6,072	22,500	21,910	28,243
IMF reserve position (IMF record)	0	0	0	0	0	0
Claims on government	199,074	231,842	221,520	175,864	201,724	159,621
Of which:						
Budget financing	181,197	209,342	199,057	171,234	196,702	153,962
Counterpart to YBRD claims[1]	17,877	22,500	22,463	4,630	5,022	5,659
Claims on public enterprises	57	0	10	50	1,108	895
Other assets	2,375	11,582	9,840	11,344	17,340	24,652
Claims on commercial banks	40	94	54	49	0	0
Fixed and other assets	2,335	11,488	9,786	11,295	17,340	24,652
Assets = Liabilities	205,794	274,531	362,815	347,507	359,099	422,854
Foreign liabilities	2,664	11,323	43,931	66,613	84,138	101,401
Of which:						
AMF	611	2,902	7,469	11,498	11,530	15,571
IMF	0	0	15,300	32,713	47,464	65,233
Other	2,053	8,421	21,162	22,402	25,144	20,597
Reserve money	143,481	163,963	179,575	154,837	175,223	211,621
Currency outside banks	111,006	129,114	120,477	126,904	139,668	166,924
Currency with banks	1,940	1,884	1,908	2,652	2,663	2,160
Commercial banks deposits	30,535	32,965	57,190	25,282	32,892	42,538
Rials	30,344	28,111	44,716	15,584	14,899	20,564
Foreign currency	192	4,811	12,475	9,698	17,993	21,974
Government deposits	3,800	9,533	16,620	17,560	16,564	24,440
Rials	3,616	7,078	10,009	10,289	7,656	9,807
Foreign currency	184	2,456	6,610	7,271	8,908	14,633
Public enterprise deposits	7,985	22,233	29,421	32,799	27,754	22,556
Demand deposits	3,313	12,036	8,869	10,606	8,769	10,624
Time deposits	3,208	4,806	6,190	9,948	8,117	137
Foreign currency deposits	1,464	5,390	14,363	12,246	10,868	11,795
Social security fund deposits	14,494	17,475	24,383	28,546	1,607	1,655
Public sector	13,081	15,757	22,008	26,298	. . .	. . .
Private sector	1,412	1,718	2,376	2,248	. . .	. . .
Other liabilities	33,370	50,004	68,886	47,153	53,813	61,181
SDR allocation	500	2,138	5,235	5,073	5,723	6,300
Claims of YBRD[1]	17,877	22,500	22,463	4,630	5,022	5,659
Exchange valuation account	2,737	4,254	11,814	12,272	13,231	9,194
Capital and reserves	600	600	600	600	600	600
Other liabilities	11,657	20,512	28,774	24,522	29,236	39,428
			(In millions of U.S. dollars)			
Memorandum items:						
Net foreign assets	135	395	690	718	387	853
Foreign currency deposits	153	253	264	224	267	303
Net foreign currency position	-28	245	535	585	270	740
Central bank gross foreign assets	357	622	1,036	1,228	980	1,488
Central bank own gross foreign assets	355	584	937	1,154	853	1,351

Source: Central Bank of Yemen.

[1]Foreign currency claims originally equivalent to US$177 million valued at the free market exchange rate, reduced to US$35 in 1997.

Table A.25. Balance Sheet of the Commercial Banks, 1994–99[1]

	1994	1995	1996	1997	1998	1999
	(In millions of Yemeni rials)					
Foreign assets	49,151	43,088	42,453	59,472	64,857	70,991
Foreign currency	5,220	5,316	2,577	3,914	3,877	4,206
Balances with banks abroad	43,387	36,863	38,554	54,320	60,342	66,726
Claims on nonresidents	127	0	0	. . .	0	0
Foreign investments	417	910	1,322	1,238	638	59
Reserves	32,899	44,055	59,903	28,052	35,714	43,630
Currency	1,940	1,884	1,908	2,652	2,663	2,160
Deposits with central bank	30,959	42,171	57,995	25,400	33,051	41,470
Rials	30,937	29,984	45,459	15,592	15,283	19,912
Foreign currency	22	12,187	12,536	9,808	17,768	21,558
(in millions of U.S. dollars)	0	96	99	75	125	135
Claims on government	390	1,295	6,963	34,873	36,267	0
Treasury bills	. . .	873	6,622	34,549	36,267	0
Credit to government	390	422	342	324	0	39,972
Claims on nongovernment sector	27,189	34,875	24,595	36,021	0	0
Credit to public enterprises	9,376	10,826	2,056	1,453	12	0
Rials	2,392	2,052	1,911	1,257	12	63,075
Foreign currency	6,984	8,774	145	196	0	0
Credit to private sector	17,619	23,865	22,358	34,380	0	0
Rials	13,684	18,840	17,212	24,631	0	0
Foreign currency	3,935	5,025	5,146	9,749	54,205	62,426
Credit to mixed enterprises	194	185	181	188	13,993	19,478
Other assets	49,244	54,831	45,338	33,070	305	649
Interbranch accounts (net)	149	0	0	151	0	0
YBRD claims on CBY[2]	17,877	22,500	22,463	4,630	20,700	24,477
Other assets[3]	31,218	32,331	22,875	28,289	0	2
Rials	8,239	11,064	20,731	24,310	10,774	5,659
Foreign currency	20,391	21,317	2,143	3,979	15,677	18,815
Assets = Liabilities	158,873	178,145	179,252	191,487	0	0
Of which:						
in foreign currency	98,422	112,966	84,886	87,834	0	0
Foreign liabilities	27,822	23,973	26,624	7,932	7,114	127,094
Deposits of foreign banks	1,268	568	1,069	440	1,265	0
Of which:						
in local currency	20	18	6	6	4	7,248
Nonresidents deposits	2,463	2,421	2,766	2,041	1,265	772
Of which:						
in local currency	1,250	1,111	1,692	1,131	4	2
Borrowing from foreign banks	24,091	20,984	22,788	5,451	950	947
Demand deposits	25,390	22,985	27,353	28,875	31,490	0
Quasi-money deposits	17,639	23,724	42,789	45,647	49,313	29,649
Time deposits	8,775	12,415	24,380	23,985	24,924	0
Savings deposits	7,653	9,333	14,747	18,122	20,705	60,293
Earmarked deposits	1,210	1,977	3,661	3,540	3,684	30,427
Foreign currency deposits	44,171	50,209	49,512	64,165	85,124	4,185
(in millions of U.S. dollars)	437	395	390	491	601	0
Government deposits	2,723	1,127	171	474	52	625
Rials	1,750	729	115	296	47	0
Foreign currency	973	397	56	178	5	30

Table A.25 *(concluded)*

	1994	1995	1996	1997	1998	1999
Other liabilities	41,129	56,127	32,804	44,395	0	0
Credit from central bank	42	4	5	26	23	0
Rials	9	4	5	21	23	45,052
Foreign currency	33	0	0	4	0	32
Capital and reserves	2,829	4,601	6,669	10,762	23,129	32
Interbranch accounts (net)	0	1,381	1,026	0	82	0
Other liabilities	15,621	37,189	25,062	30,979	14,565	0
Rials	10,615	15,964	20,121	24,504	9,534	0
Foreign currency	3,901	21,225	4,941	6,476	5,031	15,623
Exchange valuation	22,637	12,953	42	2,628	1,168	5,403
Total liabilities	158,873	178,145	179,252	191,487	173,093	161,553
Of which:						
in foreign currency	75,630	94,675	79,435	77,617	93,632	14,338
			(In millions of U.S. dollars)			
Memorandum items:						
Net foreign currency position	226	144	43	78	87	0
Net foreign assets	388	327	302	431	443	93
Foreign currency deposits (net)	163	183	259	352	356	435
			(In percent of total assets)			
Foreign assets	31.0	24.0	24.0	31.0	31.0	29.0
Treasury bills	0.0	0.0	4.0	18.0	17.0	17.0
Loans	17.0	20.0	14.0	19.0	26.0	26.0
Reserves	21.0	25.0	33.0	15.0	17.0	18.0
Other assets	31.0	31.0	25.0	17.0	10.0	10.0

Source: Central Bank of Yemen.

[1]Foreign asset, liability, and currency components are evaluated at the free market exchange rate for all periods.

[2]Foreign currency claims equivalent to US$177 million over 1993–96 and reduced to US$35 million in 1997.

[3]Also includes nonperforming loans.

Table A.26. Interest Rates, 1994–99[1]
(In percent, end-period rates)

	1994	1995	1996	1997	1998	1999
Central bank lending rates						
Government	9.0	24.1	24.0	16.0	17.1	20.0
Public enterprises	17.0	24.1	26.0	20.0	20.0	23.0
Commercial banks	16.0	24.1	23.5	16.5	20.0	23.0
Commercial bank lending rates						
Maximum rate	17.0	...	...	...	...	...
Rate range	...	25–32	25–32	15–21	17-24	23-28
Commercial bank (minimum/benchmark)						
Deposit rates[2]						
Savings deposits	10.5	20.0	20.0	11.0	15.0	18.0
Three-month time deposits	12.0	20.0	20.0	...	...	...
Six-month time deposits	13.0	21.0	21.0	...	...	...
Nine-month time deposits	14.0	21.5	21.5	...	...	...
One-year time deposits	15.0	22.0	22.0	...	...	...
Specialized banks' lending rates[3]						
Short term	7.0	7.0	7.0	7.0	...	...
Medium and long term	9–11	10–12	7–11	7–11	...	...
Treasury bill average interest rate on successful bids						
One-month	n.a.	23.1	n.a.	n.a.	n.a.	n.a.
Three-month	n.a.	n.a.	24.8	12.9	17.5	18.1
Six-month	n.a.	n.a.	25.5	12.5	17.7	17.4
Twelve-month	n.a.	n.a.	n.a.	13.3	17.8	16.2

Source: Central Bank of Yemen.

[1]Prior to July 1995, a fixed interest rate structure applied to all loans and deposit rates. The mandated minimum deposit rates were not enforced and effective deposit rates were 3–5 percent. Interest rate reform in July 1995 freed interest rates, eliminated concessional loan rates, and enforced benchmark minimum commercial bank deposit rates.

[2]In May 1997, the benchmark system was narrowed to one minimum rate for savings accounts.

[3]As of June 1998, all specialized banks have adopted the interest rate structure applying to commercial banks.

Table A.27. Distribution of Commercial Bank Credit to the Nongovernment Sector,[1] 1994–99

(End of period)

	1994	1995	1996	1997	1998	1999
			(In millions of Yemeni rials)			
Short-term loans and advances	16,264	31,242	22,676	33,058	31,417.9	33,647.4
Agriculture and fisheries	351	371	351	130	38.6	121.2
Industry	842	3,602	3,102	8,758	3,271.0	2,628.6
Construction	...	...	...	...	655.7	1,881.4
Export financing	161	72	...	43	267.8	167.2
Import financing	4,405	4,996	4,634	6,535	9,105.3	9,390.6
Trade in manufactured goods	1,861	2,881	7,038	7,636	8,767.4	4,711.1
Other	8,643	19,322	7,550	9,955	9,312.1	14,747.3
Medium- and long-term loans	1,085	3,448	1,738	2,774	4,844.1	4,724.8
Investments[2]	...	...	...	...	9,706.3	13,443.6
Total	17,349	34,690	24,414	35,832	45,968.3	51,815.8
			(In percent of total)			
Short-term loans and advances	94	90	93	92	68	65
Agriculture and fisheries	2	1	1	0	0	0
Industry	5	10	13	24	7	5
Construction	...	...	...	...	1	4
Export financing	1	0	...	0	1	0
Import financing	25	14	19	18	20	18
Trade in manufactured goods	11	8	29	21	19	9
Other	50	56	31	28	20	28
Medium- and long-term loans	6	10	7	8	11	9
Investments[2]	...	...	...	...	21	26

Source: Central Bank of Yemen.

[1]Prior to 1998, a different classification was adopted, which explains gaps in the data for the period 1994–97.

[2]Investments refer to lending by Islamic banks on Islamic principles.

Table A.28. Commercial and Specialized Banks as of December 31, 1999

	Date of Establishment	Head Office Location	Capital (Millions of Yemeni rials)	Shareholders	Shareholding (Percent)	Total Branches[1]
Commercial banks:						
Yemen Bank for Reconstruction and Development (YBRD)	1962	Sana'a	1,000.0	Government	51	37
				Yemeni private	49	
National Bank of Yemen	1969	Aden	1,915.0	Government	100	31
United Bank Ltd.	1972	Sana'a	1,000.0	Branch of United Bank (Pakistan)	100	2
Arab Bank PLC.	1972	Sana'a	1,043.0	Branch of Arab Bank (Jordan)	100	6
Banque Indosuez	1975	Sana'a	1,304.5	Branch of Banque Indosuez (France)	100	5
Yemen Commercial Bank	1993	Sana'a	1,145.0	Yemeni Private	100	8
Yemen-Kuwait Bank for Trade and Investment	1979	Sana'a	774.5	Yemeni private	100	4
International Bank of Yemen	1980	Sana'a	906.0	Yemeni private	75	5
				Saudi Arabian Banks	25	
Rafidain Bank	1982	Sana'a	60.0	Branch of Rafidain Bank (Iraq)	100	1
Islamic banks:						
Islamic Bank for Finance and Investment	1995	Sana'a	925.0	Yemeni private[2]	100	2
Altadamon Islamic Bank	1996	Sana'a	1,500.0	Yemeni private[2]	100	8
Saba Islamic Bank	1997	Sana'a	1,159.0	Yemeni private[2]	100	3
Al Watani	1998	Sana'a	750.0	Yemeni private	100	4
Specialized banks:						
Industrial Bank of Yemen	1976	Sana'a	96.5	Government	70	—
				Yemeni private	30	—
Housing Credit Bank	1977	Sana'a	200.0	Government	70	—
				Yemeni private	30	—
Cooperative and Agricultural Credit	1982	Sana'a	293.0	Government	87	34
				Yemeni cooperatives	13	

Source: Central Bank of Yemen.
[1]Including head office.
[2]With some foreign minority shareholders.

Table A.29. Indicators of Banking System Financial Soundness, 1997–99[1]

(In percent)

	1997	1998	1999
Portfolio quality:			
Problem loans/total loans	55.2	46.1	58.5
Problem loans/total assets	11.5	10.2	13.0
Provisions against problem loans/problem loans	21.7	27.8	31.0
Total capital and reserves/problem loans	46.2	83.0	62.0
Portfolio performance:			
Average return on assets	1.0	0.9	1.0
Average return on equity	13.0	15.0	14.0
Capital adequacy:			
Total capital and reserves/total assets	5.3	8.5	8.1
Risk-weighted capital adequacy ratio	0.6	2.5	5.2
Exposure to exchange rate risk:			
Total foreign currency assets (in billions of rials)	88.4	109.3	127.4
Total foreign currency liabilities (in billions of rials)	78.2	97.8	112.8
Net exposure/total capital and reserves	100	65.3	77.7
Foreign credits/foreign deposits	15.2	16.0	19.0
Estimated exposure to real estate market:			
Total real estate loans/total loans	0.3	2.0	5.2
Total construction loans/total loans	0.3	1.9	3.3

Source: Central Bank of Yemen.

[1]Data refer to the commercial banking system in aggregates, and exclude specialized banks.

Table A.30. Balance of Payments, 1994–99

	1994	1995	1996	1997	1998	Prel. 1999
	(In millions of U.S. dollars)					
Trade balance	302.1	–11.0	–30.8	–132.6	–726.8	24.5
Exports, f.o.b.	1,824.0	1,937.2	2,262.8	2,274.0	1,501.1	2,464.4
Crude oil	1,615.4	1,735.0	1,976.2	1,944.9	1,228.7	2,131.2
Government share	753.1	777.5	958.4	1,012.2	470.7	993.0
Oil companies' share	862.3	957.5	1,017.7	932.7	758.0	1,138.2
Oil products[1]	77.8	133.4	209.8	199.2	140.8	193.7
Non-oil exports	130.8	68.8	76.8	129.9	131.5	139.5
Imports	–1,521.9	–1,948.2	–2,293.5	–2,406.5	–2,227.8	–2,439.9
Oil products, f.o.b.	–207.9	–172.0	–176.5	–165.3	–116.9	–174.3
Oil sector capital goods, c.i.f.	–172.8	–113.7	–95.9	–84.5	–66.0	–70.8
Other imports, f.o.b.	–1,141.2	–1,662.5	–2,021.1	–2,156.7	–2,044.9	–2,194.8
Food	–427.4	–687.2	–915.5	–915.9	–787.2	–806.7
Nonfood	–713.8	–975.3	–1,105.6	–1,240.8	–1,257.7	–1,388.1
Services, net	–474.6	–411.1	–369.7	–469.9	–397.5	–488.8
Transportation, net	–52.5	–46.9	–50.0	–93.4	–96.7	–92.6
Freight and insurance, net	–120.3	–206.5	–233.4	–305.2	–284.2	–311.4
Tourism, net	18.5	49.9	54.9	69.7	79.0	41.6
Oil processing fees, receipts	5.0	6.0	6.2	8.0	8.0	8.0
Other services, net	13.0	–3.5	–3.0	–3.7	–5.0	–31.8
Oil companies' foreign expenditures, payments	–326.9	–202.9	–130.6	–118.5	–80.0	–80.0
Government services, net	–11.4	–7.2	–13.8	–26.7	–18.6	–22.6
Income	–578.6	–499.1	–681.6	–630.6	–359.2	–654.7
Compensation of employees	–53.4	–47.9	–47.7	–29.7	–31.0	–27.0
Investment income	–525.2	–451.2	–633.9	–600.9	–328.2	–627.7
Current transfers	1,117.0	1,103.9	1,188.4	1,255.6	1,253.5	1,314.1
General government transfers, net	71.3	40.0	60.2	89.4	59.1	90.9
Cash grants	0.0	0.0	27.5	37.1	20.2	39.0
Grants-in-kind	72.9	43.3	40.0	54.0	43.9	55.6
Payments	–1.6	–3.3	–7.3	–1.7	–5.0	–3.7
Workers' remittances, net	1,042.7	1,063.9	1,122.6	1,156.9	1,190.7	1,223.2
Other transfers (oil signature bonus)	3.0	0.0	5.6	9.3	3.8	0.0
Current account balance	365.9	182.7	106.3	22.6	–230.0	195.1
Capital account	–641.0	–876.3	–397.1	34.4	–206.6	–74.1
Medium- and long-term loans, net	–684.6	–694.1	–520.7	–66.5	–63.7	27.0
Pipeline, net	–684.6	–694.1	–520.7	–66.5	–63.7	27.0
Disbursements	82.1	53.1	138.3	151.7	161.8	231.5
Bilateral	8.9	2.2	1.3	4.1	27.1	5.0
Multilateral	73.2	50.9	137.0	147.6	134.7	226.6
Suppliers' credits	0.0	0.0	0.0	0.0	0.0	0.0
Amortization obligations	–766.7	–747.2	–659.0	–218.2	–225.4	–204.5
Bilateral	–656.1	–641.6	–550.4	–151.5	–162.5	–150.0
Multilateral	–46.2	–49.2	–64.6	–66.7	–62.9	–54.5
Short-term oil trade credits, net	1.3	–32.5	–63.7	63.5	70.7	–119.4
Oil sector direct investment, net	15.8	–217.7	–60.1	–138.5	–266.7	–318.8
Oil sector loans	–1.5	0.0	0.0	0.0	0.0	0.0
Wheat import financing, net	28.0	68.0	167.4	–79.3	–187.2	0.0
Private capital, net	0.0	0.0	80.0	255.1	240.2	337.1
Errors and omissions	–503.7	655.3	–334.0	59.6	–26.6	198.8
Overall balance	–778.8	–38.3	–624.9	116.5	–463.1	319.9

Table A.30 *(concluded)*

	1994	1995	1996	1997	1998	Prel. 1999
Financing	778.8	38.3	624.9	–116.5	463.1	–319.9
Net reserves changes (increase –)	–79.4	–713.0	–36.9	–296.7	317.1	–458.5
Official	–148.6	–260.1	–294.2	–26.9	330.0	–466.8
Commercial banks	69.2	–452.9	257.3	–269.7	–12.9	8.3
Debt relief	0.0	0.0	93.4	6,048.1	113.6	82.5
Change in overdue obligations (increase +)[1]	858.2	751.3	568.4	–5,867.9	32.4	56.2
			(In percent of GDP)			
Current account	5.6	2.8	1.7	0.3	–3.7	2.9
Exports	28.0	29.9	35.2	34.5	23.8	36.1
Crude oil	24.8	26.8	30.7	29.5	19.5	31.2
Imports	–23.4	–30.1	–35.7	–36.5	–35.4	–35.7
Capital account	–9.8	–13.5	–6.2	0.5	–3.3	–1.1
Overall balance	–12.0	–0.6	–9.7	1.8	–7.4	4.7
			(In millions of U.S. dollars, unless otherwise indicated)			
Current account including grants (percent of GDP)	5.6	2.8	1.7	0.3	–3.7	2.9
Of which:						
Official grants (percent of GDP)	1.1	0.6	0.9	1.4	0.9	1.3
Central bank own gross foreign reserves[2]	357	525	937	1,152	853	1,351
(Months of imports)[3]	2.9	3.1	4.6	5.3	4.2	6.0
Official external debt[4]	10,876	11,017	11,135	5,359	5,373	5,490
(In percent of GDP)	167	170	173	81	85	80
Debt service (percent of exports of goods and services)[4]						
Obligations basis	47	42	32	13	17	10
Actual	3	7	9	10	14	8
Change in outstanding IMF credit (increase +)	0	0	121	130	85	74

Source: Central Bank of Yemen.

[1]Includes debt to non-Paris Club creditors under discussion to ensure comparable treatment.

[2]Includes central bank SDR holdings, foreign exchange held abroad, foreign securities, gold, silver, and foreign currencies; excludes commercial bank required foreign exchange reserves with the central bank against their foreign currency deposits.

[3]Imports are c.i.f for current year and exclude imports of oil sector capital goods.

[4]Public and publicly guaranteed debt including central bank foreign liabilities. Debt and debt service reflect the 1996 and 1997 Paris Club rescheduling, including the 80 percent upfront discount provided by the Russian Federation.

Table A.31. Composition of Exports and Reexports, 1994–99[1]

	1994	1995	1996	1997	1998	Prel. 1999
			(In millions of Yemeni rials)			
Crude oil[2]	19,401	71,271	224,140	251,436	166,953	331,993
Petroleum products[2]	934	3,637	23,804	25,748	19,134	30,428
Other exports and reexports	1,237	4,522	9,659	16,798	17,869	17,014
Coffee	453	1,096	1,985	1,760	2,658	1,953
Fish	103	471	1,392	4,852	2,401	1,912
Hides and skins	113	163	602	1,202	1,137	841
Fruits and vegetables	22	128	334	674	664	709
Honey	31	67	80	223	192	148
Metal ore	27	306	317	578	430	245
Perfumes and cosmetics	60	83	198	378	750	225
Other	429	2,209	4,753	7,132	9,638	10,981
Total, f.o.b.	21,573	79,431	257,603	293,982	203,956	379,435
			(In millions of U.S. dollars)[3]			
Crude oil[2]	1,615.4	1,735.0	1,976.2	1,944.9	1,228.7	2,131.2
Petroleum products[2]	77.8	133.4	209.8	199.2	140.8	195.4
Other exports and reexports	103.0	111.7	85.1	130.3	131.6	109.2
Coffee	37.7	27.1	17.5	14.0	19.6	12.5
Fish	8.5	11.6	12.3	37.5	17.7	12.3
Hides and skins	9.4	4.0	5.3	9.3	8.4	5.4
Fruits and vegetables	1.9	3.2	2.9	5.2	4.9	4.5
Honey	2.6	1.6	0.7	1.7	1.4	1.0
Metal ore	2.3	7.5	2.8	4.5	3.2	1.6
Perfumes and cosmetics	5.0	2.1	1.7	2.9	5.5	1.4
Other	35.7	54.5	41.9	55.2	70.9	70.5
Total, f.o.b.	1,796.2	1,980.1	2,271.1	2,274.4	1,501.1	2,435.8

Sources: Central Statistics Organization; Ministry of Oil and Mineral Resources.

[1]Customs data except for crude oil. Includes oil companies' share of crude oil exports.

[2]Data provided by Ministry of Oil and Mineral Resources and Aden Refinery. Excludes reexports from Aden Refinery under processing arrangements, and includes oil companies' share of crude oil exports.

[3]Converted from Yemeni rials at the average customs exchange rate.

Table A.32. Direction of Exports and Reexports, 1994–99[1,2]
(In percent of total)

	1994	1995	1996	1997	1998	Prel. 1999
Arab countries	19.4	11.9	7.3	3.7	11.0	3.9
Djibouti	0.1	0.1	0.1	0.3	0.7	0.2
Egypt	6.9	6.5	1.4	0.0	2.0	0.3
Kuwait	0.9	0.3	0.1	1.3	4.0	0.8
Saudi Arabia	4.0	1.7	1.9	1.2	2.2	0.4
United Arab Emirates	1.5	1.0	0.4	0.5	0.8	0.3
Other	6.1	2.3	3.4	0.4	1.3	1.9
Africa	1.0	3.2	3.1	1.9	2.7	0.2
Ethiopia	0.7	0.1	0.1	0.2	0.0	0.1
South Africa	0.0	3.0	2.2	1.6	2.4	0.0
Other	0.3	0.2	0.8	0.1	0.3	0.1
Asia	42.7	61.8	55.8	75.9	67.0	89.0
China, People's Republic of	2.5	23.3	20.6	30.6	24.9	28.8
Singapore	14.3	10.1	3.6	2.7	5.9	8.6
South Korea	20.8	1.9	17.8	19.1	11.3	14.5
Thailand	0.0	6.8	13.0	16.9	22.1	25.5
Other	5.1	19.7	0.8	6.6	2.8	11.6
Industrial countries	33.3	13.7	22.3	13.1	18.3	5.5
France	3.1	0.5	2.4	2.8	1.5	0.2
Germany	0.0	0.0	0.0	0.1	2.1	0.1
Italy	2.4	0.3	3.6	3.2	0.8	0.2
Japan	13.3	12.3	12.5	5.3	3.7	1.1
Netherlands	1.1	0.2	0.0	0.0	0.4	0.0
United Kingdom	0.1	0.1	0.2	0.3	2.7	0.1
United States	12.3	0.2	0.4	0.2	5.6	0.5
Other	1.0	0.1	3.2	1.2	1.5	3.3
Other countries	3.0	8.6	11.4	5.4	1.0	0.0
Of which:						
Brazil	1.8	8.6	11.4	5.4	0.0	0.0
Bulgaria	1.2	0.0	0.0	0.0	0.0	0.0
Bunkering (ships)	0.0	0.0	0.0	0.0	0.0	0.0
Bunkering (aircraft)	0.3	0.0	0.0	0.0	0.0	0.0
Not classified	0.3	0.7	0.0	0.0	0.0	1.4
Total, f.o.b.	100.0	100.0	100.0	100.0	100.0	100.0

Sources: Central Statistics Organization; Ministry of Oil and Mineral Resources; and IMF staff estimates.
[1]Customs data except for crude oil. Includes oil companies' share of crude oil exports.
[2]Excludes reexports from Aden Refinery under processing arrangements.

Table A.33. Composition of Imports, 1994–99[1,2]

(In millions of U.S. dollars)

	1994	1995	1996	1997	1998	Prel. 1999
Food and live animals	450.3	542.8	941.3	802.0	776.2	555.5
Meat and live animals	70.9	48.8	39.5	48.8	80.0	69.1
Live animals	31.4	24.2	13.4	17.7	37.5	33.9
Meat and meat products	39.5	24.6	26.1	31.1	42.5	35.2
Dairy products and eggs	50.3	36.2	61.3	75.3	83.9	53.2
Cereals and their products[3]	198.5	315.2	648.7	445.9	414.5	263.3
Vegetables and fruits	29.4	26.8	40.0	41.0	50.5	31.1
Sugar and its products, and honey	59.1	80.1	111.9	137.4	98.6	105.7
Coffee, tea, and spices	20.7	20.5	19.1	18.3	18.2	13
Other	21.3	15.2	20.8	35.3	30.5	20.2
Beverages and tobacco	32.7	32.4	33.2	35.8	43.6	36.4
Beverages	0.7	0.9	1.7	4.8	9.8	5.1
Tobacco	32.0	31.5	31.5	31.0	33.8	31.3
Raw materials	41.4	43.8	45.5	51.7	48.6	33.6
Oilseeds	7.1	4.3	7.1	15.5	11.4	7.7
Wood and cork	26.7	30.4	26.0	24.7	26.7	18.9
Other	7.6	9.2	12.3	11.5	10.5	7
Minerals, fuels, and lubricants[3]	236.3	121.3	165.8	223.4	139.4	113.6
Animal and vegetable oils	26.4	66.7	50.8	73.1	83	55.2
Chemicals	107.8	126.3	136.2	166.5	211.1	130.4
Manufactured goods, classified by materials	296.3	353.3	298.8	353.1	374.9	234.0
Rubber manufactures	28.9	32.9	32.5	38.3	33.5	21.6
Wood and cork	14.0	11.4	10.5	16.4	18.6	6.5
Paper manufactures	27.6	42.3	34.6	34.5	48.6	32.1
Textiles	33.6	37.2	33.8	37.2	38.1	25.8
Nonmetallic mineral manufactures	39.0	39.7	45.7	44.4	44.1	28.6
Iron and steel	96.7	117.1	83.0	107.0	115.8	73.7
Metal manufactures	34.0	52.4	40.8	48.9	48.4	27.9
Other	22.5	20.3	17.8	26.4	27.8	17.8
Machinery and transport equipment	285.5	355.2	373.1	424.9	525.1	312.8
Machinery	192.9	245.3	244.1	316.7	396.6	235.6
Road vehicles	87.1	101.8	120.7	103.0	106.5	71.1
Other transport equipment	5.5	8.1	8.3	5.3	22	6.1
Other	0.0	0.0	0.0	0	0	0
Miscellaneous manufactured articles	80.0	96.7	83.8	96.9	114.4	61.5
Furniture	3.7	7.4	8.5	6.8	8.6	5.8
Clothing	27.1	22.4	15.7	20.0	25.9	11.5
Footwear	9.1	9.8	7.6	10.6	11.2	4.7
Professional and scientific instruments	9.4	8.2	9.4	12.8	24.1	13
Other	30.7	48.9	42.6	46.7	44.6	26.5
Other commodities	0.1	0.4	1.0	4.4	11.3	2.9
Total imports, c.i.f.	1,556.9	1,739.0	2,129.5	2,231.8	2,327.6	1,535.9

Source: Central Statistics Organization.

[1]Customs data. Excludes oil company investment goods imports. The sharp fall recorded for total imports in 1999 reflects preliminary and incomplete data reports for the year.

[2]Converted from Yemeni rial data at the average customs exchange rate, except for mineral fuels and lubricants, which are converted at the official rate.

[3]Data for 1994–96 are Central Bank of Yemen estimates.

Table A.34. Sources of Imports, 1994–99[1]
(In percent of total)

	1994	1995	1996	1997	1998	Prel. 1999
Arab countries	27.2	24.9	27.6	27.2	28.8	34.5
Djibouti	2.2	0.4	0.8	1.3	1.4	1.8
Egypt	1.2	1.0	1.9	1.0	1.2	1.2
Jordan	0.6	1.0	1.2	0.9	0.7	0.6
Kuwait	0.3	2.8	4.2	4.0	2.3	4.6
Saudi Arabia	9.8	7.4	9.1	9.4	11.7	10.2
Somalia	1.3	1.1	1.0	0.9	1.7	2.1
United Arab Emirates	9.9	10.8	7.7	8.5	9	11.7
Other	1.9	0.4	1.7	1.2	0.8	2.3
Asia	20.3	18.4	24.8	24.1	18.3	20.1
China, People's Republic of	2.0	2.7	3.5	3.4	3.1	2.8
Hong Kong SAR	0.5	0.6	0.5	0.4	0.4	0.2
India	1.4	1.2	3.8	2.6	2.2	2.5
Malaysia	4.5	4.9	5.6	3.5	0.4	3.6
Singapore	3.4	2.7	2.0	1.7	3.2	3.7
South Korea	1.3	1.1	1.8	1.6	1.9	1.5
Thailand	0.8	0.5	3.1	1.4	1.3	2
Other	6.4	4.7	4.5	9.5	5.8	3.8
Industrial countries	44.5	28.0	45.1	46.9	47.1	43.1
Australia	2.3	0.3	0.9	2.0	2.4	4.8
Austria	0.3	0.2	0.4	0.3	0.2	0.3
Belgium	4.2	1.6	1.5	1.6	2.1	1.2
Canada	0.4	0.2	0.6	0.6	0.6	0.4
Denmark	0.5	0.5	0.9	0.9	0.6	0.6
France	5.6	3.2	6.3	6.0	5.6	4.1
Germany	2.8	2.5	3.3	3.1	3.6	2.9
Greece	1.2	0.7	0.5	0.5	0.3	0.1
Italy	3.9	2.6	3.6	3.4	4.3	4.1
Japan	4.2	3.0	5.1	3.0	3.5	2.7
Netherlands	3.9	1.5	1.8	1.8	2.2	1.3
Spain	0.1	0.3	0.6	0.5	0.5	0.3
Sweden	0.4	0.6	0.5	0.7	0.5	0.7
Switzerland	0.2	0.2	1.5	4.7	2.8	2.5
United Kingdom	5.3	3.7	4.7	4.9	5.1	4.7
United States	8.5	5.8	6.9	6.8	5.8	5.5
Other	0.6	0.9	6.0	6.1	7	6.9
Other countries	1.3	1.0	1.1	1.7	0.9	0.4
Bulgaria	0.0	0.2	0.1	0.1	0.1	0
Czech Republic	0.0	0.0	0.1	0.1	0.1	0
Hungary	0.2	0.2	0.3	0.2	0.2	0
Poland	0.0	0.0	0.1	0.2	0.1	0.2
Romania	0.8	0.3	0.2	0.2	0.1	0
Russian Federation	0.3	0.3	0.3	0.5	0.2	0.1
Yugoslavia	0.0	0.0	0.0	0.4	0.1	0.1
Unidentified	6.7	27.6	1.4	0.1	4.9	1.9
Total imports, c.i.f.	100.0	100.0	100.0	100.0	100.0	100.0

Sources: Central Statistics Organization.
[1]Excludes oil company investment goods imports.

Table A.35. Enterprises Privatized/Liquidated, 1997–99

Name	Privatization Method	Timing	Remarks
Industrial Sector			
1. Al-Thawra metal products	30-year lease	Implemented in 1997	Lessee hires 35 of original staff and MOF continues to pay salaries/benefits of remaining workers.
2. Agriculture and metal products	30-year lease	Implemented in 1997, 1/1/1998	Lessee hires all of the 96 effective original staff.
3. Leather shoe factory	Land and building restituted; equipment sold and new land rented to purchaser for 30 years	Implemented in 1997, effective 1/1/1998	Purchaser hires 15 of original staff and MOF continues to pay salaries/benefits of remaining 78 employees.
4. Leather products	Same as (3)	Implemented in 1997	Purchaser keeps five staff and MOF continues to pay salaries/benefits of remaining 73 employees.
5. Martyrs' garment factory	Same as (3)	Implemented in 1997, effective 1/1/1998	Purchaser keeps 10 staff and MOF continues to pay salaries/benefits of remaining 98.
6. Vegetable oil factory	Equipment sold and land leased for 30 years	Implemented in 1998	The three employees were retained by purchaser of equipment.
7. Soap factory	Equipment sold but no deal concluded on leasing the site	Sale of equipment done in 1997	Technical Privatization Office will take over in handling the fate of the site
8. The public bakery	Equipment sold and the building and land rented for other purposes	Sale of equipment finished in 1998, and land leased	Owner keeps 12 staff and MOF continues to pay salaries/benefits of remaining 75 employees.
9. Women's sewing cooperative	Liquidation	Completed in 1999	
Agricultural Sector			
10. Hammam Ali state farm (Dhamar government)	Privatized by rent	Implemented in 1999	
11. Dar Sa'ad poultry (Aden gov.)	Privatized by rent	Implemented in 1999	
12. Old Fowah poultry (Hadramout)	Privatized by rent	Implemented in 1999	
13. New Fowah poultry (Hadramout)	Privatized by rent	Implemented in 1999	
14. Agricultural machinery rental Station–Saiyoun Hadramout (government)	Privatized by management buyout under new name, Saiyoun Company for Agricultural and Industrial Machinery	Implemented in 1999	This is the only enterprise that has been privatized through Technical Privatization Office.
15. Al-Mashhad Farm (Hadramout)	Not available	Implemented in 1999	
Transport Sector			
16. National Shipping Agency (Natship)	Not available	Implemented in 1999	Directly privatized by ministry. It was one of the two major activities (shipping) undertaken by the National Shipping Company.
17. Stevedoring operations	Not available	Implemented in 1999	Directly privatized by ministry. It was the second major activity (loading/ unloading cargoes) of the National Shipping Company.
Supply and Trade Sector			
18. Consumption society for state, process public, and mixed sectors employees	Liquidation	Implementation was still ongoing in 1999	Might not have been completed by year-end.

Source: The Yemeni authorities.

Table A.36. Enterprises To Be Privatized/Liquidated

Name	Status in Process	Remarks
Large Enterprises:		
1. Aden refinery	Short-listed consultant started evaluation in mid-January 2000, completion of study was expected in July 2000	Oil sector
2. Airport ground handling services	Short-lists of consultants approved; invitation letter to them in preparation	Transport sector
3. General corporation for land transport	Same as above	Transport sector
4. General corporation for cement and marketing production (Sana'a)	Same as above	Industrial sector
5. Yemen drug company (Sana'a)	Same as above	Industrial sector
Small and Medium Enterprises: Industrial Sector		
6. The biscuit and candies factory (Aden)	Short-list of consultants ready for HC approval	As of February 1998, had been tendered three times; very low bids each time
7. Automatic bakery (Aden)	Same as above	Same as above
8. Dairy factory (Aden)	Same as above	Same as above
9. Canada Dry factory (Aden)	Same as above	
10. National tanning factory (Aden)	Same as above	
11. Tomato paste factory (Lahaj)	Same as above	Labor force estimate in 1997: 118
12. Textile and spinning factory (Aden)	Same as above	
13. Textile and spinning factory (Sana'a)	Negotiation with the Chinese government ongoing for capital share	
14. The National Company for Aluminum Manufacturing	Cabinet decree just issued for privatization	
15. The National Company for Sponge and Metal Furniture Manufacturing Ltd.	Same as above	
Agricultural Sector		
16. Agricultural machinery rental station in Al-Dale (Lahaj government)	Short-list ready for HC approval.	Labor force estimate in 1997: 51
17. Agricultural machinery rental station in Jear (Abyan government)	Same as above	Labor force estimate in 1997: 111
18. Agricultural machinery rental station in Behan (Shabwah government)	Same as above	Labor force estimate in 1997: 56
19. Agricultural machinery rental station in Laboos (Lahaj government)	Same as above	Labor force estimate in 1997: 34
20. Agricultural machinery rental station in Saber (Lahaj government)	Same as above	Labor force estimate in 1997: 91
21. Agricultural machinery rental station in Loder (Abyan government)	Same as above	
22. Agricultural machinery rental station in Mefah (Shabwah government)	Same as above	
23. Agricultural machinery rental station in Nisab (Shabwah government)	Same as above	
24. General corporation for fruit and vegetables marketing (Aden government)	Same as above	

Table A.36 *(continued)*

Name	Status in Process	Remarks
25. Date packing unit (Hadramout government)	Short-list ready for HC approval	
26. Agricultural machinery rental station (Al Habilin, Lahaj government)	Same as above	
27. General corporation for agricultural services (Sana'a)	Same as above	
28. General corporation for poultries (Aden)	Same as above	
Fisheries Sector		
29. Central unit for maintenance and services—subsidiary of the general corporation for fish services and marketing (Aden government)	Short-list ready for HC approval	
30. Shograh fish canning factory (Abyan government)	Same as above	Labor force estimate in 1997: 147
31. Ice factory in Midi (Hajjah government)	Same as above	
32. Ice factory in Ahwar (Abyan government)	Same as above	
33. Ice factory in Bear Ali (Shabwah government)	Same as above	
34. Ice factory in Kosia'ar (Hadramout government)	Same as above	
Transport Sector		
35. Yemen navigation lines	Short-list ready for HC approval	
36. Aden dockyards company	Same as above	Labor force estimate in 1997: 366
37. Port of Nashtoun	Consultant's report was submitted	One of the three semi-large enterprises whose pre-privatization strategy is covered by the IDA Project
Supply and Trade Sector		
38. Public corporation for building material trade (Aden)	HC approved sale of assets in June 2000	Labor force estimate in 1997: 612; Evaluation finished prior to 10/98
39. Public corporation for textiles and electric supplies	Same as above	Labor force estimate in 1997: 793
40. Yemen company for free trade—Al-Nasr, Aden	Same as above	Labor force estimate in 1997: 331 Evaluation finished by 3/99
41. Caltex silos complex—subsidiary of the Yemen trade corporation (Aden)	HC approved privatization in June 2000	Labor force estimate in 1997: 60
42. Central refrigeration plant—subsidiary of the Yemen trade corporation (Aden)	Short-list ready for HC approval	Labor force estimate in 1997: 192
43. Central bakery and mills in Taiz—subsidiary of the public trade corporation for foreign trade and grains	Same as above	Labor force estimate in 1997: 86
44. Central bakery and mills in Sana'a—subsidiary of the public trade corporation for foreign trade and grains	A contract was signed with a local consultant company for performing the evaluation	Labor force estimate in 1997: 73

Table A.36 *(concluded)*

Name	Status in Process	Remarks
45. Central refrigeration plants in Lahaj, Abyan, Shabwah and Al-Mahrah—subsidiaries of the Yemen Trade Corporation	Short-list ready for HC approval	
46. Public corporation for building material trade in Lahaj, Abyan, Shabwah and Hadramout.	HC approved sale of assets in June 2000	Evaluation completed by 3/99
Telecommunications Sector		
47. Mobile services company (GSM)	The High Tendering Committee is evaluating bidding offers to choose the most successful two bids	
48. Telephone booths	Work in progress	
Financial Sector		
49. National Bank of Yemen	Sale procedures to be decided in June HC meeting	
50. Yemen Bank for Reconstruction and Development	Restructuring projected to be completed by end 2000, at which time sales procedures could start	
51. Housing bank	Strategy still under preparation	Recently turned over to TPO to carry out process
52. Industrial bank	Committee to liquidate the bank appointed in October 1999	
53. Agriculture bank	Restructuring plan approved by cabinet. Bids being taken (until mid-February) from companies recommended by the World Bank to conduct the restructuring	

Source: Technical Privatization Office.

Table A.37. Social Fund for Development: Total Investment and Disbursement up to September 30, 1999
(According to Governorates)

Governorate	Number of Projects	Committed ($)	Disbursed ($)	Percentage of Disbursement
Sana'a (Capital)	54	3,291,222	890,231	27
Sana'a	121	5,431,381	2,513,345	46
Aden	32	3,671,454	712,367	19
Taiz	102	5,293,416	3,275,606	62
Hodiedah	52	4,442,188	2,092,508	47
Lahj	30	1,954,712	775,143	40
Ibb	58	3,539,637	1,667,917	47
Abian	16	1,083,369	513,663	47
Dhamar	62	3,994,849	1,204,412	30
Shabwah	26	1,168,441	341,743	29
Hajjah	58	3,139,445	1,109,249	35
Baidhaa	24	1,476,077	532,932	36
Hadhramout	44	2,347,406	1,802,782	77
Saadah	16	1,034,072	396,874	38
Mahweet	29	2,229,693	692,781	31
Maharah	17	1,045,587	589,106	56
Maareb	16	875,422	527,438	60
Al-Jawf	9	524,656	171,040	33
More governorates	19	495,886	189,997	38
Total	785	47,038,913	19,999,135	43

Source: Social Fund for Development Newsletter-Issue No. 8 (October–December, 1999).

Recent Occasional Papers of the International Monetary Fund

208. Yemen in the 1990s: From Unification to Economic Reform, by Klaus Enders, Sherwyn Williams, Nada Choueiri, Yuri Sobolev, and Jan Walliser. 2002.
207. Malaysia: From Crisis to Recovery, by Kanitta Meesook, Il Houng Lee, Olin Liu, Yougesh Khatri, Natalia Tamirisa, Michael Moore, and Mark H. Krysl. 2001.
206. The Dominican Republic: Stabilization, Structural Reform, and Economic Growth, by Alessandro Giustiniani, Werner C. Keller, and Randa E. Sab. 2001.
205. Stabilization and Savings Funds for Nonrenewable Resources, by Jeffrey Davis, Rolando Ossowski, James Daniel, and Steven Barnett. 2001.
204. Monetary Union in West Africa (ECOWAS): Is It Desirable and How Could It Be Achieved? by Paul Masson and Catherine Pattillo. 2001.
203. Modern Banking and OTC Derivatives Markets: The Transformation of Global Finance and Its Implications for Systemic Risk, by Garry J. Schinasi, R. Sean Craig, Burkhard Drees, and Charles Kramer. 2000.
202. Adopting Inflation Targeting: Practical Issues for Emerging Market Countries, by Andrea Schaechter, Mark R. Stone, and Mark Zelmer. 2000.
201. Developments and Challenges in the Caribbean Region, by Samuel Itam, Simon Cueva, Erik Lundback, Janet Stotsky, and Stephen Tokarick. 2000.
200. Pension Reform in the Baltics: Issues and Prospects, by Jerald Schiff, Niko Hobdari, Axel Schimmelpfennig, and Roman Zytek. 2000.
199. Ghana: Economic Development in a Democratic Environment, by Sérgio Pereira Leite, Anthony Pellechio, Luisa Zanforlin, Girma Begashaw, Stefania Fabrizio, and Joachim Harnack. 2000.
198. Setting Up Treasuries in the Baltics, Russia, and Other Countries of the Former Soviet Union: An Assessment of IMF Technical Assistance, by Barry H. Potter and Jack Diamond. 2000.
197. Deposit Insurance: Actual and Good Practices, by Gillian G.H. Garcia. 2000.
196. Trade and Trade Policies in Eastern and Southern Africa, by a staff team led by Arvind Subramanian, with Enrique Gelbard, Richard Harmsen, Katrin Elborgh-Woytek, and Piroska Nagy. 2000.
195. The Eastern Caribbean Currency Union—Institutions, Performance, and Policy Issues, by Frits van Beek, José Roberto Rosales, Mayra Zermeño, Ruby Randall, and Jorge Shepherd. 2000.
194. Fiscal and Macroeconomic Impact of Privatization, by Jeffrey Davis, Rolando Ossowski, Thomas Richardson, and Steven Barnett. 2000.
193. Exchange Rate Regimes in an Increasingly Integrated World Economy, by Michael Mussa, Paul Masson, Alexander Swoboda, Esteban Jadresic, Paolo Mauro, and Andy Berg. 2000.
192. Macroprudential Indicators of Financial System Soundness, by a staff team led by Owen Evans, Alfredo M. Leone, Mahinder Gill, and Paul Hilbers. 2000.
191. Social Issues in IMF-Supported Programs, by Sanjeev Gupta, Louis Dicks-Mireaux, Ritha Khemani, Calvin McDonald, and Marijn Verhoeven. 2000.
190. Capital Controls: Country Experiences with Their Use and Liberalization, by Akira Ariyoshi, Karl Habermeier, Bernard Laurens, Inci Ötker-Robe, Jorge Iván Canales Kriljenko, and Andrei Kirilenko. 2000.
189. Current Account and External Sustainability in the Baltics, Russia, and Other Countries of the Former Soviet Union, by Donal McGettigan. 2000.
188. Financial Sector Crisis and Restructuring: Lessons from Asia, by Carl-Johan Lindgren, Tomás J.T. Baliño, Charles Enoch, Anne-Marie Gulde, Marc Quintyn, and Leslie Teo. 1999.
187. Philippines: Toward Sustainable and Rapid Growth, Recent Developments and the Agenda Ahead, by Markus Rodlauer, Prakash Loungani, Vivek Arora, Charalambos Christofides, Enrique G. De la Piedra, Piyabha Kongsamut, Kristina Kostial, Victoria Summers, and Athanasios Vamvakidis. 2000.
186. Anticipating Balance of Payments Crises: The Role of Early Warning Systems, by Andrew Berg, Eduardo Borensztein, Gian Maria Milesi-Ferretti, and Catherine Pattillo. 1999.
185. Oman Beyond the Oil Horizon: Policies Toward Sustainable Growth, edited by Ahsan Mansur and Volker Treichel. 1999.

184. Growth Experience in Transition Countries, 1990–98, by Oleh Havrylyshyn, Thomas Wolf, Julian Berengaut, Marta Castello-Branco, Ron van Rooden, and Valerie Mercer-Blackman. 1999.

183. Economic Reforms in Kazakhstan, Kyrgyz Republic, Tajikistan, Turkmenistan, and Uzbekistan, by Emine Gürgen, Harry Snoek, Jon Craig, Jimmy McHugh, Ivailo Izvorski, and Ron van Rooden. 1999.

182. Tax Reform in the Baltics, Russia, and Other Countries of the Former Soviet Union, by a staff team led by Liam Ebrill and Oleh Havrylyshyn. 1999.

181. The Netherlands: Transforming a Market Economy, by C. Maxwell Watson, Bas B. Bakker, Jan Kees Martijn, and Ioannis Halikias. 1999.

180. Revenue Implications of Trade Liberalization, by Liam Ebrill, Janet Stotsky, and Reint Gropp. 1999.

179. Disinflation in Transition: 1993–97, by Carlo Cottarelli and Peter Doyle. 1999.

178. IMF-Supported Programs in Indonesia, Korea, and Thailand: A Preliminary Assessment, by Timothy Lane, Atish Ghosh, Javier Hamann, Steven Phillips, Marianne Schulze-Ghattas, and Tsidi Tsikata. 1999.

177. Perspectives on Regional Unemployment in Europe, by Paolo Mauro, Eswar Prasad, and Antonio Spilimbergo. 1999.

176. Back to the Future: Postwar Reconstruction and Stabilization in Lebanon, edited by Sena Eken and Thomas Helbling. 1999.

175. Macroeconomic Developments in the Baltics, Russia, and Other Countries of the Former Soviet Union, 1992–97, by Luis M. Valdivieso. 1998.

174. Impact of EMU on Selected Non–European Union Countries, by R. Feldman, K. Nashashibi, R. Nord, P. Allum, D. Desruelle, K. Enders, R. Kahn, and H. Temprano-Arroyo. 1998.

173. The Baltic Countries: From Economic Stabilization to EU Accession, by Julian Berengaut, Augusto Lopez-Claros, Françoise Le Gall, Dennis Jones, Richard Stern, Ann-Margret Westin, Effie Psalida, Pietro Garibaldi. 1998.

172. Capital Account Liberalization: Theoretical and Practical Aspects, by a staff team led by Barry Eichengreen and Michael Mussa, with Giovanni Dell'Ariccia, Enrica Detragiache, Gian Maria Milesi-Ferretti, and Andrew Tweedie. 1998.

171. Monetary Policy in Dollarized Economies, by Tomás Baliño, Adam Bennett, and Eduardo Borensztein. 1998.

170. The West African Economic and Monetary Union: Recent Developments and Policy Issues, by a staff team led by Ernesto Hernández-Catá and comprising Christian A. François, Paul Masson, Pascal Bouvier, Patrick Peroz, Dominique Desruelle, and Athanasios Vamvakidis. 1998.

169. Financial Sector Development in Sub-Saharan African Countries, by Hassanali Mehran, Piero Ugolini, Jean Phillipe Briffaux, George Iden, Tonny Lybek, Stephen Swaray, and Peter Hayward. 1998.

168. Exit Strategies: Policy Options for Countries Seeking Greater Exchange Rate Flexibility, by a staff team led by Barry Eichengreen and Paul Masson with Hugh Bredenkamp, Barry Johnston, Javier Hamann, Esteban Jadresic, and Inci Ötker. 1998.

167. Exchange Rate Assessment: Extensions of the Macroeconomic Balance Approach, edited by Peter Isard and Hamid Faruqee. 1998

166. Hedge Funds and Financial Market Dynamics, by a staff team led by Barry Eichengreen and Donald Mathieson with Bankim Chadha, Anne Jansen, Laura Kodres, and Sunil Sharma. 1998.

165. Algeria: Stabilization and Transition to the Market, by Karim Nashashibi, Patricia Alonso-Gamo, Stefania Bazzoni, Alain Féler, Nicole Laframboise, and Sebastian Paris Horvitz. 1998.

164. MULTIMOD Mark III: The Core Dynamic and Steady-State Model, by Douglas Laxton, Peter Isard, Hamid Faruqee, Eswar Prasad, and Bart Turtelboom. 1998.

163. Egypt: Beyond Stabilization, Toward a Dynamic Market Economy, by a staff team led by Howard Handy. 1998.

Note: For information on the title and availability of Occasional Papers not listed, please consult the IMF Publications Catalog or contact IMF Publication Services.